Just Go

GRAND CANYON

A COMPLETE GUIDE TO THE GRAND CANYON NATIONAL PARK AND SURROUNDING AREAS

Eric Henze

GONE BEYOND GUIDES

Gone Beyond Guides
Publisher

How to Use This Guide

This travel guide does much of the planning research for you so you can spend more time in the enjoyment of not working and having fun! You see, nearly every one of us wants to GO on a vacation, we just don't want to PLAN a vacation. This travel guide solves that dilemma by taking a tremendous amount of the burden out of the vacation planning aspects for a trip to the Grand Canyon and all the cool surrounding sites.

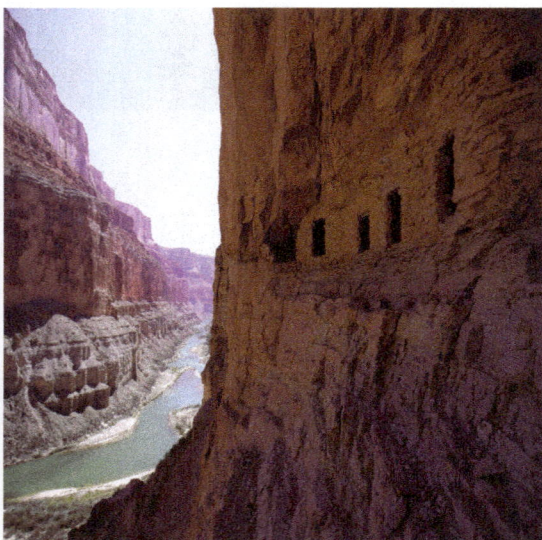

Grand Canyon and the Colorado River

First off, this guidebook gives you everything you need to know in order to have a truly wonderful stay within Grand Canyon National Park. This includes all the various things to see and do, where to go, both on the road and off, plus tips on best lodging and dining. Whether you want to peer over the rim, take a hike, or embark on a multi-day rafting adventure, this book has these and many other scenarios covered.

Next, most folks do not come *just* to see the Grand Canyon, as there are dozens of other incredible things to do in the Southwest that are relatively close to the park. We've gathered all of these different places and bundled them into easy to discover Side Trips that you can take either before or after you've completed your visit to the Grand Canyon. There are twelve side trips in all. Each of these trips is designed as a step by step package, but with enough choices built in to allow you to customize your own trip.

Each side trip is complete and has all the details you need, including full descriptions of the places to visit along the way, tips on how to make the most of each side journey, how much time to allow, and again, a list of suggested places for lodging and dining. We also recommend which side trips can be combined. Nearly all of the research has been done for you, making it a lot easier to create your own vacation.

This book is designed to make you an expert in creating your own perfect Grand Canyon vacation! I sincerely hope you have the time of your lives in whatever you do and wherever you go!

Happy Travels,

Eric Henze

WHAT IS THE GRAND CIRCLE?

This travel guide makes reference not only to the Grand Canyon, but a few times to something called "The Grand Circle." Since you will be traveling within this so-called circle, it makes sense to fill in the details on what the term means.

The Grand Circle encompasses five southwestern US states but more importantly, is so named because it contains the highest concentration of national and state parks in the United States. Within this imaginary 500 mile-diameter area, there are almost 80 parks and hundreds of other attractions. Simply put, the Grand Circle is a bounty of fun and adventure.

By the numbers, most of the parks that make up the Grand Circle are within Utah and Arizona, but the full magnitude of the circle encompasses lands within Nevada, New Mexico, and Colorado as well. The imaginary circle is about 500 miles in diameter or roughly 126 million acres of land. This book covers a subset of this larger circle, describing 27 parks and attractions along with 10 towns and cities, in full detail. With this book, it will take as far north as Zion National Park, west to Las Vegas, south to Phoenix, and east to the Four Corners.

Historically, the Grand Circle was a term created when the Southwest National Parks was just beginning. The NPS worked with the Union Pacific Railway and created trips by rail and bus up until the 1970's. Back then, a trip to the Grand Circle was a time of great adventure and romance. There were dance bands at the stops, and as your tour bus would drive away from the lodge, employees would line up and "sing away" the visitors. Today, it remains one of the best vacations in North America that one can take. This is a vacation destination for adventure, relaxation, and wonder. It is a land that humbles, inspires, and refreshes the spirit and for those that know it, they have the Grand Circle as a bucket list place to experience at least once in their lives.

WHEN TO GO

There are really only two factors on when to go, do you like temperate climates or would you prefer fewer people. Weather plays a hand in both but in different ways.

In general, the Grand Canyon and all of the Grand Circle is a hot place in the summer, starting in mid to late June and going full force through August. That doesn't seem to keep folks away, particularly if you have kids out for the school year. Temperature wise though, the best time to go is during the spring/early summer and fall/early winter. The elevation is another consideration. The weather can be quite pleasant at the rim of the Grand Canyon, but oppressively hot down at the canyon's river bottom. Monsoon season typically starts around mid-September. The warm and dramatic thunderstorms are both one of nature's finest shows and a death warrant if you are in a slot canyon at the wrong time during a storm.

Grand Canyon National Park

PARKS OF THE GRAND CIRCLE

NP	National Park	**NRA**	National Recreation Area
NM	National Monument	**SP**	State Park
NHP	National Historic Park	**SHP**	State Historic Park

Sandy
Heber City
PROVO
40
Nephi
89
Mt. Pleasant
Delta
6
10
CAVE LAKE SP
WARD CHARCOAL OVENS SHP
Ely
50
93
6
50
Sevier Lake
Richfield
GREAT BASIN NP
93
24
72
70
GOBLIN VALLEY SP
318
21
15
Beaver
Torrey
24
UTAH
CAPITOL REEF NP
BASIN AND RANGE NM
Piocha
SPRING VALLEY SP
ECHO CANYON SP
CEDAR BREAKS NM
89
12
ANASAZI SP
CATHEDRAL GORGE SP
FRONTIER HOMESTEAD SP
Parowan
Caliente
Cedar City
KERSHAW-RYAN SP/ EELGIN SCHOOLHOUSE
BEAVER DAM SP
ZION NP
14
BRYCE NP
KODACHROME SP
GLEN CANYON NRA
NEVADA
GUNLOCK SP
SNOW CANYON SP
18
Springdale
St. George
9
GRAND STAIRCASE-ESCALANTE NM
89
RAINBOW BRIDGE
SAND HOLLOW SP
QUAIL CREEK SP
CORAL PINK SAND DUNES SP
Kanab
VERMILION CLIFFS NM
Page
ANTELOPE CANYON
58
Mesquite
389
PIPE SPRING NM
Jacob Lake
89A
NAVAJO
VALLEY OF FIRE SP
95
Indian Springs
67
89
160
LAS VEGAS
GRAND CANYON-PARASHANT NM
GRAND CANYON NP
Tuba City
127
Henderson
Lake Mead
Colorado River
Tusayan
Little
LAKE MEAD NRA
95
ARIZONA
WUPATKI NM
SUNSET CRATER VOLCANO NM
15
93
66
64
180
Flagstaff
40
Colorado
Laughlin
Bullhead City
Kingman
Verde
Williams
SLIDE ROCK SP
WALNUT CANYON NM
Needles
Sedona
TUZIGOOT NM
RED ROCK SP
DEAD HORSE RANCH SP
MONTEZUMA CASTLE NM
CALIFORNIA
95
Lake Havasu City
93
Prescott
89
River
260
17
Payson
AGUA FRIA NM
87
188
10
Blythe
Quartzsite
60
Wickenburg
60
Salt River
Salton Sea
95
PHOENIX
Tempe
Scottsdale
TONTO NM

COLORADO

NEW MEXICO

DINOSAUR NM

Vernal

oosevelt

Craig

Steamboat Springs

Fort Collins

Greeley

Fort Mor

13

Estes Park

34

64

Meeker

40

River

Boulder

DENVER

139

Silverthorne

70

RIFLE FALLS SP

Rifle

Colorado

Glenwood Springs

Vail

Aspen

285

Castle Rock

70

Fruita

70

Grand Junction

COLORADO NM

133

82

Silverthorne

24

24

COLORADO SPRING

Delta

Gunnison

550

BLACK CANYON OF THE GUNNISON NP

Gunnison

Salida

Cañon City

46

Moab

Montrose

River

CURECANTI NRA

50

285

Arkansas

River

PUEBLO

50

Ro

141

RIDGWAY SP

62

COLORADO

17

GREAT SAND DUNES NP

Walsenburg

90

Telluride

145

Del Norte

160

Monte Vista

150

25

350

191

Monticello

141

NATURAL BRIDGES NM

CANYON OF THE ANCIENTS NM

Cortez

160

Alamosa

1

EDGE OF CEDARS SP

Blanding

MANCOS SP

160

Durango

CHIMNEY ROCK NM

84

Trinidad

HOVENWEEP NM

162

MESA VERDE NP

550

GOOSENECKS SP

Bluff

YUCCA HOUSE NM

491

AZTEC RUINS NM

Aztec

San

84

Raton

87

FOUR CORNERS MONUMENT

64

491

64

Juan

Tierra Amarilla

64

Cimarron

64

Farmington

550

EL VADO AND HERON LAKE SP

Taos

Springer

NUMENT
LEY
VAJO
BAL
K

NEW MEXICO

84

285

412

CANYON DE CHELLY NM

Chinle

CHACO CULTURE NHP

518

Española

191

371

57

197

126

BANDELIER NM

SANTA FE

264

Window Rock

509

KASHA-KATUWE TENT ROCKS NM

Las Vegas

BBELL
ADING
T NHS

Gallup

550

PECOS NHP

40

285

84

Grants

PETROGLYPH NM

ALBUQUERQUE

Pecos

Tucumc

53

EL MORRO NM

Zuni

191

EL MALPAIS NM

36

Los Lunas

40

117

PETRIFIED FOREST NP

River

180

St. Johns

60

N

w Low

Eager

191

Quemado

60

Socorro

380

Alpine

25

380

0   100 mi

0   100 km

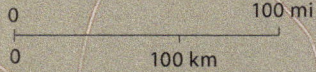

© GONE BEYOND GUIDES 2015-2019

Roswell

Fort S

If you want to go at a time when the crowds have thinned, the best times to go are the "shoulder seasons." These are the short periods between the normal peak travel periods. These are currently between March and May and October to November. Often, this is the best time to get a deal on a hotel. If you are a hiker, the best times are between September and June, which is another way of saying anytime except the dead of summer. Also, remember that full access to the *entire* park is from May to October. The North Rim closes around mid-October or after the first snowfall, whichever comes first. That said, the South Rim is open year round.

The dead of summer is for many, the only choice as this is the time everyone can get time off. You won't be alone, and the Grand Canyon and surrounding parks get a lot of summer traffic. The parks in summer can be too hot to hike in during the heat of mid-day, so for those that take go in the summer, get in the habit of hitting the trails in the cool of early morning.

WHERE TO GO

If you think about it, there is a fair amount of irony in guidebooks that tell you the best places to go to avoid crowds. They are basically saying, we've learned all these secret cool places that no one goes to, and we are now publishing this information in a globally available guidebook for anyone to read. If you see one of these sections, don't believe it, the word is already out on all these "secret places." In fact, places such as Havasu Falls are so impacted, it is quite difficult to get a permit to hike the trail.

That said, there are some general tips to getting an otherwise crowded national park or monument to yourself. Take the Grand Canyon for example. This park receives some 4.5 million visitors to the South Rim alone. The vast majority of these folks don't hike any farther than to the overlooks. So simply getting out on any trail cuts the population of the park down by about 90%. Getting out on a trail also helps you connect with the park and really experience it.

There are other tips to share. In general, I've found that the more strenuous the hike is, the harder the trail is to get to, and the longer the trail's length, the greater the chances you will have the trail to yourself. If the trail is a short little-paved walkway with interpretive signs, be prepared to share it. If it is one of the routes described in these guides, so rugged there is barely a trail, be prepared to survive on your own because you are likely the only one out that way.

The same can be said about the weather. Heat, rain, snow, and cold tend to filter out a fair amount of people. What's amazing about this is sometimes inclement weather will bring out the most unique views of a trail you will likely ever see. Now keep you in mind that you should add in a large degree of common sense. You don't want to have a slot canyon "all to yourself" in a thunderstorm or hike in the direct heat of a summer's day unless you are fully prepared and acclimated. Don't be stupid in your quest to have the place to yourself. The point here is, in general, I've found a rather obvious truth. If a guidebook says it's secret, it isn't. The more remote a place is, the longer the hike, the steeper the inclines, the more extreme the journey, these all act as filters to minimizing the crowd factor.

ENTRANCE FEES

If you are planning on traveling to several national parks in a given year, it makes sense to purchase the Annual Pass. This will save you money in the long run, especially if you buy it at the first National Park you visit. For example, the entrance fees at the Grand Canyon National Park and Zion National Park is $35 per park for a private vehicle, $30 for motorcycles, and $20 per person for an individual permit. Petrified Forest National Park has a $20 entrance fee for vehicles and $10 for motorcycle as well as walk/bike in permits. The Annual Pass is $80 and allows you entrance to all National Parks in the United States.

HOURS, RATES, AND AVAILABILITY

This travel guide describes over 200 places to eat and sleep. Every attempt has been made to provide as accurate information as possible. That said, when hours open are shown, they typically represent summer hours. Hotel rates were intentionally left off because they vary widely depending on the time one travels. In short, this travel guide should be used as a guideline only. Double check everything once you narrow down your own travel plans. We aren't responsible for any incorrect information in this book, but all the same, no one wants you to have a bad vacation, so double check.

Most of Arizona is on Mountain Standard Time year round and does not observe Daylight Savings Time. The biggest exception to this is within the Navajo Nation, which does honor Daylight Savings Time.

BEING PREPARED

Hiking in the Grand Circle can be highly rewarding. However, don't let the desert fool you. This is an extreme environment, and one shouldn't just venture out without some forethought and preparation. This section seems straightforward, but as the rangers at the Grand Canyon can attest to, there are literally dozens of people that venture out into the wilderness with nothing more than enthusiasm. Since enthusiasm alone can really put a damper on your hike, here are some tips to make your hikes safer and more enjoyable.

Fall Colors at Oak Creek Canyon

WATER

Rule of thumb; bring three quarts per person per day. Some folks prefer two 1.5-liter bottles; some find they can balance their day or backpacks out better with three 1.0-liter bottles. Make sure the bottles do not leak by turning them upside down to see if water comes out. If it's only a drip, it's still a problem.

Water is pretty heavy, but bringing more rather than less keeps you hydrated and allows you to go farther.

If you are traveling with small children, you will likely need to carry their water for them beyond one quart. Keep this in mind as you are packing.

CLOTHING

Bring layers as appropriate for the hike. This means if the temperatures are cooler when you are at rest; bring a layer or two to keep you warm. Windbreakers are great allies in keeping warmth in and cold out and are also lightweight. In really cold temps a good beanie helps as well, as some 15% of your body temperature is lost through your head. If it looks like rain, bring a waterproof version of that windbreaker.

In the heat, most folks go with the t-shirt and shorts, which is fine, but also bring a hat for shade. The heat can be oppressing, especially with no shade and that hat will definitely help. I also recommend a full brimmed hat over a baseball cap. This will provide more shade and definitely helps keep the back of your neck from getting sunburned.

In either hot or cold weather, bring another warm layer if you can, even if you don't think you will need it. This is your emergency backup layer should you find yourself having to spend the night in the wilderness for whatever reason. A windbreaker that can be rolled up or a long sleeve shirt can make a big difference if you find yourself facing the setting sun with nothing but a t-shirt and shorts on a summer trip. It's also a good thing to have on hand for others that may need some warmth when you don't.

BOOTS, TENNIS AND WATER SHOES

Most people will tend to go for their tennis shoes because they are comfortable and easier to lace up. That said, boots are preferred because they offer a lot more protection, especially around the ankles. Tennis shoes are great for flat surfaces, but boots are made for uneven terrain. It's like taking a sedan car tire on a 4WD road instead of an all-terrain tire. You wouldn't do it to your car, don't do it to your feet. Where a good boot and also, be the boot. Wear it in before you start your hiking adventures, so you don't get blisters.

If the trail involves some hiking in water, it really helps to have a pair of water shoes. They are lightweight and keep your boots dry. A dry boot makes for a happy hiker, whereas a wet boot can destroy your feet in short order.

DAYPACK

A decent no-nonsense day back to hold everything is essential. At the end of the day, you just want something that will last a long time. The more parts the pack has the more parts there are that can fail. Zipper quality is number one. Most otherwise solid daypacks fail because of the zipper.

Also, a little tip on the daypack. If you get one that zips like an upside-down U, put the zippers on one side or the other, not at the top. I have personally had a branch find its way between the two zippers at top and open the entire contents of the pack onto the trail. In my case, it opened on a brushy 30-degree incline I was scrambling up, and I watched my lunch and water roll downhill and out of sight forever.

OTHER GEAR

At this point, you have three quarts of water, a bunch of layers, some food, and no room for anything else right. Well, it can seem that way. What to bring is a balancing act. On the one hand, you want to be lightweight. The more stuff you have on your back, the more burdensome it will feel. On the other hand, you do want to be prepared. In the excellent book, *Climbing Ice by Yvon Chouinard*, he says something that is about as true a piece of advice I've ever heard in this context:

If you bring it, you will use it.

What this means is if you bring a sleeping bag, you will likely spend the night in it. If you bring a rope, you will likely use that rope. So, start with packing only what you need for the hike.

ESSENTIALS INCLUDE:

- Water and some food
- A hat
- Extra clothing as appropriate
- Sunscreen
- A map and possibly this trail guide (if you feel you will need it to navigate the trail)

On top of this, I would seriously consider also bringing:

- Some form of fire, a lighter, or fire starter of some kind
- Compass
- Small first aid kit, a whistle, and reflector mirror (for emergencies)
- A sharp knife
- Moleskin (for blisters)
- Ibuprofen (to help if you aren't acclimated to the heat)
- Water purification tablets
- Small flashlight or headlamp (I prefer Coast LED headlamps, heavy duty, long lasting, and powerful).
- Smart phone
- GPS device

It's hard to come up with a list that works under all conditions, and the above list is more geared towards summer hiking than winter, so adjust what you bring for cold, rain, or snow. Also, be sure to bring something fun, a little treat goes a long way and is much better appreciated on the trail.

Grand Canyon National Park

WHAT MAKES GRAND CANYON SPECIAL

For many, the Grand Canyon is the pinnacle of natural beauty. It hides nothing, standing before the viewer in its humble magnificence. Each glance brings a unique experience, each play of shadow by passing cloud a different lighting. It is a masterpiece, some 17 million years in the making, one of the seven natural wonders of the world, up with the likes of Mount Everest and the Great Barrier Reef. It is one of the most recognized and most visited natural landscapes on the planet.

What makes the Grand Canyon special is its non-boastful presence. It overwhelms the viewer but does not try. It amazes the eye and even soothes the soul simply by gazing at it, yet it has no mandate or imposition in approach. Each viewer can take in the Grand Canyon on his or her own terms, meet it wherever they are in their own life, and the view takes in all that baggage, weariness, and imposition and returns a warm sense of life. Considered a holy land by the original inhabitants of the area and a solemn bringer of peace by most that gaze upon it, the Grand Canyon simply is.

It is one of the few places that doesn't create an expectation to travel within it; one can gain much by simply viewing it, by scanning the horizon, peering down its canyon walls, watching the tiny thread of the Colorado and wonder as to how that little ribbon of water created all this. The Grand Canyon creates a sense of awe, an assertion of the divine, a wellness of being simply in gazing upon it. Whether during the heat of summer or the snowy accent of winter, whether from the light of sunset or the spotlit rays of sunshine pouring through the thunder clouds of a mid-day storm, each view gives comfort.

Think of the times in your life when you felt special. Those singular moments when everything went just so, that you risked the impossible and it actually worked in your favor. When you decided to do something not for yourself, but for someone else. You did that something even when it meant that only you would know of the benefit provided, an unconditional presence of selflessness. This is the Grand Canyon, providing inspiration and warm takeaways for 5 million visitors every year, giving of itself, inducing respectful wonder simply by its own manifestation. What makes the Grand Canyon special is that it gives; it gives openly, generously and without asking anything at all in return. You leave a better person having simply looked at it. Few places in this world can make this claim.

PLANNING YOUR VISIT

There are lots of things to do in Grand Canyon National Park, and there is something for everyone. Whether you are an active outdoor enthusiast or just want to look over the rim, it's recommended to spend at least one night in the park or in the nearby town of Tusayan, Arizona. Part of enjoying the Grand Canyon and most of the Southwest is slowing down to the pace of the land. Staying a night will allow you to wake up to one of the typically amazing mornings that the Grand Canyon has to offer.

GRAND CANYON IN 1-2 DAYS

If you only have a day or so, your best bet is to head to the South Rim. Start at the Grand Canyon Visitor Center to get your bearings or park at the Grand Canyon Village and walk to the rim for a view. Other recommended highlights in the village are the El Tovar Hotel, Yavapai Geology Museum, and Kolb Studio.

Sunlight after a heavy rain

From here you can drive east to Desert View and check out the Tusayan Museum and Ruin and the Desert View Watchtower. Along with this drive, the Grandview Point offers a slightly less crowded overlook and its possible to do a partial hike along Grandview Trail if you are looking to get a more immersive experience within the park. Another hiking recommendation is to hike a portion of the Rim Trail and take in the different views from the top. Hermit Road Shuttle is another convenient and fantastic option.

GRAND CANYON IN 3 DAYS

Beyond including everything mentioned in the above list, think about doing a planned or permitted hike to the bottom of the canyon from the South Rim. You can rent a mule and have it take you to Phantom Ranch or if you are in good physical condition, hike to the bottom and spend the night. The round trip for this trip is close to 18 miles round trip, which takes most folks about 8 hours or more to complete. Other hikes include the entire Grandview Trail and partially hiking all of the other formal trails, except Hermit's Rest, which requires extra time to get to. The Bright Angel Trail to Plateau Point is 6 miles round trip and is an excellent choice. You will feel like you've made it into the Grand Canyon without having to commit to the full hike to the Colorado River, plus the views are amazing here. Also, think about doing a half day or full day river rafting trip.

You can also think about enjoying the Grand Canyon from the North Rim and everything that side has to offer, including driving to Point Imperial and Cape Royal or staying at the Grand Canyon Lodge. Keep in mind that the North Rim closes in winter. The North Rim offers a quieter and more tranquil experience but requires a full six hours more driving to get there.

GRAND CANYON IN 4 + DAYS

If you want to spend more time just in the Grand Canyon, Side Trip 6 – "Rim to Rim and Beyond" offers a complete Grand Canyon itinerary to both the North and South rims with a couple of fun additions in between. That said, most people that spend more than 3 days in the park are here to do some extensive hiking or join in on a rafting trip. Full service guided rafting trips are offered and range from 3 – 18 days. Overnight camping in the Grand Canyon requires a backcountry permit. See the details on getting one above. Both get the visitor into an immersive experience in the park and is highly recommended if you have the time.

WHEN THE PARK IS OPEN

The South Rim is open year round. The North Rim is closed from mid October through mid May each year. The entrance fee to the park is $35 per vehicle for a seven day stay. This allows entry to either rim, when open.

THINGS TO DO - SOUTH RIM

The plus for having so many visitors is the park can support a larger variety of programs. The Park Service does a very good job at catering to the broad range of visitors to the area, from casual tourists who are content to step out of their car and look over the edge to hardcore whitewater river rafters, and from art enthusiasts to geocaching fans. There is something for just about everybody in the Grand Canyon. The below are a few of the highlighted activities.

Grand Canyon's Three Sets of Rocks

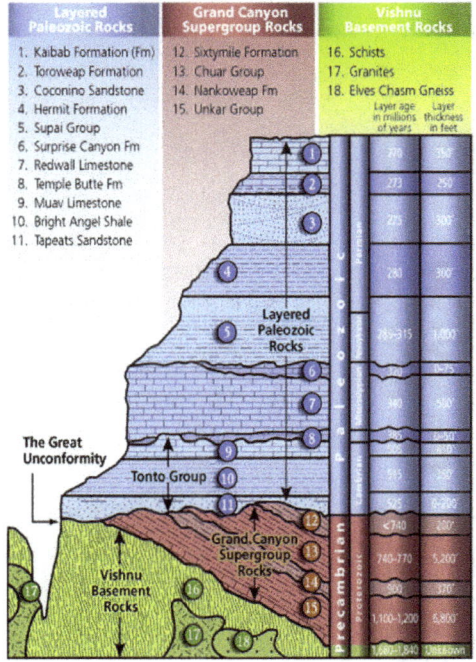

Grand Canyon geology

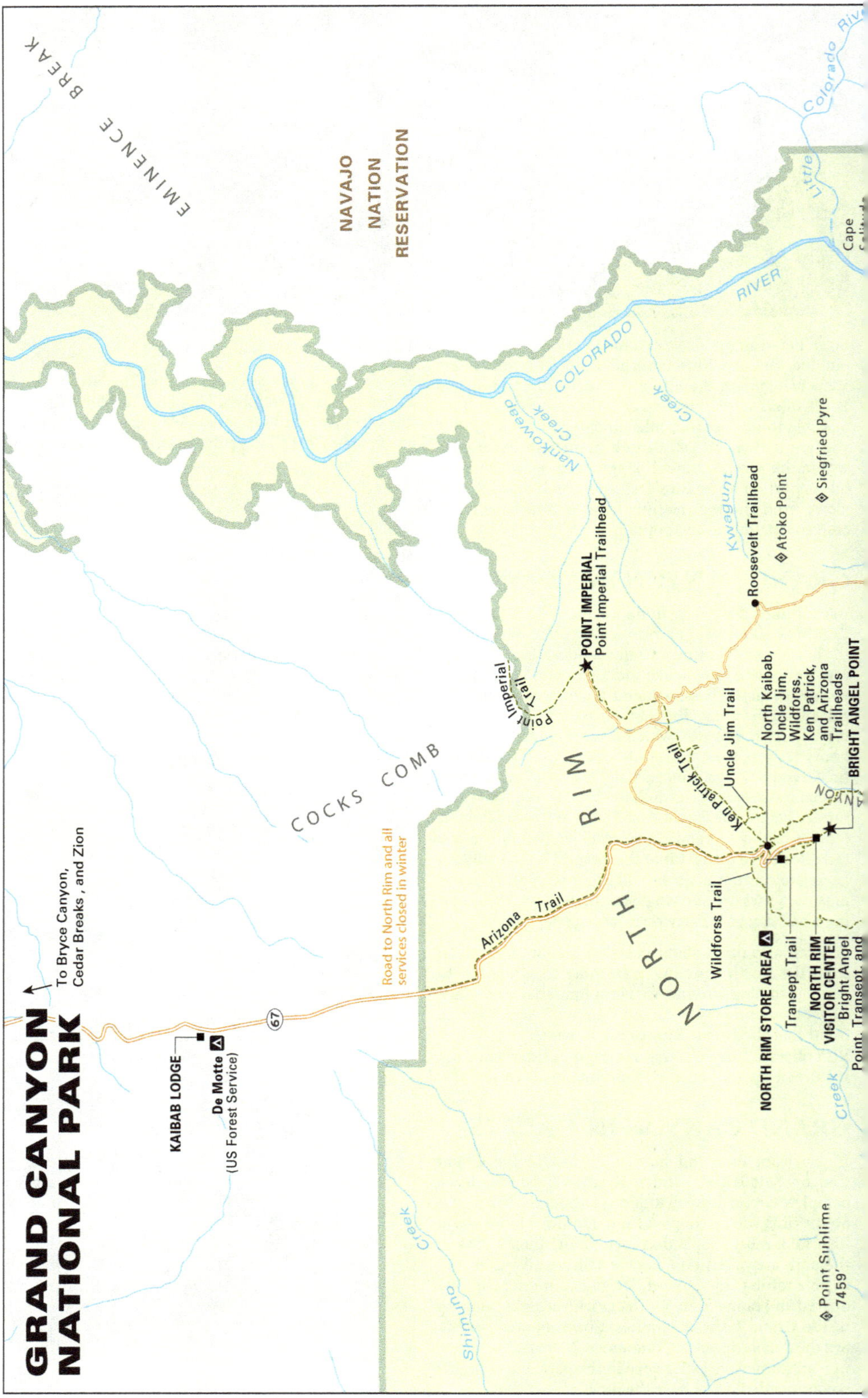

GRAND CANYON
NATIONAL PARK

EMINENCE BREAK

NAVAJO
NATION
RESERVATION

Colorado River
Little Colorado River

COLORADO RIVER

Nankoweap Creek

Kwagunt Creek

Cape
Solitude

◈ Siegfried Pyre

● Roosevelt Trailhead
◈ Atoko Point

★ POINT IMPERIAL
Point Imperial Trailhead

Point Imperial Trail

Uncle Jim Trail

Ken Patrick Trail

North Kaibab,
Uncle Jim,
Wildforss,
Ken Patrick,
and Arizona
Trailheads

BRIGHT ANGEL POINT

KAIBAB

COCKS COMB

NORTH RIM

Arizona Trail

Wildforss Trail

Transept Trail

NORTH RIM STORE AREA ▲

NORTH RIM
VISITOR CENTER

Bright Angel
Point, Transept, and

Road to North Rim and all
services closed in winter

67

KAIBAB LODGE

De Motte ▲
(US Forest Service)

To Bryce Canyon,
Cedar Breaks , and Zion

◈ Point Sublime
7459'

Shinumo Creek

Creek

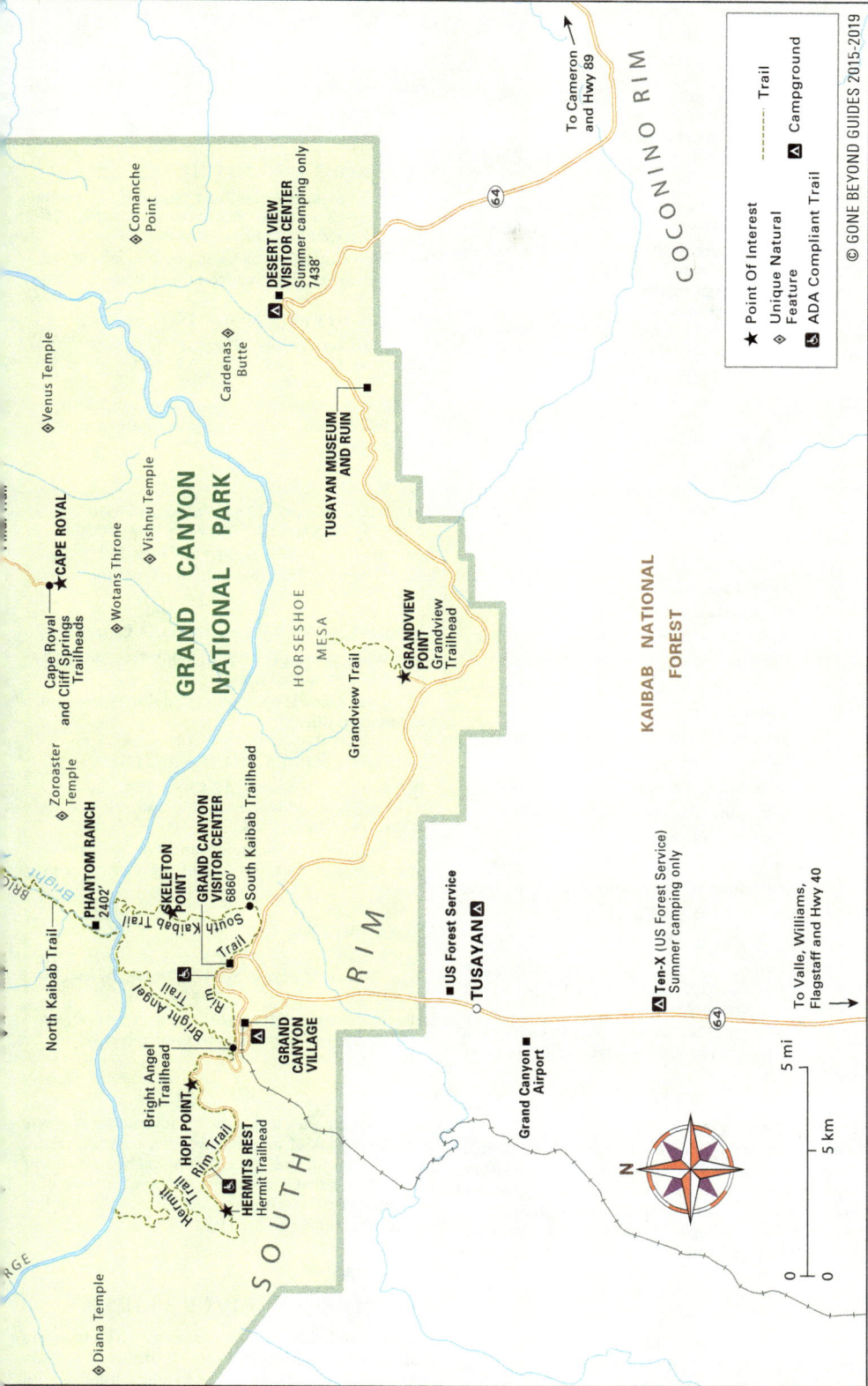

Map Legend

★ Point Of Interest
◈ Unique Natural Feature
♿ ADA Compliant Trail
- - - - - Trail
⚊ Campground

© GONE BEYOND GUIDES 2015-2019

GRAND CANYON NATIONAL PARK

KAIBAB NATIONAL FOREST

COCONINO RIM

SOUTH RIM

HORSESHOE MESA

To Cameron and Hwy 89

64

DESERT VIEW VISITOR CENTER
Summer camping only
7438'

◈ Comanche Point

◈ Venus Temple

Cardenas Butte

TUSAYAN MUSEUM AND RUIN

◈ Vishnu Temple

◈ Wotans Throne

CAPE ROYAL

Cape Royal and Cliff Springs Trailheads

Grandview Trail

GRANDVIEW POINT
Grandview Trailhead

◈ Zoroaster Temple

PHANTOM RANCH 2402'

North Kaibab Trail

Bright Angel

SKELETON POINT

GRAND CANYON VISITOR CENTER 6860'
South Kaibab Trailhead

South Kaibab Trail

■ US Forest Service

TUSAYAN ♿

Rim Trail

Bright Angel Trail

Bright Angel Trailhead

GRAND CANYON VILLAGE ♿

HOPI POINT ★

Rim Trail

HERMITS REST
Hermit Trailhead

Hermit Trail

◈ Diana Temple

Grand Canyon Airport ■

♿ **Ten-X** (US Forest Service)
Summer camping only

To Valle, Williams, Flagstaff and Hwy 40

64

N

0   5 mi
0   5 km

11

Choosing a Rafting Tour Operator

The commercial permit route is the quickest way to get a rafting trip within the Grand Canyon. Non-Commercial permits are handed out by a weighted lottery, and it typically takes years to get one unless you are extremely lucky.

There are so many river rafting operators and while the National Park Service is considering limiting the number of operators in the future, to date, finding one can be a weary exercise. Below are the ones that get consistently high marks, have been around the longest, and are recommended to explore further first: If you don't see one that may be a favorite, the full list is located here: https://www.nps.gov/grca/planyourvisit/river-concessioners.htm.

First, let's review some rafting jargon.

- Trips that begin at Lee's Ferry and end at Phantom Ranch are considered the top or upper half of the Canyon.
- Trips that begin at Phantom Ranch (Pipe Springs) are considered the lower or bottom half of the Canyon.
- Bottom also refers to trips that start from the bottom and go up river. Top refers to starting at the top and working downriver.
- Motor trips use a motor to get around the river and are the fastest way to see the Grand Canyon.
- Oar and dory trips are with smaller rafts, piloted by a single boatman, and offer a more intimate experience. The run is at the pace of the river and carried out without the sounds of a motor.
- Paddles are like an oar or dory trip except you get one of the paddles and get to play a part in the sport of rafting.

Western River Expeditions, Inc.

7258 Racquet Club Drive, Salt Lake City, UT 84121 (866) 904-1160, (801) 942-6669, FAX (801) 942-8514, www.westernriver.com

In business since 1958, motor only, full canyon and bottom half of canyon tours offered. Ability to create custom trips.

O.A.R.S. Grand Canyon, Inc.

P.O. Box 67, Angles Camp, CA 95222, (800) 346-6277, (209) 736-2924, FAX (209) 736-2902, www.oars.com/grandcanyon/

In business since 1969, oars and dories, full canyon, upper and lower half of canyon tours offered.

Outdoors Unlimited

6900 Townsend Winona Road, Flagstaff, AZ 86004 (800) 637-7238, (928) 526-4546, FAX (928) 526-6185, www.outdoorsunlimited.com

In business since 1969, oars and paddles, full canyon, upper and lower half of canyon tours offered.

Hatch River Expeditions, Inc.

5348 East Burris Lane, Flagstaff, AZ 86004, (800) 856-8966 (928) 526-4700 FAX (928) 526-4703, www.hatchriverexpeditions.com

In business since 1929, motor, oars, and custom trips, full canyon, upper and lower half of canyon tours offered.

Tour West, Inc.

P.O. Box 333, Orem, UT 84059, (800) 453-9107, (801) 225-0755, FAX (801) 225-7979, www.twriver.com

In business since 1969, motors and oars, full canyon, bottom, upper and lower half of canyon tours offered.

Grand Canyon Expeditions Company

P.O. Box 0, Kanab, UT 84741, (800) 544-2691, (435) 644-2691, www.gcex.com

In business since 1964, motors and dories, only full canyon tours offered.

Arizona River Runners, Inc.

P.O. Box 47788, Phoenix, AZ 85068-7788, (800) 477-7238, (602) 867-4866, FAX (602) 867-2174, www.raftarizona.com

In business since 1970, motors and oars, full canyon, bottom, upper and lower half of canyon tours offered.

Canyoneers, Inc.

P.O. Box 2997, Flagstaff, AZ 86003, (800) 525-0924, (928) 526-0924, FAX (928) 527-9398, www.canyoneers.com

In business since 1936, motors and oars, full canyon, upper and lower half of canyon tours offered.

River Rafting

Rafting down the Colorado is not only a popular activity, for many it is a bucket list item, something they have to do before they head on to the big national park in the sky. As a result, don't expect to show up and get on the river. Rafting is by permit only in the Grand Canyon and, depending on the activity, can take one to two years to receive a permit. The Park has made an effort to streamline the types of trips available and the permitting process for each.

That said, rafting down the Colorado through the Grand Canyon is truly a defining moment in anyone's life. It is an experience that moves beyond words, resets your definitions of awe and wonder, brings a restful peace to the soul and at times puts you in moments of unholy terror that—on getting to the other side of—help remind you just how awesome it is to be alive. It is worth the planning and the wait.

ONE DAY
COMMERCIAL RIVER TRIPS:

Half day and full day smooth water river trips are available through park concessionaire Colorado River Discovery or from the vendors listed above.

You can purchase tickets at any of the park's lodges. The smooth water river trips are the only trips that do not require a permit and as the trip never encounters rapids, is open to all ages from four years old and up.

While these trips are gentle and without the excitement of white water, they are a wonderful way to see the park and are highly recommended. Bring food and water, sunscreen, a hat and, of course, your camera. On a side note about the camera, yes, it's okay to bring a camera on the trip that isn't waterproof as it is unlikely you will get wet. That said, use caution. In the summer, you won't need a towel as in the heat of the day you will dry off pretty quickly. In the spring and cooler seasons, bring layers. As you will be entering at the Glen Canyon Dam, which is inside the protection of Homeland Security, you will be checked for weapons, including pepper spray and pocket knives. These will not be allowed, so don't bring them.

Transportation from the lodge to the Dam is included.

3- TO 18-DAY
COMMERCIAL RIVER TRIPS

For those who are looking for whitewater rapids and adventure, use the list of river concessionaires on previous page that provide full service guided trips. Each company offers its own suite of trips, and many cater to the different experiences visitors are looking for. Trips can last for as little as a few days to up to 18 days.

The upside of a guided trip is that, first and foremost, you don't need to become an expert in whitewater rafting. The domain of the rafter is a world unto itself. They have their own language, and while they are a friendly, tightly knitted group, it's an investment of time and money to enter their world and walk, err—paddle—among them. A guided trip comes with the security that you are riding down the Colorado with an expert at the helm.

Plus, the thoughts of where to camp, what to eat, and even where to do your business are pretty much taken care of for you. The downside is the cost and the fact that reservations need to be made one to two years in advance.

Details on what trips are offered, in what type of raft, duration, and other amenities are numerous. The best place to start is the Grand Canyon NPS page, which lists all of the river concessionaires. Go to: http://www.nps.gov/grca/planyourvisit/river-concessioners.htm

2- TO 5-DAY
NONCOMMERCIAL RIVER TRIPS

Permits are available to the general public starting one year in advance and are assigned on a first come, first served basis. Two non-commercial permits are authorized each day launching from Diamond Creek. Each trip is limited to a maximum of 16 people. There is no fee for the permits, and they can be obtained by filling out a permit application and mailing it to the NPS permits department. While the NPS does not charge a fee for the permit, the Hualapai Tribe does charge a fee for crossing their land.

The permit can be found by going to http://www.nps.gov/grca/planyourvisit/upload/Diamond_Creek_Application.pdf

You can also call directly: (800) 959-9164, fax (928) 638-7843.

As mentioned above, you are crossing both National Park Service land and Hualapai tribal land. Hualapai means "people of the tall trees" in reference to the Ponderosa Pine. This small community of about 2000 individuals primarily bases its economy on tourism. One way they do that is to charge a fee for each person (including drivers) and each vehicle traveling Diamond Creek Road, which they own. Cost is $100 for each person and vehicle, (example: 16 passengers, 2 drivers,

Shooting the Rapids down the Colorado

and 2 vehicles will cost $1800 total). Camping on the south side of the river (river left) above the high-water mark will also require a permit from the Hualapai. More information can be had by calling the Hualapai directly at (928) 769-2219.

The NPS permits authorize you and your group to travel for 2 to 5 days from Diamond Creek in the Lower Gorge of the Colorado River. This 52-mile (84 km) section is spectacular and includes both smooth water and some decent rapids to shoot as well as culturally significant areas. River users are asked to treat these cultural areas with respect so that future generations can enjoy them. Camping is limited but is free on the north side (river right).

One word of note: acceptance. The river has changed since the days of Powell. You will be sharing the river with many other users, especially at the launch and take-out areas. You will find motorized upstream and downstream travel from Lake Mead and even see a helicopter or two. There will be moments that are all yours, but there will also be moments that are shared with others.

12- TO 25-DAY
14 ## NONCOMMERCIAL RIVER TRIPS

This type of self-guided river trip travels among the rugged section between Lees Ferry to Diamond Creek and is for those fully experienced in river rafting. The permits are made available through a weighted lottery. For more information, start here: http://www.nps.gov/grca/planyourvisit/overview-lees-ferry-diamond-ck.htm.

HIKING SOUTH RIM

There are many hiking trails within the South Rim of the Grand Canyon. Hikes range from pleasant to steep, and all offer exceptional views. Exploring the canyon from the rim is a very nice way to enjoy the canyon's scenery if you are looking for a non-strenuous hike. Bright Angel Trail is much steeper but gets you down further into the canyon itself. Backpacking is also available via permit.

While you can go down to the river and back in one day, it is an all-day hike and is typically not recommended. The hike down and back up is often underestimated. At the rim, it is pleasantly cool, and the distance perception is heavily skewed. Objects don't look that far away and look smaller than they really are. It is only when hikers get to the bottom of the river that they fully understand the enormity of the Grand Canyon. At the river's edge, it is often very hot, and while the water looks tempting, it could carry you away if you get in it, so it doesn't offer the reprieve you hoped to get. From the river's bottom, the rim is a never-ending uphill journey that you will likely feel for a day or so afterward. If you do go, start early, and bring lots of water and pleasant little comfort foods and drinks to help you enjoy the journey.

RIM TRAIL

Easy – (13.0 mi / 21.0 km), one way, time varies on the route taken, elev. Δ: 200 ft / 61m, trailhead at viewpoint at Grand Canyon Village and along Hermit Road

The Rim Trail is great for just strolling in the Grand Canyon with the view slowly changing before you. The trail starts at the South Kaibab Trailhead and extends to Hermit's Rest. It can be picked up from any overlook, and by utilizing the shuttle system, one can pick up the trail and drop off it with a great deal of convenience. The trail is mostly paved and well-traveled. For quieter moments, try walking it in tune to the sunrise or meander along its route in the late afternoon into dusk.

BRIGHT ANGEL TRAIL

Strenuous – (12.0 mi / 19.3 km to Plateau Point), round trip, allow 5-8 hours, elev. Δ: 3,039 ft / 926 m, trailhead west of Bright Angel Lodge

Strenuous – (17.6 mi / 28.3 km to Colorado River), round trip, allow 5-8 hours, elev. Δ: 4,888 ft / 1,490 m, trailhead west of Bright Angel Lodge

Bright Angel is a very well-defined trail that ultimately leads to the Colorado River itself. While it is possible to do this in one day, as mentioned above, this is an all-day hike and not for the casual hiker. The thing to realize about Bright Angel is it is very inviting and gives wonderful views as you immerse yourself into the depths of the canyon. However, the trail is steep, which gives you the impression that you are "cooking with gas" as you travel downward. It is only on the return that you realize just how steep this trail is. Allow twice as much time for the return trip and bring twice as much water for this hot, exposed trail.

For groups with small children, going to the first switchback offers a pleasant experience without subjecting little feet to the steeper bits just ahead. For those not looking to do a full 12-mile (19 km) hike,

Bright Angel Trail

One of the many tranquil moments on the Colorado

going to Indian Gardens offers great views and a nice stopping point before turning around. There is water to refill your canteen and even a ranger on duty most of the time. Indian Gardens is 9 miles (14.5 km) round trip. If you decide to go the 1.5 miles (2.4 km) farther to Plateau Point, you won't be disappointed. This fairly level trail takes you to a nice viewpoint of the Colorado River and surrounding canyon. This is a great spot to get a good understanding of the immensity, grandeur, and beauty of the Grand Canyon. You'll see how far you've traveled, and upon looking at the river below, you'll see how far you would still need to go, which is humbling.

SOUTH KAIBAB TRAIL

Strenuous – (6.0 mi / 9.7 km to Skeleton Point), round trip, allow 4 -5 hours, elev. Δ: 2,011 ft / 613 m, trailhead at Yaki Point off Desert View Drive

Strenuous – (12.0 mi / 19.3 km to Colorado River), round trip, allow 8 -10 hours, elev. Δ: 4,800 ft / 1,463 m,

From South Rim to Phantom Ranch: 6.9 mi / 11.1 km, to North Rim: 20.9 mi / 33.6 km

It is possible to take the South Kaibab Trail to the river and even connect over to Bright Angel, but most people do this as a multi-day trip due to the strenuous nature of the journey. Just like Bright Angel Trail, South Kaibab is steep, offers incredible views, and is very exposed. The first destination along the trail is Ooh-Aah Point, which offers an expansive view of the canyon and is less than 2 miles (3.2 km) round trip.

By the way, Ooh-Aah Point gets its name from an uncommon, nearly prehistoric language that is hotly debated by linguists as to its exact meaning. This is a rough translation, but most agree that "Ooh-Aah" means either "Wow!" or "The-Place-of-Amazing-Selfie-with-View-of-Grand-Canyon-About-One-Mile-From-Rim." You decide which translation works best for you.

There is a restroom at Cedar Ridge, but that is the extent of the facilities on the South Kaibab Trail. Cedar Ridge is about 1.5 miles (2.4 km) from the rim. Skeleton Point offers great views of the river and the surrounding area and is the recommended turnaround for day hikers.

On the question of South Kaibab versus Bright Angel, South Kaibab's fewer amenities means it is slightly less traveled than Bright Angel. That said there are very few hikers on these trails relative to the vast number of people looking over the canyon's edge at the rim. If you are looking to escape into your own personal experience of the canyon, either trail will get you there.

HERMIT TRAIL

Strenuous – (17.8 mi / 28.6 km to Colorado River), round trip, allow 8-12 hours, elev. Δ: 4,340 ft / 1,323 m, trailhead at Hermits Rest

The Hermit Trail begins at Hermit's Rest and, like all the trails described here, is accessed via shuttle. This trail is great for many reasons if you are an experienced hiker looking for something a little more rugged. It was originally built by horse thieves during the nineteenth century and is today considered a threshold trail, which means the National Park doesn't actively maintain it. There is water to be found along the trail, but it needs to be treated. Some of the trail has rutted out in areas and, in some cases, rock slides covering the trail require one to do a little scrambling to navigate around them. The point here is, if you are an experienced hiker, the Hermit Trail offers just about everything, including an endpoint worthy of the journey. It is 8.9 miles (14 km) down to the river, but if you are able to make it, you are rewarded with Hermit Rapids, perhaps the strongest hydraulics and biggest waves of any set of rapids in the canyon. The Hermit Rapids help to motivate any hiker and do not disappoint. You hear them before you see them and in seeing them, there is nothing but gushing awe and respect.

It cannot be overstated that this is a trail to be taken seriously. Plan—bring the right gear, including plenty of food and water, and start early if you do plan to take on this all-day hike. There is a primitive campground at the river's edge, and most folks do this as an overnight trip.

GRANDVIEW TRAIL

Strenuous – (6.0 mi / 9.7 km to Horseshoe Mesa / Toilet Junction), round trip, allow 4-5 hours, elev. Δ: 2,500 ft / 762 m, trailhead at Grandview Point along Desert View Drive

Grandview is one of the quickest ways to get down into the canyon. It is very steep in some places and during the winter is dangerously icy. Crampons or some other means of traction for your footwear is required in winter. The trail offers deep views into the canyon as well as ruins of historic mining structures. Another feature of the trail is the placement of log "cribs" in some of the vertical sections of the Kaibab/Toroweap section. Many of these log supports were swept away during a landslide in the winter of 2005, but there are a few examples of these historical trail structures still around.

The Grandview Trail is not as well maintained as either Bright Angel or South Kaibab Trails. There are steep drop-offs in some areas. Use caution when hiking this trail.

MULE TRIPS

The mule rides offered by park concessionaire Xanterra are a classic way of seeing the Grand Canyon. The day trips offered change seasonally, and new offerings open up at the whim of the concessionaire. Most rides are typically 3-hour, 4-mile (6.4 km) rides. You don't need prior experience riding a mule, and your tour will include a fair amount of interesting interpretation about the geology and human history along the trail.

Overnight tours are also offered, and this ride is on par with rafting down the Colorado River in terms of generating incredible memories. You will ride your mule to Phantom Ranch located near the river. Lunch is provided, and the steak dinner at the ranch is hearty and very welcome after the day's journey. As with the day trips, the overnight trips are full of interpretive narration on nearly all aspects of the park. The overnight trip to Phantom Ranch has been a high-water mark for many visitors.

The downsides to the mule trips are the expense and the fact that you need to reserve the event well in advance. There is a wait list for day-before cancellations; however, the chances of people canceling are very slim.

This is a great place to work for a mule

For the 2017 season, it cost $588.43 for one person or $1027.86 for two to ride a mule to Phantom Ranch and spend the night there.

Mule rides from the South Rim can be reserved through: Xanterra Parks & Resorts, (303) 297-2757, (888) 297-2757

VIRTUAL CACHING

For those who have never heard of this, virtual caching is the delightful marriage of treasure hunting and technology. Specifically, a "cache" is a term that denotes a bunch of stuff stowed somewhere in the wilderness. With virtual caching, a visitor uses his or her GPS system to find the cache. The reward is in part the journey and in part finding the cache, which— being virtual—means what you find is a cool location.

The National Park Service has done a wonderful job of offering an interesting way to explore the park.

You will need a GPS device (or smartphone with GPS), the park map, which is located inside the park's official newspaper, and a copy of the instruction for their EarthCache Program. The instructions can be picked up at the Grand Canyon Visitor Center, where different coordinates are listed. Input the coordinates into your GPS device and take the shuttle or walk to the various destinations. None of the virtual caching is done off trail; everything can be found on the paved rim of the park and on the trails. Along the way, the instruction sheet acts as an educational pamphlet on different aspects of the park. Virtual caching is a cool way to discover new things about the park, and if you are navigationally challenged, perhaps a way of discovering a bit about yourself as well!

You will need to keep a record of all your coordinates, which will be necessary to solve the final clue. It takes about 4–6 hours to complete this puzzle, and the tour will take you over a good deal of the park along the way. You can, in the end, receive a certificate of completion. See the visitor center for more details.

HOPI HOUSE

Built in 1904 by architect Mary Colter, the Hopi House houses native crafts for sale in a building in the Hopi style.

GRAND CANYON RAILWAY

The Grand Canyon Railway is an excellent way to get to the Grand Canyon. The train starts in Williams and ends at the Grand Canyon Village. Run by Xanterra Resorts, the train offers a taste of the old west with mock train robberies and refurbished period cars. The train takes about 2 hours and 15 minutes each way. They have many offerings to choose, including lodging packages. For more information call (800) 843-8724.

KOLB STUDIO

Art gallery, photo gallery, bookstore and place of historical interest run by the Grand Canyon Association. The studio is near the Bright Angel Lodge.

EL TOVAR HOTEL

Built in 1905, this hotel is on the National Register of Historic Places. It is noted for its Arts and Crafts as well as Mission style interior and exterior and is an incredible example of early twentieth century National Park lodge architecture.

YAVAPAI GEOLOGY MUSEUM

A great place to learn everything you wanted to know about the geology of the Grand Canyon. Many exhibits, three-dimensional models, and photographs along with the outdoor nature and geology "Trail of Time" where each meter traveled on the trail represents one million years of the geology of the Grand Canyon. If you think about it, the "Trail of Time" took about 2 billion years to make, so it is well worth seeing.

TUSAYAN RUIN AND MUSEUM

The Tusayan Pueblo Ruins allow you to get a close look at an Ancestral Puebloan village ruins along a relatively flat 1-mile trail. The accompanying museum has supporting exhibits and is open from 9am – 5pm in the summer months. There is also a small bookstore inside the museum.

DESERT VIEW WATCHTOWER

Located on the East Rim of the park, the four-story, 70-foot-high (21m) stone building was built in 1932 by Fred Harvey Architect Mary Colter. Mary Colter designed many of the buildings in the Grand Canyon, including Hopi House, Lookout Studio, Bright Angel Lodge, the Phantom Ranch buildings, and Hermit's Rest (but not El Tovar Lodge). Patterned after the Pueblo kivas and watchtowers, the Watchtower has a unique touch in its design.

SKYWALK

The Skywalk is managed by the Hualapai Tribe and is located on their tribal lands. It is a horseshoe-shaped walkway securely bolted into the canyon walls such that is juts out over the canyon itself. With the floors and sides made of glass, the structure juts out about 70 feet (21m) from the canyon rim, giving the feeling that you are suspended in air over the canyon. It is one of the most famous attractions within the western portion of the Grand Canyon. This attraction is about a 4 hour drive from the Grand Canyon Village. There is a separate fee for this attraction. Skywalk reservations: 1-888-868-9378 or 1-928-769-2636.

Kolb Studio

DRIVING AROUND THE SOUTH RIM

Like Zion NP and Bryce NP, Grand Canyon receives too many visitors to make driving around the park practical. The NPS offers a fairly robust shuttle system to get you around, and it is not only highly recommended to use the shuttle system; it is the only method year-round for some roads and during peak season for others.

In general, the shuttle system is divided into two loops, the Village Route and Kaibab Rim Route. The Village Route goes to the west and stops at Mather Campground, Trailer Village, Market Plaza, Grand Canyon Visitor Center, Shrine of the Ages, Train Depot, Bright Angel Lodge and Trailhead, and Maswik Lodge. The Village Route also stops at the Hermit's Rest Transfer, which is where you pick up the Hermit's Rest shuttle during peak season.

The Kaibab Route winds to the east and stops at the Grand Canyon Visitor Center, South Kaibab Trailhead, Yaki Point, Pipe Creek Vista, Mather Point, and Yavapai Geology Museum.

The Hermit Road Shuttle is a great way to see the western side of the park. It offers stops at multiple overlooks, including Hermits Rest, Pima, Mohave, and Powell Points You can drive on Hermit Road during the winter months. To the east, the Desert View Road is a wonderful drive that ultimately takes you to the Desert View Wattchtower and the East Rim of the Grand Canyon.

THINGS TO DO - NORTH RIM

If forty is the new twenty, then the North Rim of the Grand Canyon is the new South Rim. It is harder to get to, not open year-round and, as a result, it has an energy of peace, tranquility, and overall slowness of pace. The North Rim gets a mere 10 percent of the overall visitor traffic to the Grand Canyon, offering more chances to feel you have the park to yourself. On the South Rim, there are more amenities, and it is open year-round; however, if you are going during peak season, the North Rim becomes an attractive option if you aren't prepared to share your experience with literally bus loads of fellow visitors. It is the view less photographed, the road less traveled and the experience less shared, but it is still everything the Grand Canyon is known for, just from the other side of the river.

There are a couple of other things to know about the North Rim. It is at a higher elevation, ranging from 8000 to 8800 feet (2438 to 2682m). This is 1000 to 1800 feet higher than the South Rim. This means the weather will be cooler and the snow deeper, hence the closure of the park in winter. The other thing to note is fewer trails are going into the canyon on the North Rim and the only one going to the river is longer and thus more strenuous because of the elevation gain.

HIKING NORTH RIM

BRIGHT ANGEL POINT TRAIL

Easy – (0.5 mi / 0.8 km), round trip, allow 30 minutes, elev. Δ: 200 ft / 61m, trailhead near visitor center

Bright Angel Point is a nice walk from Grand Canyon Lodge and nearby visitor center. There are examples of marine fossils within the rocks along the way. Be sure to pick a park brochure, which shows the location of the fossils and gives a good historical back story of the lodge and this historic trail.

TRANSEPT TRAIL

18

Easy – (3.0 mi / 4.8 km), round trip, allow 1 - 2 hours, elev. Δ: 150 ft / 46 m, trailhead near North Rim Lodge

The Transept Trail starts at the Grand Canyon Lodge and follows the rim of the canyon to the North Rim Campground. There are great views along the way.

KEN PATRICK TRAIL

Strenuous – (10.0 mi / 16.0 km), one way, 5 - 6 hours, elev. Δ: 600 ft / 183 m, trailhead north of visitor center at North Kaibab Trailhead

The Ken Patrick Trail is named after a ranger killed in the line of duty. He is buried within the Grand Canyon, but worked at Point Reyes National Seashore and was killed by poachers in 1973.

This there and back trail is best accomplished with two cars. Starting from the North Kaibab Trailhead, the Ken Patrick Trail starts off clearly for the first 2 ½ miles but can become very difficult to find after reaching the Old Bright Angel Trail signpost. If you are an experienced hiker and this sounds appealing, simply keep north, and don't go too far from the rim. Once you pick up the Cape Royal Road, the trail becomes easier to find and maintains close to the rim all the way to Point Imperial.

UNCLE JIM TRAIL

Moderate – (5.0 mi / 8.0 km), round trip, allow 2 - 3 hours, elev. Δ: 100 ft / 30 m, trailhead north of visitor center at North Kaibab Trailhead

This trail starts from the same parking lot as the North Kaibab Trailhead and meanders through the Kaibab Plateau forest to Uncle Jim's Point, which overlooks Bright Angel, Roaring Springs, and an overall spectacular view of the canyon.

BRIDLE TRAIL

Easy – (1.2 mi / 2.0 km), one way, allow 1 hour, elev. Δ: 161 ft / 49m, trailheads at viewpoint at North Rim Lodge and at North Kaibab Trailhead

A gentle trail that parallels the road from the Grand Canyon Lodge to the North Kaibab Trailhead. The Bridle Trail is a great after dinner hike to take in the peace of the canyon.

NORTH KAIBAB TRAIL

Strenuous – (14.0 mi / 22.5 km), one way, allow 6-10 hours, elev. Δ: 5,780 ft / 1,762 m, trailhead north of visitor center at North Kaibab Trailhead

Note that while the total distance to the river is shown, it does not include the distance back. This is because the total distance to the Colorado River and back is 28 miles and is definitely not recommended as a day hike. Folks do use the North Kaibab Trail as the starting point for a rim-to-rim hike, primarily because the trip for the longer leg of the two sides is downhill if you start on from the North Rim.

Lower Ribbon Falls

Panorama from North Rim

The North Kaibab Trail is special because it starts at a higher elevation than either South Kaibab or Bright Angel trails. The 1000-foot increase in elevation is such that a hike down the North Kaibab Trail to the Colorado River means you will pass through every ecosystem found between Canada and Mexico. It is the least visited of the maintained trails and is also the most strenuous. It is definitely a serious day hike at 28 miles (45 km) round trip and is typically done as a backpacking trip. There are a few restroom facilities and seasonal water available, though the water will need to be treated.

The trail heads steeply down at first until it flattens out a bit as you enter into the base of Bright Angel Canyon. At 5.0 miles (8.0 km), you encounter Roaring Springs, which is a short side trip that is easily visible from the trail. Here you can see water coming directly out of the cliff, typically with a nice flow, creating a little island of moss and ferns within the desert. Roaring Springs flows into Bright Angel Creek as you continue down the trail. This is an important water source, delivering the drinking water for every visitor within Grand Canyon NP. If you make it to the Colorado River, you can see the pipe going over the river on the underside of Bright Angel Trail's Silver Bridge.

Just a little farther down at 5.4 miles (8.7 km) is a structure known as the Pumphouse Residence or Aiken Residence. From 1973 to 2006, Bruce Aiken was an artist, NP employee, and pump master, overseeing the water supply for the park. He and his wife Mary raised three children at the canyon bottom, and lucky hikers were greeted with lemonade from the children from time to time. Aiken's work reflects a fine-tuned harmony with the area of the Grand Canyon. Working mainly in oil, the light, balance, and overall portrayal of rock and water are testimonies to living within the Grand Canyon, raising a family, and experiencing nearly each day of one's life for 33 years inside its walls.

Another treasure on the North Kaibab is Ribbon Falls at 8.5 miles (13.7 km). It is a little grotto in the desert cascading gently on the west side of Bright Angel Creek. It is a great place to get out of the heat of the day, which can be intense in the summer. Between the Cottonwood

Campground and Bright Angel Campground, you enter the Inner Gorge, which is a narrow canyon of the 2 billion-year-old Vishnu Schist. If you make it this far, you are now walking on rock roughly half as old as the earth itself. You can connect to either the South Kaibab or Bright Angel Trail over the two bridges that cross the Colorado at the canyon bottom.

At this point, you may be thinking North Kaibab is a gem of a trail, (which it is), and thus wondering if you could do a rim-to-rim adventure. The good news is you can. Trans Canyon Shuttle offers two rim-to-rim shuttles daily (go to http://www.trans-canyonshuttle.com for more info). The not-so-good news is getting reservations at one of the primitive campgrounds is a challenge. Also, the shuttles depart early morning and early afternoon, so factor in an overnight stay at the opposing rim or hoofing it out to make the shuttle on the last day.

19

WIDFORSS TRAIL

Strenuous – (10.0 mi / 16.0 km), round trip allow 4 – 5 hours, elev. Δ: 400 ft / 122 m, trailhead north of visitor center west of North Kaibab Trailhead

The Widforss Trail may just be the longest interpretative trail in the entire Grand Circle. Be sure to pick up a brochure at the trailhead. The trail hugs the canyon rim for the first half of the hike and then heads into a forested area to end at Widforss Point. The expansiveness of the Grand Canyon from this vista is impressive, and it was a favorite of Gunnar Widforss, an early twentieth-century landscape artist.

ARIZONA TRAIL

Strenuous – (12.6 mi / 20.3 km), one way, allow 5 - 6 hours, trailheads at North Kaibab trailhead and Kaibab National Forest boundary

The Arizona Trail is an 800-mile adventure that starts in Mexico and heads northward until it ends in Utah. A part of the trail leverages the existing north and south rim to rim trails of Grand Canyon NP. From the North Kaibab Trail, it continues through the park for another 10 miles before hitting the park's boundary. This portion roughly follows Highway 67, traveling through the forest canopy and Harvey Meadow.

GRAND CANYON VILLAGE

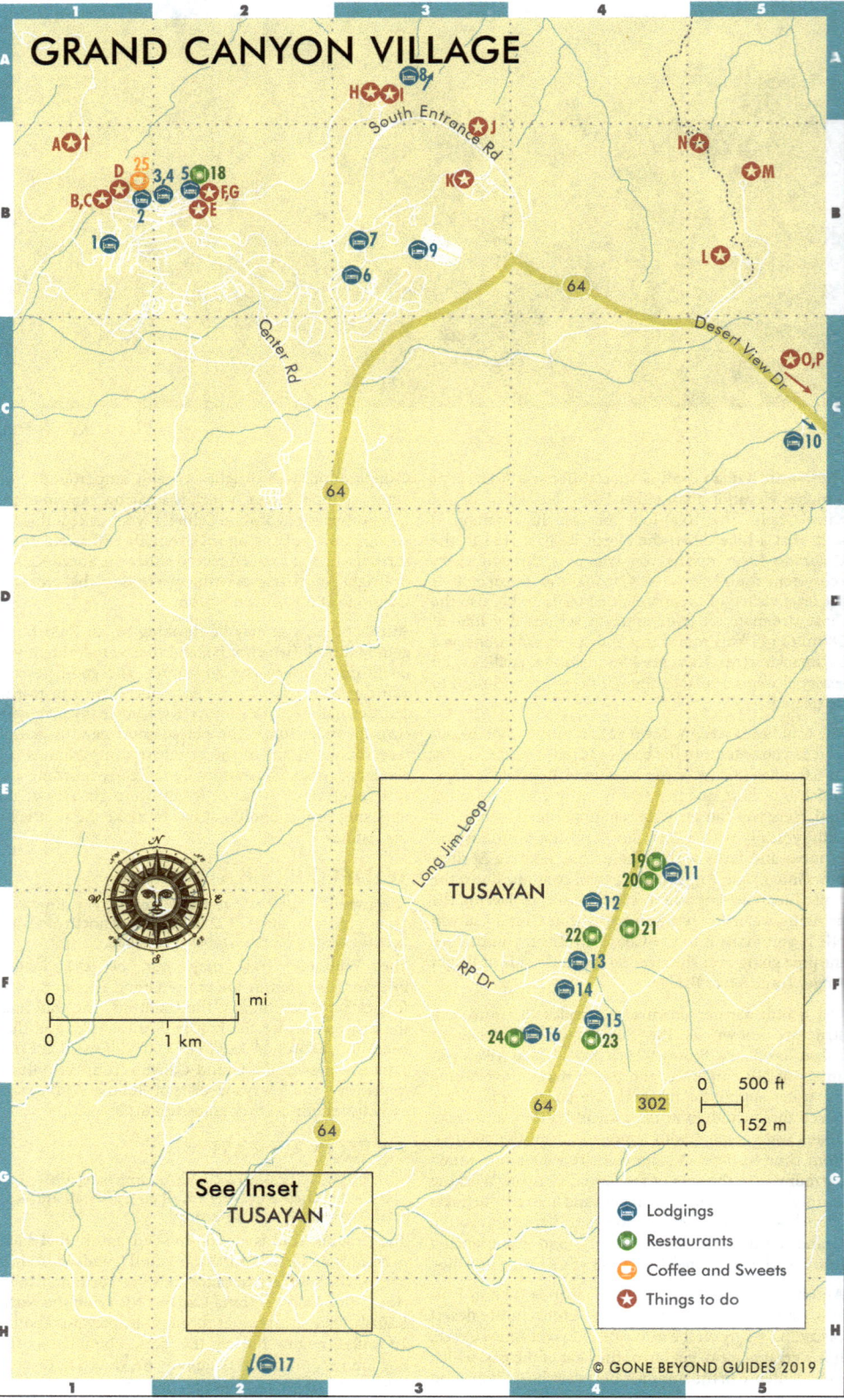

A ☆ ↑

D 25
B,C ☆ 3,4 5 18
2 F,G
E ☆

1

H ☆ ☆ I ⌂ 8
South Entrance Rd
J ☆

K ☆

7
9
6

N ☆

M ☆

L ☆

64

Desert View Dr

O,P ☆

10

Center Rd

64

20

TUSAYAN

Long Jim Loop

19
20 11
12
RP Dr
22 21
13
14
24 16 15
23

64
302

500 ft

0   1 mi

0   1 km

See Inset
TUSAYAN

64

Lodgings
Restaurants
Coffee and Sweets
Things to do

17

© GONE BEYOND GUIDES 2019

View of Grand Canyon from the South Rim

POINT IMPERIAL TRAIL

Easy – (4.0 mi / 6.4 km), round trip, allow 1.5 - 2 hours, elev. Δ: negligible, trailhead at the end of Point Imperial Road

This is an easy hike through an area recovering from a wildfire in 2000 and is a great way to take in the tenacity of nature recovering from devastation. On the way, one will see young Aspens and innocent wildflowers starting anew from the aftermath of the fire. This is a great hike for a sunrise at Point Imperial.

ROOSEVELT POINT TRAIL

Easy – (0.2 mi / 0.3 km), round trip, allow 30 minutes, elev. Δ: negligible, trailhead at Cape Royal Road

More of a pleasant walk than a hike, this little ditty leads to a nice bench with great views of the canyon.

CAPE FINAL TRAIL

Easy – (4.0 mi / 6.4 km), round trip, allow 1.5 - 2 hours, elev. Δ: 150 ft / 46 m, trailhead at Cape Royal Road

An easy trail that ends at one of the higher elevation views of the Grand Canyon at Cape Final. As this trail is not often used, it provides good promise if you are looking for a secluded and peaceful hike. Cape Final is at 7850 feet. Be careful if you decide to go onto the ledge's edge, it's a long way down.

CAPE ROYAL TRAIL

Easy – (0.6 mi / 1.0 km), round trip, allow 30 minutes, elev. Δ: 40 ft / 12 m, trailhead at the end of Cape Royal Road

An easy, flat walk that allows views of Angels Window arch, the Colorado River, and if you look through the arch at the right angle, you can see both at the same time! Great photo opportunity and easy to access. There are interpretative markers along the way.

GRAND CANYON VILLAGE - SOUTH RIM

Lodging and Camping

1 Maswik Lodge..B1
2 Bright Angel Lodge..B1
3 Thunderbird Lodge..B2
4 Kachina Lodge...B2
5 El Tovar..B2
6 Mather Campground..B3
7 Yavapai Lodge..B3
8 Phantom Ranch...A3
9 Trailer Village RV Park....................................B3
10 Desert View Campground...............................C5
11 Camper Village..E4
12 Grand Canyon Plaza Hotel.............................F4
13 Red Feather Lodge..F4
14 Holiday Inn Express..F4
15 The Grand Hotel at the Grand Canyon.........F4
16 Best Western Premier Grand Canyon...........F4
17 TenX Campground..H2

Restaurants

18 El Tovar Dining Room.....................................B2
19 We Cook Pizza and Pasta................................E4
20 Yippee-Ei-O! Steakhouse................................E4
21 Big E Steakhouse & Saloon.............................F4
22 Plaza Bonita...F4
23 Canyon Star Steakhouse and Saloon.............F4
24 The Coronado Room...F4

Coffee and Sweets

25 Bright Angel Fountain......................................B1

Things To Do

A Hermit Road Shuttle Bus Route.....................B1
B Bright Angel Trailhead.....................................B1
C Rim Trail...B1
D Kolb Studio...B1
E Grand Canyon Railway Depot.........................B2
F Hopi House...B2
G Verkamp's Visitor Center.................................B2
H Yavapai Geology Museum................................A3
I Yavapai Point...A3
J Mather Point..A3
K Grand Canyon Visitor Center..........................B3
L South Kaibab Trailhead....................................B5
M Yaki Point...B5
N Ooh Ahh Point...B5
O Tusayan Ruin and Museum..............................C5
P Desert View Watchtower..................................C5

CLIFF SPRINGS TRAIL

Easy – (1.0 mi / 1.6 km), round trip, allow 45 – 60 minutes, elev. Δ: 150 ft / 46 m, trailhead at the end of Cape Royal Road

A refreshing hike through a wooded ravine to a rocky overhang containing a seeping spring. The water is not suitable for drinking directly as tempting as it may seem. The spring holds an ecosystem for ferns and moss and can provide some nice shade from the day's sun. Look for the remains of a granary from the original inhabitants of the area early into the hike.

Driving Around the North Rim

There are two main drives from the visitor center and Grand Canyon Lodge that takes you to canyon rim overlooks. The drives are very scenic and offer many pullouts to get out and explore the panorama of the canyon. Visiting both points can take half a day.

POINT IMPERIAL

(3 miles / 4.8 km)

Point Imperial is the highest point on the North Rim at 8,803 feet (2,683 meters). From this high vantage point, you get an overview of the eastern end of the Grand Canyon, starting at the narrow walls of Marble Canyon and opening up profoundly into the Grand Canyon proper. The Painted Desert lies farther in the distance.

CAPE ROYAL

(15 miles / 24.1 km)

Cape Royal is arguably the most panoramic drive in the entire Grand Canyon. It offers views up and down the canyon as well as across, providing ample opportunities for amazing photos or simply breathtaking memories. It is a popular destination both at sunrise and at sunset for this reason. There is a natural arch known as Angels Window, where, from the right angle, one can see through the arch to the Colorado River itself. It is also possible to see the Desert View Watchtower on the South Rim.

El Tovar Hotel

GRAND CANYON LODGING

There are two main areas to stay within Grand Canyon National Park. The most accessible, with the most accommodations and amenities, is the South Rim, including Desert View. The South Rim is also the most popular, receiving nearly 90 percent of the park's 5 million annual visitors. The remaining 500,000 visitors head to the North Rim. Of the two, the South Rim is open year-round, and both offer the most lodging and camping options of any of the national parks described in this book but is also the most visited.

SOUTH RIM LODGING

Within the South Rim of the Grand Canyon are six lodges, one ranch, and three main camping destinations. If you are coming during the off-season, South Rim contains the only campgrounds and lodging that are open year-round. Desert View and North Rim campgrounds close during the fall and winter months. All lodges and campgrounds book up so make sure you reserve far in advance, especially if you are vacationing during the summer months.

EL TOVAR HOTEL

This is the flagship of the entire set of lodges in the Grand Canyon. El Tovar opened its doors in January 1905 under the design of Charles Whittlesey, who was the Chief Architect for the Atchison, Topeka, and Santa Fe Railway. Unlike the rustic, grand, Arts and Craft designs of Stanley Gilbert Underwood, the inspirations for the El Tovar came from European descent, which gives the lodge a look reminiscent of a Swiss chalet. This was done intentionally to appeal to the vacationing elite of the era, which saw Europe and its culture as the reference for elegance. The hotel has seen all manner of the rich and famous, from President Theodore Roosevelt to Sir Paul McCartney. If you don't get a chance to stay in the El Tovar, definitely drop in to check it out. It is a remarkable and historic place.

All prices are as stated for 2019 with standard rooms starting at $226.45 for one double and $274.52 for one queen. For families needing two queen beds, set your sights and pocketbook on the deluxe rooms at $369.52. That said if you are okay with spending three hundred dollars on a room, time to up-sell you to the suite. Many of the 78 rooms within this property are suites containing minor differences and ranging from $462 to $562. The suites offer more square footage, a sitting room and some have a private balcony. Extra persons for the standard and deluxe rooms only are $14.

KACHINA LODGE

The Kachina Lodge has a much more contemporary feel than Bright Angel or El Tovar but also offers incredible

Bighorn checking out the view

views. The rooms are decent, basic, and typically show some wear. Folks staying in this hotel need to check in at the El Tovar Hotel Front Desk. All rooms offer a king or two queens, plus your own bathroom. Street side rooms run at $234.81 while canyon rooms run $253.62with a charge of $9 per each extra person.

THUNDERBIRD LODGE

Similar to the Kachina Lodge in both form and function, the Thunderbird Lodge offers suitable clean basic rooms, some with spectacular views. The pricing structure is also equivalent to the Kachina Lodge. To check into the Thunderbird Lodge, you need to head to the Bright Angel Lodge Front Desk.

BRIGHT ANGEL LODGE

Regarding magnificent views of the Grand Canyon right from your room, Bright Angel Lodge is a top pick. This is not a five-star hotel, the rooms typically show wear from being constantly at capacity. However, the staff is exceptional, and the views are amazing. The lodge has something for every budget, from lodge rooms with a shared bathroom, private cabins and rooms and even historical cabins. The two historic cabins, the Red Horse, and Buckey O'Neill Cabin, are double in price and are better suited for couples. The Bright Angel Lodge was designed by Southwest architect Mary Jane Colter in 1935 and has a warm rustic feel inside and out. Rooms are $88.51-226.45 per night with a charge of $9 per each extra person.

MASWIK LODGE

Maswik Lodge is a large 278 room complex set back from the canyon's edge. The overall design and architecture reflect the 1960's, which is when the facility was built. Maswik is a Hopi name for the kachina that guards all of the Grand Canyon. One thing the Maswik lodge does do is guard the family pocketbook.

South Rooms are an affordable $116.73 for two queens, with the North Rooms fetching $224.36. Extra persons are $9. Overall, the Maswik lodge gets consistently complimentary reviews. Whether it's the price to value or the kachina Maswik helping to make for a pleasant stay, folks tend to leave satisfied.

YAVAPAI LODGE

The Yavapai Lodge is the largest of the lodges at 378 rooms separated into two wings of multistory structures. The best thing going for Yavapai Lodge is its proximity to the nearby Market Plaza, where a general store, deli, post office and bank can be found. It is also within walking distance of the Visitor Center, and coin-operated laundry. The lodge is a bit more pricey than the Maswik Lodge for this reason, with West rooms containing two queen beds coming in at $167.25. Extra persons are again $9 each.

PHANTOM RANCH

The Phantom Ranch accommodates in a manner unlike any of the other lodges or campgrounds. The ranch and the rancher's name was created from the mind of Mary Jane Colter in the 1920's. The cabins are rustic and look right out of a western movie set, built with a nice mixture of wood and native stones.

What makes the Phantom Ranch cabins special is the journey involved in getting to them. One cannot just pull up to the Phantom Ranch and roll the suitcases across the parking lot. The ranch is at the bottom of the Grand Canyon, so the only way to get to it is by mule, foot or via the Colorado River itself. For hikers, there are dormitories separated by gender for $53 per night. For families, consider the complete trip combination which includes getting down to the ranch by mule, full meal options (including a steak dinner) and the cabin. Each cabin holds two people, so if you are traveling as a family, expect to reserve two cabins if you go this route. Full details on the ranch can be found here: www.grandcanyonlodges.com/lodging/phantom-ranch/

One thing to note on staying at the Phantom Ranch, you can't simply drop in, and you can't announce you have extra folks out of the blue and expect them to get a place to stay. You need to reserve everything ahead of time, and if you are hiking down, you need to let the ranch know you are on your way. This is one of the most popular things to do in the Grand Canyon, so plan accordingly.

SOUTH RIM CAMPING

MATHER CAMPGROUND

Mather Campground is centrally located in the South Rim park area and is run by the National Park Service. There are 319 campsites available that accommodate RVs up to 30 feet. There are no hookups. If you have a larger RV or need hookups, head to Trailer Village.

Mather Campground is named for the national park's first director and is the largest campground in Grand Canyon. There is firewood for sale, there are laundry and shower facilities, and a dump and water station is available. Generators are allowed from 7 am to 9 am and again from 6 pm to 8 pm. Pine Loop is geared toward tent camping, so if you find yourself in Pine Loop, generators are not allowed. Quiet hours for the entire campground are from 10 pm to 6 am.

All sites are reservable and assigned. It is highly recommended you reserve your site before arriving. Reservations are taken up to six months in advance. You can stay at the campground for up to seven consecutive days and a total of 30 days per year, though if wanting to stay longer than that is a problem you are trying to

23

solve, I'm envious! Check-in starts at noon, check-out is at 11 am. If the site is available, you can renew for another day after 9 am.

The park generally receives good marks from every aspect. It has hot showers for $2 and is close to nearby Market Plaza, which contains a cafeteria, delicatessen, and grocery store. It is also close to the shuttle system, which has drop-offs at every overlook in the South Rim short of Desert View. You can take the shuttle to the visitor center and Bright Angel Lodge.

TRAILER VILLAGE

Trailer Village is close to Mather Campground and about ½ mile (0.8 km) from the rim of the Grand Canyon. While it is located within the National Park, it is operated by the Xanterra concessionaire. Here you will find 80 pull-through, paved sites with full hookups. RVs up to 50 feet long can be accommodated. Each site has the usual picnic table, barbecue grill and 30 and 50-amp electrical service. You can also hook into cable TV, water, and sewage if desired. The Trailer Village is open all year and starts at $49 a night. It shares the shower and laundry facility with Mather Campground at the Camper Services area, which is located farther from Trailer Village and close to the Mather Campground. Besides this downside, the Trailer Village otherwise receives similar praise to that of Mather Campground. You are in the center of the park near the rim of the Grand Canyon. It will be difficult to not be pleased with your stay.

DESERT VIEW

The Desert View section of the park is about 25 miles (41 km) from the South Rim proper, tucked away to the east of the park. While it does get a little less traffic than the main South Rim, the Desert View Drive is typically included as part of the journey for many Grand Canyon visits. There are 50 sites available for tents and RVs up to 30 feet long. Unlike the Mather Campground, Desert View is offered on a first come, first served basis. The campground is closed by late fall and opens in the late spring, typically between October and May.

During the summer months, the campground is filled by early afternoon. The site does have a self-serve registration kiosk that accepts credit cards, though there is something kind of quaint about filling out those little campsite envelopes and having to find exact change for the $12-a-night fee.

There are bathrooms and water, but no dumping or water station, and no showers. The Desert View section has many of the same amenities as the South Rim, including its own visitor center, marketplace, and Desert View Indian Watchtower, which is modeled after ancient Anasazi watchtowers and is a unique architectural feature within the park.

OTHER CAMPING

The nearby town of Tusayan has a couple of campgrounds. Ten-X Campground is open from May through September and is operated by the U.S. Forest Service. There are 70 sites available with 15 of them reservable through Recreation.gov. The fee is $10 per night. There is one group site that can be reserved for a party of 100 people.

Camper Village is commercially operated and is located about 7 miles (11 km) south of the Grand Canyon Village in Tusayan. It is open seasonally and offers hook-ups and coin-operated showers. The site offers a general store and convenient pizza; however, this should be considered as a place of last resort. It is consistently given bad reviews on the advisor sites. Call (928) 638-2887.

LODGING OUTSIDE THE SOUTH RIM

GRAND CANYON PLAZA HOTEL

406 Canyon Plaza Ln, Tusayan, AZ 86023, (928) 638-2673, grandcanyonplaza.com

The Grand Canyon Plaza Hotel does an exceptional job of staying on top of keeping their property refreshed and up to date. Plus, they just opened a new sports bar called the Wagon Wheel Saloon. The hotel is family

The Colorado River cutting through the Grand Canyon

owned and managed with pride. They offer friendly customer service, double vanities, an outdoor pool and jacuzzi, Wi-Fi, and a breakfast buffet. The property also has some nice touches for those coming from out of the country, including multilingual support, and Japanese and Chinese television stations. The hotel just underwent a name change (from Canyon Plaza Resort) and complete remodel of a third of their rooms. This location is a good value overall.

RED FEATHER LODGE

300 AZ-64, Tusayan, AZ 86023, (928) 638-2414, redfeatherlodge.com

Red Feather Lodge is a family owned and operated the property and has been around for over 50 years. The rooms are clean, the staff incredibly friendly, and they have a large sized swimming pool with adjoining hot tub. While the rooms have been updated, a stay here is a bit nostalgic. They have kept just enough of the retro style ambiance to bring back memories of past family trips.

HOLIDAY INN EXPRESS GRAND CANYON

226 AZ-64, Tusayan, AZ 86023, (928) 638-3000, ihg.com

Another one of the Grand Canyon's mid-range hotels. The rooms at this Holiday Inn aren't as glamorous as some of the other similar hotels in the area, but they do have a huge indoor pool with massive panes of glass alongside a mural of the Grand Canyon. Their hot tub is also on the larger side.

THE GRAND HOTEL AT THE GRAND CANYON

149 AZ-64, Tusayan, AZ 86023, (928) 638-3333, grandcanyongrandhotel.com

The Grand Hotel has an impressive lobby that matches its names. The rooms are comfortable with big fluffy mattresses. A larger suite is also available. The indoor pool and hot tube are on the smaller side. Overall, a nice choice.

BEST WESTERN PREMIER GRAND CANYON SQUIRE INN

74 AZ-64, Tusayan, AZ 86023, (928) 638-2681, www.bestwestern.com

Best Western offers a range of property types and their Premiere inns are a solid 3-star hotel. While there is no pool here, they do have a fitness center, hot tub, a fine dining restaurant, room service, laundry facilities, and free Wi-Fi. They also offer family rooms and suites along with standard rooms. Overall, a stay here is consistently pleasant and meets expectations.

NORTH RIM LODGING

The North Rim receives much less traffic, is harder to get to and has limited seasons of operation. It is a mere 10 miles (16 km) from the South Rim as the raven flies but a 220-mile (354 km) journey to drive from rim to rim. Given that this side of the canyon gets closer to 500,000 visitors versus the 4.5 million on the South Rim, the pace is much more relaxed and steady. Getting to the North Rim is doable in an RV and can be a rewarding way to see the Grand Canyon. There are one main campground on the rim and one lodge on this side of the park. The North Rim of the Grand Canyon, including the campground, is not open year-round. They close for winter typically in October and reopen in mid-May.

GRAND CANYON LODGE

The Grand Canyon Lodge was originally built from the design of Gilbert Stanley Underwood in 1927/28 but was severely burned in 1932 and rebuilt shortly after, though whether Underwood had a hand in the new design is under debate. It does carry a fair amount of Underwood's style. The lodge is located at Bright Angel Point and is typically an excellent alternative to the hustle and bustle happening at the South Rim.

For families, the best bet is staying in the Western Cabins, which offer two queen beds, full-size bath, and porch. Be sure to ask for the Rim View Cabins as opposed to the Standard Cabins. Another great option are the Pioneer Cabins, which were recently remodeled in 2009. These cabins offer two rooms with bunk beds or twin beds in one room and a queen-sized bed in the other room.

NORTH RIM CAMPING

NORTH RIM CAMPGROUND

There are 74 standard sites available for RVs and tents plus several more for tent only and group sites. There are no hookups, but there is a water and dump station at the campground. Firewood is available for sale at the nearby General Store.

As the campground is run by the National Park Service, many of the same rules apply as they do in the South Rim. Generators are allowed from 7 am to 9 am and again from 6 pm to 8 pm. Quiet hours for the entire campground are from 10 pm to 6 am. All sites are reservable and assigned. It is highly recommended that you reserve your site before arriving. Reservations are taken up to six months in advance. You can stay at the campground for up to seven consecutive days and a total of 30 days per year. Check-in starts at noon, check-out is at 11 am. If the site is available, you can renew for another day after 9 am. There are laundry and shower facilities as well as change machines nearby.

GRAND CANYON DINING

DINING INSIDE THE PARK

There are many choices within the park, including options for sit down dining, grocery markets, casual cafes, snack bars, lounges, and places to grab food to go. On the south rim, these are open year-round. On the north rim, all food services (and lodging) are closed in the winter. For a full list of dining options within the park, go here: www.nps.gov/grca/planyourvisit/restaurants.htm. The options are too numerous to list in full, but a few are described that truly stand out.

SOUTH RIM DINING

EL TOVAR DINING ROOM

AMERICAN, $$, Village Loop Dr, Grand Canyon, AZ 86023, (928) 638-2631, open daily for breakfast, 6:30am–10:30am, lunch from 11am–2pm, and dinner from 4:30pm–10pm, under renovations from April to December 2018.

The South Rim's El Tovar dining room and the lodge first opened in 1905 as a place to be for those traveling to the Grand Canyon. Today the dining room's timeless architecture is still just as magnificent. The service and food are consistently exceptional, making this one of the top dining destinations within the Grand Circle. This is a world class dining experience at the edge of the Grand Canyon.

PHANTOM RANCH CANTEEN

AMERICAN, $$, North Kaibab Trail, Grand Canyon National Park, AZ, (888) 297-2757, www.grandcanyonlodges.com/dining/phantom-ranch-canteen, open seasonally, specific seating times

This is one of the most unique dining experiences in the Grand Canyon. For those adventurous enough, you can dine at the bottom of the canyon. Whether you are

camping overnight or doing a rim to rim hike, Phantom Ranch will be a welcome rest stop and place to fill up before moving on. They serve breakfast and dinner only, and there are specific seating times for meals (so don't be late, they will close the doors during the service). Reservations are absolutely required; walk-in service is not an option here.

NORTH RIM DINING

GRAND CANYON LODGE DINING ROOM

AMERICAN, $$, North Rim, Grand Canyon National Park, AZ, (928) 638-2611, www.grandcanyonforever.com/dining, open seasonally 6:30am - 9:30pm, (closed in winter)

From the dining room to the food, the dining room at the Grand Canyon Lodge is simply amazing. The architecture is big and bold, with great viewing opportunities. The service is awesome, and the food is delicious as well. Dining here is a truly great experience. Hours vary and reservations recommended.

DINING OUTSIDE THE PARK

WE COOK PIZZA AND PASTA

PIZZA AND PASTA, $, 605 N Hwy 64, Grand Canyon Village, AZ 86023, (928) 638-2278, open daily 11am - 9pm

Quick service, fresh salad bar, and the usual assortment of pizza and pasta offerings.

YIPPEE-EI-O! STEAKHOUSE

AMERICAN, $$, 541 Hwy 64, Grand Canyon Village, AZ 86023, (928) 638-2780, open daily 11am - 10pm

Like many of the restaurants near the Grand Canyon Village, Yippee-ei-o! is a touristy, jam-packed, get 'em in, get 'em out, order and do not complain kinda place. I'm sure somewhere, some owner really wants to provide a better experience, but there are just so many darn tourists. All of these establishments do try their best, but the volume of people makes it hard to create a personal experience for everyone. There are exceptions though. If you go really early, especially for dinner, say 4:30 - 5:30, you get a fresh staff and not as many people. I have had some good experiences here, combined with many more where you just feel like a part of the tourist herd.

BIG E STEAKHOUSE & SALOON

AMERICAN, $$, 395 Hwy 64, Grand Canyon Village, AZ 86023, (928) 638-0333, bigesteakhouse.com, open daily 1pm - 9pm

The food at Big E is hearty, hot, and delicious, with lots of choices. The ambiance is fun and definitely adds to the feeling you are on vacation. Big E is a good choice overall.

PLAZA BONITA

MEXICAN, $, 352 Hwy 64, Grand Canyon Village, AZ 86023, (928) 638-8900, open daily 7am - 10pm

Plaza Bonita offers a good selection within the genre of Mexican cuisine. The atmosphere is done nicely in a southwest style, and prices are reasonable.

View from Desert Tower

THE CANYON STAR RESTAURANT AND SALOON

STEAKHOUSE, $$, 149 Hwy 64, Grand Canyon Village, AZ 86023, (928) 638-3333, grandcanyongrandhotel.com, open daily 2pm - 11pm

Be prepared for long wait times during the long busy season. Once seated, the food is very good. They serve up a large selection of menu items, and there should be something for everyone. The ambiance is warm and bright. Overall a good place to get a late lunch or dinner. This restaurant is part of the Grand Hotel at the Grand Canyon.

THE CORONADO ROOM

AMERICAN, $$, 74 Hwy 64, Grand Canyon Village, AZ 86023, (928) 638-2681, grandcanyonsquire.com, open daily 5pm - 10pm

Part of the Best Western Premier Squire Inn, The Coronado Room offers a fine dining experience. They have a wide selection of starters, soups, salads, entrées, and deserts. It's a bit pricey for the overall experience.

COFFEE AND SWEETS!

BRIGHT ANGEL FOUNTAIN

ICE CREAM, Rim side of Bright Angel Lodge, Grand Canyon, AZ 86023, (928) 638-2631, open daily 6:30am - 10pm

The Fountain at Bright Angel is a place to get ice cream right at the edge of the Grand Canyon, and the portions are generous. The downsides are long lines, poor inventory control (they keep running out of the most popular flavors) and they serve the same stuff you could buy at a store. Still, there is something very cool in being handed your own cone and getting to sit and take in the view of the Grand Canyon.

SIDE TRIPS OF THE GRAND CANYON

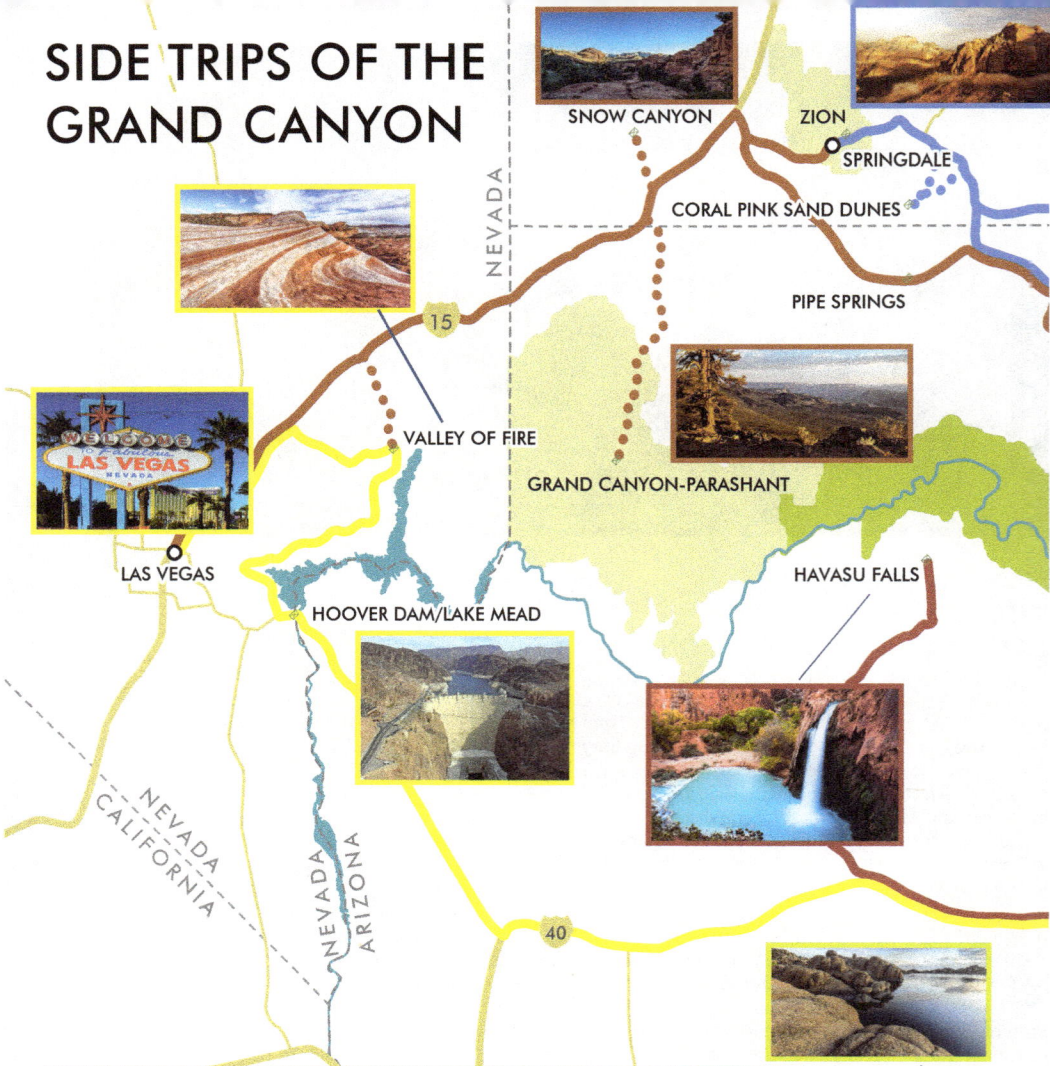

SNOW CANYON

ZION
SPRINGDALE

CORAL PINK SAND DUNES

PIPE SPRINGS

NEVADA

15

VALLEY OF FIRE

LAS VEGAS

GRAND CANYON-PARASHANT

HAVASU FALLS

HOOVER DAM/LAKE MEAD

HAVASU FALLS

NEVADA
CALIFORNIA

NEVADA
ARIZONA

40

PRESCOTT

Legend

ANCIENT LANDS -*pg 30*		GRAND CANYON NATIONAL PARK
MYSTICAL SEDONA -*pg 42*		
HISTORICAL SOUTHWEST -*pg 56*		PARKS
PHOENIX ON THE RISE -*pg 72*		
PETRIFIED FORESTS -*pg 82*		CITIES + TOWNS
RIM TO RIM AND BEYOND -*pg 92*		
MONUMENT VALLEY -*pg 102*		
INTO ZION AND UTAH -*pg 108*		
THE LIVING PAST -*pg 126*		
VEGAS BABY! -*pg 132*		
HAVASU FALLS -*pg 146*		
THE SECRET GRAND CANYON -*pg 150*		

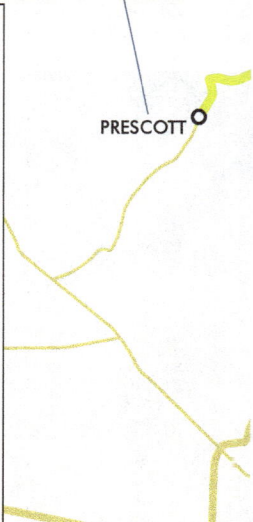

N

0   20 mi

0   20 km

UTAH
ARIZONA

MONUMENT VALLEY

FOUR CORNERS

89

VERMILION
CLIFFS

ANTELOPE CANYON

NAVAJO NATIONAL
MONUMENT

67

160

CANYON DE CHELLY

NORTH RIM

GRAND CANYON VILLAGE

89

64

HUBBELL TRADING POST

WUPATKI

64

SUNSET CRATER VOLCANO

PETRIFIED FOREST

FLAGSTAFF

WALNUT
CANYON

SLIDE ROCK

SEDONA

JEROME

RED ROCK

METEOR CRATER

40

MONTEZUMA WELL
MONTEZUMA CASTLE

COTTONWOOD
DEAD HORSE RANCH

TUZIGOOT

AGUA FRIA

17

Grand Canyon National Park

PHOENIX

Side Trip 1 – Ancient Lands

BEST FROM

Starting from the South Rim Grand Canyon is shortest distance for this side trip. Tack on an additional 3-hour drive if coming from the North Rim.

WHAT YOU WILL SEE

- Wupatki National Monument
- Sunset Crater National Monument
- Walnut Canyon National Monument
- Flagstaff

WHY CHOOSE THIS SIDE TRIP

The Ancient Lands side trip is educational, hip, and laid back all at the same time. The journey starts with a trip back in time through unspoiled high desert prairies to Wupatki National Monument. Here you will see and walk among the multiple ruins of a once flourishing culture. The remoteness of Wupatki is part of its charm, as it feels as if you are seeing it as it was 800 years ago when the area was inhabited. Just 25 miles away the 12,000 foot San Francisco Peaks seem larger than life, providing an enticing contrast to the surrounding high desert ponderosa.

Just down the road from Wupatki is Sunset Crater National Monument, a geological destination set in an environment of pinyon pine forest. This park contains a rather perfect and picturesque set of cinder cones, again with the backdrop of the San Francisco Peaks nearby. The cinder cone itself is off limits to hikers, but there are a few hikes around the park that one can take.

Next, just east of Flagstaff is Walnut Canyon National Monument. The environment again changes, this time to limestone canyons within a dense forest of pine. Inside the monument are a collection of ancestral cliff dwellings abandoned some 700 years ago that one can explore.

The end destination is Flagstaff and as a college town, it is progressive enough to challenge the stereotypes of a "typical mountain town." Just outside of the city limits are a number of forest hikes and even cross-country skiing in the winter.

ALLOW

- Recommended – 2 days.
- Total Drive Time: 3 hours
- Wupatki National Monument: 2 – 3 hours
- Sunset Crater: 30 minutes – 2 hours
- Walnut Canyon: 2 – 3 hours
- Flagstaff: This trip can easily be completed in 2 days with an overnight in Flagstaff. If you are pressed for time, choose 1-2 of the three state parks listed to or get an early start to make this a day trip.

CAN BE COMBINED WITH

Side Trip 2 - "Mystical Sedona," Side Trip 3 – "Historical Southwest," Side Trip 4 – "Phoenix on the Rise," and Side Trip 5 – "Petrified Forests."

WUPATKI NATIONAL MONUMENT

It is the landscape that these ruins reside in that really makes this a special place. The land encapsulates the raw austerity of the high desert. The sagebrush covers the red land as a dotted green tapestry of nature. Typically, the skies are a deep blue, and the clouds float above in an explosion of pure white, massive, giant things, beautiful and magical to the eye. The sapphire blue color of the sky is due to the altitude, and in the late afternoon, the land comes alive in colors that are rich and simply beyond description.

Wupatki Ruins

ANCIENT LANDS

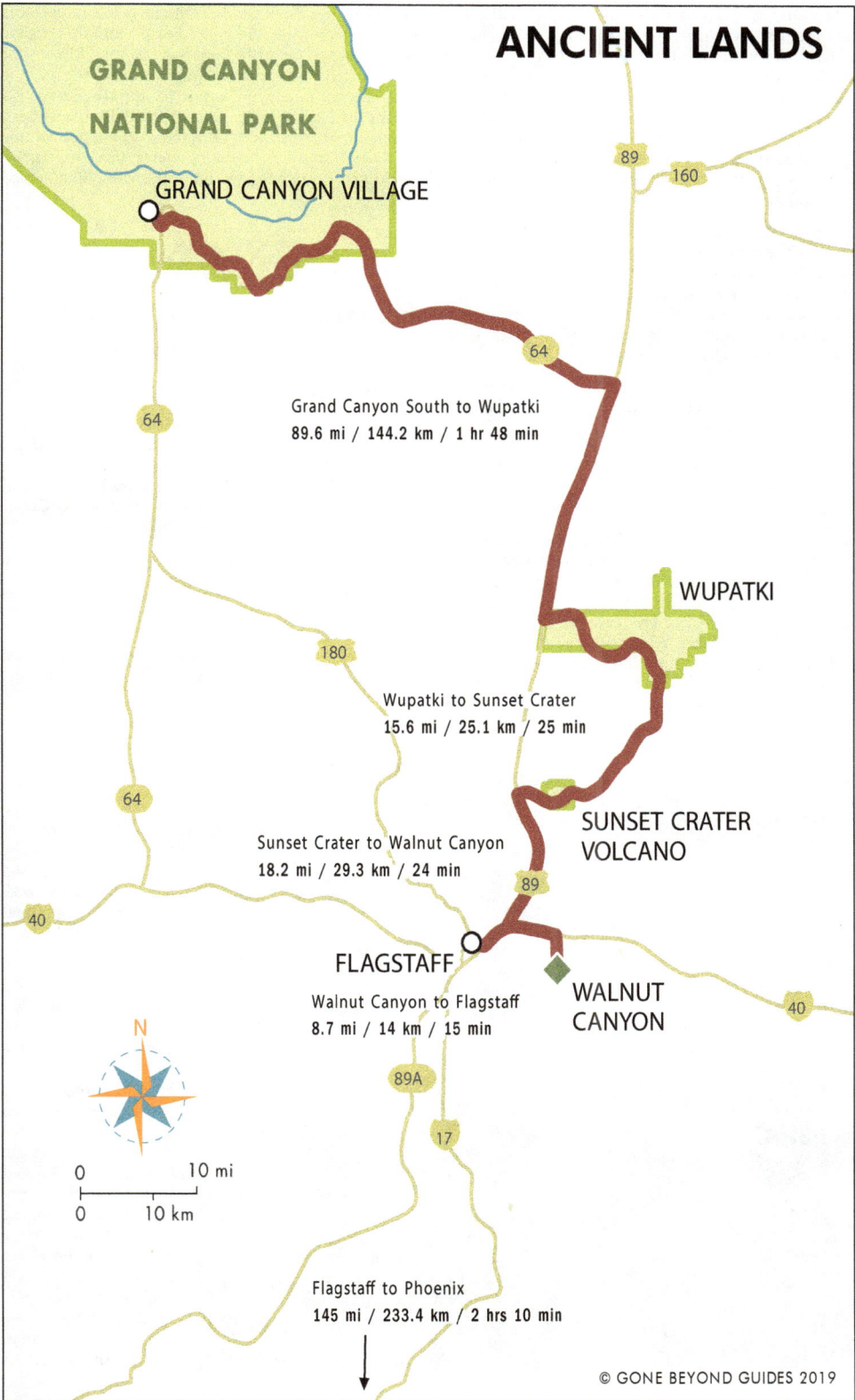

GRAND CANYON NATIONAL PARK

GRAND CANYON VILLAGE

89

160

89

64

Grand Canyon South to Wupatki
89.6 mi / 144.2 km / 1 hr 48 min

64

WUPATKI

180

Wupatki to Sunset Crater
15.6 mi / 25.1 km / 25 min

64

SUNSET CRATER
VOLCANO

Sunset Crater to Walnut Canyon
18.2 mi / 29.3 km / 24 min

89

40

FLAGSTAFF

40

Walnut Canyon to Flagstaff
8.7 mi / 14 km / 15 min

WALNUT
CANYON

N

0   10 mi

0   10 km

89A

17

Flagstaff to Phoenix
145 mi / 233.4 km / 2 hrs 10 min

© GONE BEYOND GUIDES 2019

The ruins themselves are also special, with ball courts and multi-storied structures. The park is small enough to feel that you can explore it completely, yet spread out to parallel the vastness of the land that surrounds it. There is a scenic drive leading to many different interpretative sites, where one can learn about the lifeways of these people, such as how they grew corn by planting a single seed about six inches into a hole. This brought the roots closer to water and protected the young seedling from harm.

The park offers ranger-led Discovery Hikes for up-close views of the ruins and petroglyphs. Details can be found at www.nps.gov/wupa/planyourvisit/guidedtours.htm. Reservations are required, and group size is limited to 12 people. Please call 928-679-2365 to reserve a spot. There is an additional fee for some of the hikes. Hikes are offered from October through April.

Wupatki National Monument is a day use area open from sunrise to sunset year-round. The visitor center is open typically from 9am to 5pm.

SUNSET CRATER NATIONAL MONUMENT

Sunset Crater is a 900-year young cinder cone created as the result of volcanic activity. The area has undergone a smattering of volcanic activity, but Sunset Crater is unique in that it occurred very recently from a geologic perspective. There are lava caves to explore, cinder cones to climb and lava fields one can walk within. The red and yellow color of the cinders creates a wonderful offset to the tortured blacks and greys of the surrounding lava and is a favorite spot for photographers. Typically, the snow-capped the San Francisco Peaks frame the background of these shots.

Sunset Crater sits at 7000 feet, and the altitude does have an effect on hiking if you aren't acclimated. The crater itself is closed to climbing, but there are other hikes in the area.

Sunset Crater National Monument is a day use area open from sunrise to sunset year-round. The visitor center is open typically from 9am to 5pm. The visitor center opens at 8am from June to October. There is camping at the nearby Bonito Campground which is run by the Forest Service and is just outside the western boundary of the park. Campground amenities include 44 T/RV campsites, drinking water, flush toilets, no hookups, and is operated on a first come-first served basis.

HIKING SUNSET CRATER NATIONAL MONUMENT

LAVA FLOW TRAIL

Easy – (1.0 mi / 1.6 km), round trip, allow 30 minutes

Be sure to pick up a brochure for this self-guided interpretive trail. The trail covers a small loop at the base of the crater. A one-quarter mile of the trail is paved and accessible. There are some great views of Sunset Crater and the San Francisco Peaks along the way.

LENOX CRATER TRAIL

Strenuous – (1.0 mi / 1.6 km), round trip, allow 30 – 45 minutes

This trail allows access to a lava field that was once an ancient volcano. Though the trail is but one mile round trip, it is steep with loose cinders that make for laborious walking.

O'LEARY PEAK TRAIL

Strenuous – (10.0 mi / 16.1 km), round trip, allow 3 – 4 hours

This is a there and back trail that climbs a lava dome volcano. The trail is an old roadbed and is very evident from a distance. The old forest service road climbs six switchbacks to obtain the top. Great views and a radio tower are at the top to greet you.

This trail doesn't get too much traffic but offers some really commanding views. From the top, you get an amazing shot of the San Francisco Peaks as well as into Sunset Crater. The Painted Desert is to the north. As ho-hum as hiking an old forest service road to a radio tower might sound, this is a cool hike from the perspective of the views. They are spectacular, making this a hidden gem.

Sunset Crater

Walnut Canyon

WALNUT CANYON NATIONAL MONUMENT

Though relatively close to Wupatki NM and Flagstaff, the terrain is much different here. The cliff dwellings were built within Kaibab limestone, which also forms the rim of the Grand Canyon. Here the land is dry with some high desert scrub fauna and the limestone is a mud white, which provides a unique contrast to the usual red sandstones. The limestone also allows for the creation of alcoves, which offered protected building locations for the ancestral people.

The park is very small, about 3500 acres, but don't let that fool you, there are over 300 cliff dwellings here. There is also a visitor center and two trails. The ruins are situated along the cliff walls of Walnut Canyon, at a deeply striated gooseneck that has formed within the canyon. The ruins share a similarity to those at Mesa Verde in that they both make use of the naturally formed limestone alcoves.

Walnut Canyon National Monument is open from 9am - 5pm November to June and 8am - 5pm during the summer season. All times are Mountain Standard Time.

HIKING WALNUT CANYON NATIONAL MONUMENT

RIM TRAIL

Easy – (0.7 mi / 1.1 km), round trip, allow 45 - 60 minutes

This trail offers a paved and wheelchair accessible self-guided tour of the ruins and surrounding canyon. There are two overlooks with benches and several ruins to see, with descriptions along the way. It is possible to see ruins off in the canyon from the overlooks as well as several sites right along the path.

ISLAND TRAIL

Strenuous – (1.0 mi / 1.6 km), round trip, allow 1 hour

This is a paved trail that travels along the rim of the park's main gooseneck and down into the canyon to observe some cliff dwellings first hand. The trail is steep in sections, with many steps as well. There are many sites to see along the way, including some rooms built into the alcove that is intact enough for shelter today. The trail brings the visitor remarkably close to the sites, which allows for an up close and personal view of these rooms.

Walnut Canyon ruins

FLAGSTAFF

Flagstaff, Arizona or "Flag" as the locals call it, is a mix of cultures. As the home of Northern Arizona University (NAU), Flagstaff is a college town. It is also a town built on the backbone of the lumber, ranching, and railroad industries, which together create a city that somehow gets along. It is hip, young, liberal, and environmentally friendly combining with folks trying to put food on the table in the same way their dad and grandad did. The mountain town is thus a mix of new influence and older customs.

The other factor that weighs on Flagstaff is the weather. The winters are snowy and harsh by Arizona standards, and the wear and tear of winter shows once the city snow melts into a more temperate spring. This same factor is also a unique quality, allowing Flag to be one of the only ski destinations in the state. The higher elevation also favors the marvel of cool mountain air, the wind through the Ponderosa pines and the sprays of seasonal wildflowers. It is in the winter, a wonderland. In the summer, it is a bustling, get things done, but glad to be here kind of place for the folks that call the city their home.

THINGS TO DO IN FLAGSTAFF

MUSEUMS
Those looking to explore the wonders of the Colorado Plateau, head to The Museum of Northern Arizona (3101 N. Fort Valley Rd., (928) 774-5213). The museum has been around since the late 1920's and offers exhibits in anthropology, geology, biology, and fine art. Much of the art is by Zuni, Hopi, and Navajo artists and is worth a visit. For admission, children under 10 are free, ages 10-17 are $8, and adults are $12.

The Arboretum at Flagstaff (4001 S. Woody Mountain Rd., (928) 774-1442) is more than a diverse array of over 750 species of plants, they also hold summer concerts and other events such as "Shakespeare Under the Pines" and "Wine in the Woods – AZ style." Check out their website for what's happening currently (http://www.thearb.org/events/).

For budding astronomers, head to the place where Pluto was discovered! Lowell Observatory, (1400 W. Mars Hill Rd., (928) 233-3212) has telescope viewings day and night, multimedia shows, exhibits, and an immersive space theater called SlipherVision. The brand new Giovale Open Deck Observatory will open in 2019 offering viewers glimpses of the heavens through a suite of six sophisticated telescopes.

If watching stars and planets aren't your thing, then try the Pioneer Museum sponsored by the Arizona Historical Society (2340 N. Fort Valley Rd., (928) 774-6272). Here you can discover the history of northern Arizona and Flagstaff. The museum is housed inside what was once a county hospital at the turn of the 1900's and has three acres to explore. For a completely different experience, get a guided tour of the Riordan Mansion State Historic Park (409 W. Riordan Rd., (928) 779-4395). This Arts and Craft style home was built in 1904 by lumber tycoons, Timothy and Michael Riordan. The property gives a great example of pre-depression opulence. The interior of the mansion is by guided tour only and reservations are recommended.

OUTDOOR ACTIVITIES
Located in the beautiful San Francisco Peaks, the Arizona Snowbowl (9300 N. Snowbowl Rd., (928) 779-1951) offers many things to do in the summer, including chairlift rides, mountaintop dining, disc golf, and family activities. For the winter season, the Snowbowl is the place to go for snowboarding and downhill skiing. There are terrains for every level, from beginner to double black diamond. The Snowbowl offers food, lodging, ski instructors, and six lifts.

Bearizona (I-40 Exit 165, (928) 635-2289) is a wild animal park that gives up-close views of bighorn sheep, wolves, bison, black bears and many other birds and animals. One highlight is the High Country Raptors show, where you get to see owls, falcons, hawks and other birds of prey in close action. You can also catch a ride on one of their touring buses, that take visitors through guided tours of the drive-through portion of the park.

Many people visiting Flagstaff head out to Meteor Crater (35 miles east of Flagstaff on I 40E, (928) 289-2362). This roadside attraction is described in greater detail within the Side Trip 5 - "Petrified Forests" route.

Area view of Flagstaff

SHOPPING

Historic Downtown has a wide variety of boutique shops and restaurants located within a late 1890 architectural setting. The area is between Humphrey's Street and Verde Street off Route 66. This is a great place to stroll around, get a snack, and window shop. Beyond downtown, the shopping experience is aimed more at the locals. This includes the 4th Street District (North 4th St. from Route 66 to Linda Vista) offering a few boutique shops and eateries and Aspen Place at the Sawmill at the corner of Butler Avenue and Lone Tree Road.

HIKING

Note that all hikes around the Flagstaff are at elevations of 8000 feet or greater. Most of these hikes are best done from early spring to late fall and may have snow even in the summer.

VEIT SPRINGS

Easy – (1.5 mi / 3.4 km), round trip, allow 60 minutes

Veit Springs Trail is more of a stroll than a hike, making this a great way to just relax in the outdoors. The wide path travels through Aspen forests, an old log cabin and a pond depression with pictographs. To get here, take HWY 180 to Snowbowl Rd and make a right on this road, traveling about 4.4 miles to the Lamar Haines parking area.

KACHINA TRAIL

Moderate – (12.2 mi / 19.6 km), round trip, allow 6 hours

Kachina Trail is a great way to experience the San Francisco Peaks, especially in the fall, when the aspen leaves turn color. Given this hike is 5.7 miles long one way with elevation, the ideal way to hike this is with a two-car shuttle system, starting the hike at the top (9300 feet) and heading down to the end at 8800 feet. On this hike, you will experience the full breadth of fir, spruce, and aspen, delightful meadows, great views down into Flagstaff and surrounding mountains, and crisp mountain air. It doesn't get much better than this hike. Allow 3 hours if you can do the shuttle system. This trail is accessed by taking HWY 180 to the end of Sugarbowl Road at first parking lot on your right. The other end of the trail can be picked up at the Weatherford Trail, found off of FR420.

FATMANS LOOP

Moderate – (2.5 mi / 4.0 km), round trip, allow 1 -1.5 hours

Located on Elden Mountain off of Route 66, Fatmans is a typically easy hike with segments of short steep climbs. Here there are scenic views of Flagstaff as you walk among a diverse community of plant life on the now dormant volcano. The hike gets its name because you will have to navigate around huge rocks that narrow the trail down to 4 feet gaps in some parts. Take Route 66/Hwy 89 past the entrance to the Flagstaff Mall where you will see a sign for "Mt Elden Trailhead" that leads to the trail parking lot. You can take a connector trail to the top of 2900-foot Mt Elden. This hike is popular on weekends.

LAVA RIVER CAVE

Moderate – (0.8 mi / 1.3 km), round trip, allow 1 -1.5 hours

Looking for something completely different? Hike inside a lava tube nearly one mile long! This vent was formed nearly 700,000 years ago and today offers a great underground adventure. Navigation requires a few areas where you need to bend down to keep from bumping your head. You'll also want to bring 2-3 light sources and warm clothing. The cave does get very dark and can be as cool as 42° F, even in the summer. To get here, take US 180 North to FR245 and turn left. Drive on this road for 3 miles and turn onto FR171 to FR171B. The caves are a short distance after this turn.

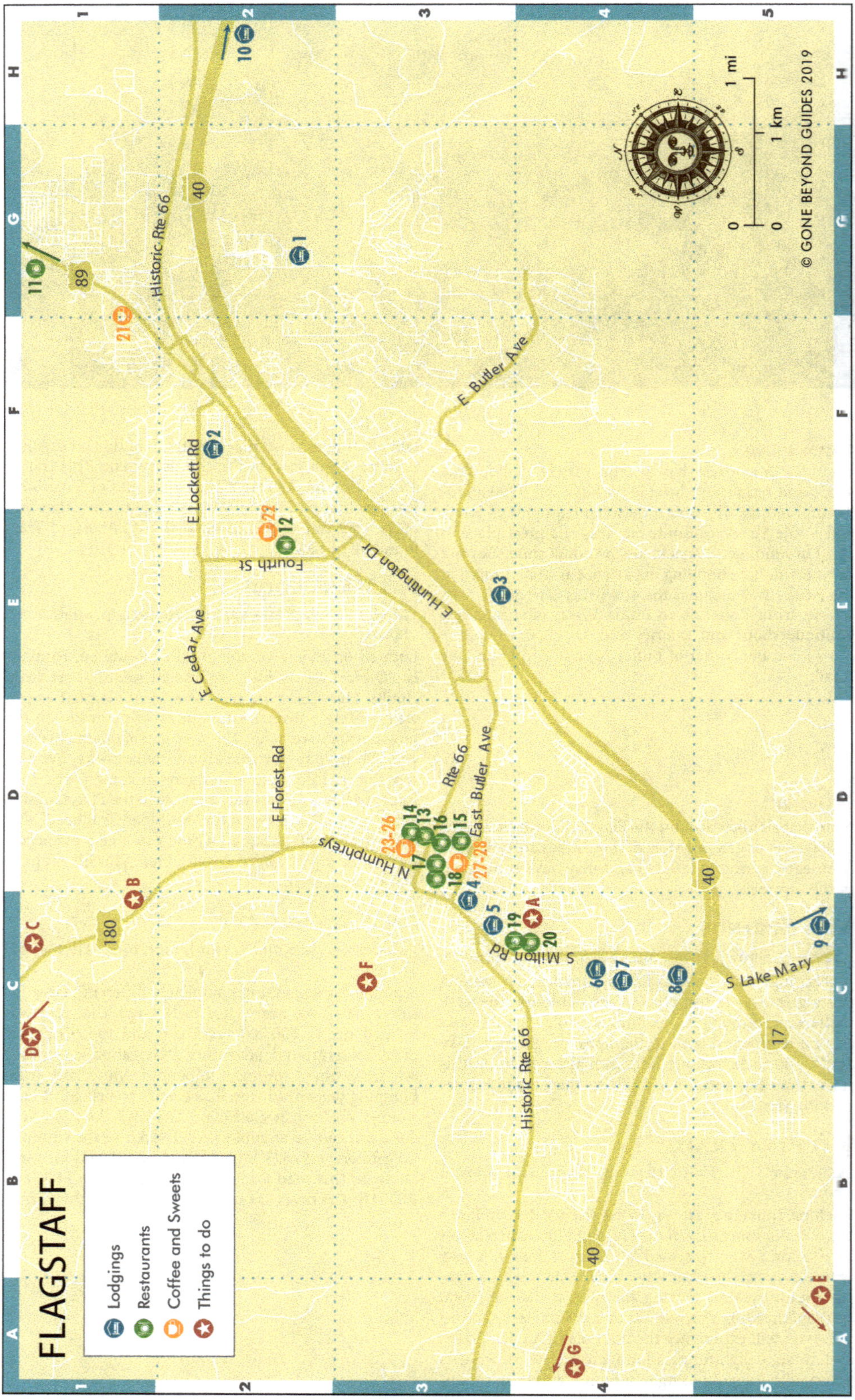

FLAGSTAFF
Lodgings
Restaurants
Coffee and Sweets
Things to do
Historic Rte 66
E Lockett Rd
Fourth St
E Huntington Dr
E Butler Ave
E Cedar Ave
E Forest Rd
N Humphreys
Rte 66
East Butler Ave
S Milton Rd
S Lake Mary
1 mi
1 km
© GONE BEYOND GUIDES 2019

LODGING

SONESTA ES SUITES FLAGSTAFF

1400 N Country Club Dr, Flagstaff, AZ 86004, (928) 526-5555, sonesta.com

The Sonesta is tucked away across the street from the rolling greens of the Continental Golf Club. The hotel offers tranquility combined with solid customer service. They have sizeable suites with a full kitchen along with free Wi-Fi and breakfast, along with a small gym and outdoor pool.

COUNTRY INN & SUITES BY CARLSON, FLAGSTAFF

3501 E Lockett Rd, Flagstaff, AZ 86004-4044, (928) 526-1878, countryinns.com

The Country Inns by Carlson is on the eastern edge of town, but still on the primary business and historic route 66. This is a clean and simple 3-star hotel, offering free breakfast. Indoor pool, and room service.

LITTLE AMERICA HOTEL FLAGSTAFF

2515 E. Butler Avenue, Flagstaff, AZ 86004-6019, (928) 779-7900, flagstaff.littleamerica.com

The Little America is a modern and recently remodeled hotel about 10 minutes from the downtown Flagstaff area. The rooms, outdoor pool, and lobby are hip and slightly upscale. They also offer breakfast, lunch, and dinner at their Silver Pine Restaurant and Bar. Overall, good value for the money.

DRURY INN & SUITES FLAGSTAFF

300 S Milton Rd, Flagstaff, AZ 86001-6259, (928) 773-4900, druryhotels.com

Close to Old Town Flagstaff, the Dury Inn is a modern multistory hotel offering a wide range of services. A big positive of the Dury is that this is a 3.5-star hotel at a reasonable price. Breakfast is included, parking is free, and they offer an indoor pool, whirlpool, fitness center and guest laundry. There's even free sodas and popcorn from 3-10pm and the "5:30 Kickback", where they offer a rotating menu of hot food and mixed drinks.

Downtown "Flag"

EMBASSY SUITES BY HILTON FLAGSTAFF

706 S Milton Rd, Flagstaff, AZ 86001-6301, (928) 774-4333, embassysuites3.hilton.com

This Hilton property is up the road closer to Route 66 and Old Town. Suites are available along with a lounge area with bar. They offer an outdoor pool, fitness center and free breakfast and Wi-Fi.

37

FLAGSTAFF

Lodging

Restaurants

Coffee and Sweets

Things To Do

Flagstaff is especially incredible in the spring and fall seasons

HILTON GARDEN INN FLAGSTAFF

350 W Forest Meadows St, Flagstaff, AZ 86001-2918, (928) 226-8888, hiltongardeninn3.hilton.com

Right on the main north-south thoroughfare of Flagstaff, the Hilton Garden is conveniently located. They offer clean rooms, good customer service, along with a breakfast buffet and indoor pool.

SPRINGHILL SUITES FLAGSTAFF

2455 S Beulah Blvd, Flagstaff, AZ 86001-8736, (928) 774-8042, marriott.com

Springhill Suites Flagstaff is a 3-star hotel offering an indoor pool, suites, small gym, and free breakfast. The hotel ambiance is basic with a touch of modern design.

COURTYARD BY MARRIOTT FLAGSTAFF

2650 S Beulah Blvd, Flagstaff, AZ 86001-8924, (928) 774-5800, marriott.com

Just north of I40, this hotel offers the same consistent quality as other Courtyard hotels. Clean rooms, modern lobby, good customer service and indoor pool. They do offer a breakfast buffet; however, you may want to look at other options for breakfast as it's not the greatest value for the cost.

ARIZONA MOUNTAIN INN & CABINS

4200 Lake Mary Rd, Flagstaff, AZ 86005-9210, (928) 774-8959, arizonamountaininn.com

This is a beautiful place to stay. Arizona Mountain Inn is off the beaten path on 13 acres within the Coconino Forest. The inn offers several options for lodging, including B&B suites and individual cabins. They even have a Hogan style tent that sleeps 16. The cabins vary in capacity, sleeping from 2 to 10 folks. Their online site shows multiple pictures of each cabin and suite. The cabins offer a rustic, western, and woodsy alternative to the cookie cutter hotel chain experience. Plus, they come with a full kitchen and living area.

The suites are more romantic, some with 2-person hot tubs, 50" HD TV's, and king size poster beds. The views from every room, whether cabin or suite or Hogan are wonderful!

TWIN ARROWS NAVAJO CASINO RESORT

22181 Resort Blvd, Exit 219, I-40, Flagstaff, AZ 86004-9715, (928) 856-7200, twinarrows.com

Twin Arrows is about 30 minutes from downtown. This hotel offers everything you might expect from an Indian Casino, including cheap rooms, several dining options, gambling, as well as events and other entertainment. The rooms and overall décor are modern and clean. They also offer an indoor pool and room service. As a 4-star hotel at 2-star prices, this is arguably one of the best deals all up for the money, as long you are open to the casino vibe that comes with the great price.

RESTAURANTS

THE HORSEMEN LODGE STEAKHOUSE

Steakhouse, $$, 8500 US-89, Flagstaff, AZ 86004, (928) 526-2655, horsemenlodge.com, open Monday thru Thursday 8am - 9pm, Friday and Saturday 7am -10pm, Sunday 7am - 9pm

The Horseman Lodge does steak, for breakfast, lunch, and dinner. For example, you can get either a boneless ribeye and eggs or those same eggs with filet mignon, sirloin, or a New York strip. That's just breakfast, which is served until 2pm. The dinner menu expands from there, offering elk chops and bison tenderloin on top of the usual steak choices. If you are looking for a steak, no matter the meal, the Horseman Lodge Steakhouse will deliver. They are found up Highway 89 in northern Flagstaff on the way to the Grand Canyon.

SATCHMO'S

Cajun/Creole/BBQ, $, 2320 N 4th St, Flagstaff, AZ 86004, (928) 774-7292, satchmosaz.com, open daily 11am - 9pm

Satchmo's has been named the best BBQ in the Southwest by Southern Living Magazine. Their take on BBQ is with a Cajun twist, adding in coleslaw to their pulled pork sandwiches and offering favorites like red beans & rice, jambalaya, and catfish. The Cajun meets BBQ menu is a great combo, making for a completely satisfying meal. The ambiance of the place is a bit lacking, chairs, tables, napkins are about it.

MARTANNE'S BURRITO PALACE

Mexican, $, 112 E Rte. 66, Flagstaff, AZ 86001, (928) 773-4701, open Monday thru Saturday 7:30am - 9pm, Sunday 7:30am - 3:30pm

Just plain delicious Mexican cuisine. They serve a mean breakfast burrito but also serve up Eggs Benedict. Lunch and dinner menu is filled with lots to choose from. The portions are hearty, hot, and served up quick.

SHIFT KITCHEN & BAR

American, $, 107 N San Francisco St, Flagstaff, AZ 86001, (928) 440-5135, shiftflg.com, open Wed thru Monday 5-10pm, closed Tuesday, open Monday thru Friday for breakfast 7:30am -11am

Shift Kitchen is gourmet food without a lot of pretenses. If you've ever experienced mind-blowing food truck dishes, aka - incredible food without the cloth tablecloths and sommelier, then you've got a good idea of what Shift has to offer. The dishes are all simply delicious, the service is friendly, but the ambiance is not over the top. The point to be made here is that the focus is on the food. They are open for breakfast but are best known for their dinners, everything is good, but if you can't choose, go for the tasting menu.

CORNISH PASTY CO

British Pub, $, 26 S San Francisco St, Flagstaff, AZ 86001, Phone number (928) 440-5196, cornishpasty-co.com, open daily 11am - midnight, closes at 2am Thursday thru Sunday

Cornish Pastry Co is a newer location serving British pub fare. This restaurant is part of an Arizona chain that offers a hip and lively backdrop to a host of British comfort foods and beers on tap. The pasties are hearty, delicious, and delightfully decadent. They also offer soups and salads and pool tables. Note that they are open till early morning.

LUMBERYARD BREWING COMPANY

American, $, 5 S San Francisco St, Flagstaff, AZ 86001, (928) 779-2739, lumberyardbrewing. com, open daily 11am - 11pm, closes at 2am Wed - Saturday

The Lumberyard offers generous portions with a menu full of comfort food along with several home-brewed beers on tap. Here you can get chicken wings, nachos, burgers, and the ever-amazing "deep fried big mac n' cheez balls." You get the idea, leave your diet at the door and say, "Why not, it's vacation time! Let's eat!"

NOMADS GLOBAL LOUNGE

Tapas, International Cuisine, $, 19 W Phoenix Ave, Flagstaff, AZ 86001, (928) 774-7958, modubeau.com, open Monday thru Thursday 4 - 10pm, open from 3 - 11pm Friday and Saturday, until 9pm on Sunday

Tucked inside the Motel Dubeau, Nomads is a fun place to have a glass of beer or wine while enjoying a few small plates of high quality, fresh food. The atmosphere is warm and inviting, making this a suitable place to kick back, relax, and just hang out with friends. They also have outdoor seating. The food is all nicely prepared, with baguettes and dips, Yucatan chicken, meat pies, and salmon cakes as examples of what the offer.

Humphreys Peak covered in snow

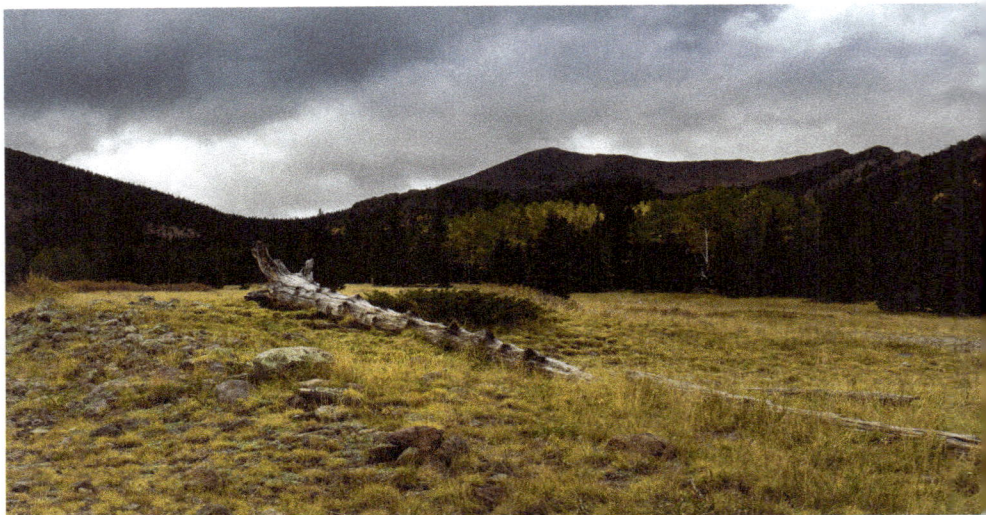

THE TOASTED OWL CAFÉ

American, meals for under $10, 12 S Mikes Pike St, Flagstaff, AZ 86001, (928) 774-5326, thetoastedowl. com, open daily 7am - 4pm

The Toasted Owl offers a go to place for a hearty breakfast as well as sandwiches and burgers for lunch. The breakfasts keep them on the map, offering breakfast burritos, omelets, scrambles, and pancakes.

OREGANO'S PIZZA BISTRO

Pizza and Pasta, $, 980 N Country Club Dr, Flagstaff, AZ 86004, (928) 233-3000, oreganos.com, open daily 11am - 10pm

There are a lot of pizza places in Flagstaff and in fact, there are two Oregano's in Flag alone. The reason this one made the grade is consistency and choice in the saturated world of sit down pizza restaurants. You can choose from pan, thin crust or stuffed pizzas, pastas, wings, and salads. Both locations are clean and well lit. The other location is close to Northern Arizona University and gets a little more of the college crowd, but is otherwise an equivalent choice.

COPPA CAFÉ

French, $$, 1300 S Milton Ave, Flagstaff, AZ 86001, (928) 637-6813, coppacafe.net, open Wed thru Saturday 3 - 9pm, Sunday 10am - 3pm

Coppa offers fine French and country French cuisine for dinner as well as a Sunday brunch. The food is of high quality similar to what you find in a high-end restaurant. The offerings are honestly hard to find anywhere in the Southwest, including steak tartare, foie gras and clay baked duck egg. Most of the ingredients are locally sourced, and it is clear there is a lot of passion for French cuisine here. The ambiance, however, is simple and a bit more like what you would find at a to-go lunch place.

COFFEE AND SWEETS

TOP OF THE MOUNTAIN COFFEE AND MILKSHAKES

ICE CREAM, COFFEE, 4705 N US Hwy 89, Flagstaff, AZ 86004, (928) 527-3031, open daily 6am -6pm

Everything you need to know about this place is in the name. They offer drive-through coffees and milkshakes that satisfy the taste buds for those on the go.

WHITE DOVE COFFEE SHOP

COFFEE, 2211 E 7th Ave, Flagstaff, AZ 86004, (928) 774-3059, open Monday thru Friday 6:30am - 6pm, Saturday 8am - 3pm

White Dove is low key and cozy, offering hot and cold coffee drinks along with a small selection of breakfast and lunch sandwiches. This is a place of humble atmosphere, yet high on quality.

FLAGSTAFF CHOCOLATE COMPANY

CHOCOLATE, 120 N Leroux St, Flagstaff, AZ 86001, (928) 779-5611, open daily 10am - 9pm, open to 8pm Sunday

Located in Old Town, the Flagstaff Chocolate Company offers one of the widest selections of chocolates and candies in the city.

STEEP LEAF LOUNGE

TEA/COFFEE, 1 E Aspen, Flagstaff, AZ 86001, (928) 440-3474, open daily 8am - 10 pm, until 11pm on Friday and Saturday

Steep is very close to Firecreek Coffee but offers more of a laid-back vibe with a twist of small-town local tea and coffee house. If you are looking for a cup of tea or espresso drink in a relaxed atmosphere, try Steep.

Hiking near Humphreys Peak and Arizona Snowbowl

SWEET SHOPPE & NUT HOUSE

CANDY, ICE CREAM, 15 E Aspen Ave, Flagstaff, AZ 86001, (928) 213-9000, sweetshoppecandy.com, open daily 10am - 8pm, except open till 10pm Friday and Saturday

Get your sweet tooth fix on with gourmet caramel apples, fudge, chocolates, and candies. Located in Old Town.

FIRECREEK COFFEE

COFFEE, 22 E Rte. 66, Flagstaff, AZ 86001, (928) 774-2266, firecreekcoffee.com, open daily 7am - 9pm

Firecreek Coffee sits in a tiny space, but with warm, lively ambiance and great espresso drinks. These folks love every bean that comes into their fold. They offer various food items to enjoy with your coffee and frequent performances to entertain their guests. They even have coffee bean subscriptions if you fancy yourself to become a home barista. Located right on Route 66, it doesn't get much cooler than Firecreek.

SINGLE SPEED COFFEE CAFÉ

COFFEE, 2 S Beaver St, Flagstaff, AZ 86001, (928) 214-7280, singlespeedcafe.com, open daily 6:30am - 4pm

When you live in a college town, there's a broad selection of coffee houses. Single Speed is one of them. Beyond the espresso drinks, they offer a nice selection of hearty breakfast and lunch items, all homemade and all well executed. Single Speed is more than coffee, they also offer a large choice of loose leaf and other assorted teas. The ambiance is warm and welcoming.

MACY'S EUROPEAN COFFEE HOUSE & BAKERY

BAKERY, COFFEE, 14 S Beaver St, Flagstaff, AZ 86001, (928) 774-2243, macyscoffee.net, open daily 6am - 6pm

Macy's is a great alternative to find healthy breakfast and lunch menu items, along with wonderfully prepared coffee and baked goods. They offer an assortment of gluten and vegan goodies all homemade. Macy's also roasts their own beans.

Views on the way down to Sedona, Arizona from Flagstaff

Side Trip 2 – Mystical Sedona

BEST FROM

Starting from the South Rim Grand Canyon is your quickest way to take this side trip. Tack on an additional 3-hour drive if coming from the North Rim.

WHAT YOU WILL SEE

- Sedona, Arizona
- Slide Rock State Park
- Red Rock State Park

WHY CHOOSE THIS SIDE TRIP

They say that once the dust of the Sedona red rocks touches your feet, it never comes off. This isn't just a fanciful statement either, many people who upon setting their gaze on the beauty of Sedona, vow never to leave. During a monsoon, the sky is an angry canvas backdrop for the towering warm monoliths. On a clear day, there is a different moment of wonder around each turn, and a cold winter's storm will leave this town of red rocks dusted with a purity of white snow that simply brings amazement that anything this beautiful could be real. And the sunsets? The sunsets here are so magnificent as to be called out by Travel and Leisure as one of the 12 best places to see one, not just in the state of Arizona mind you, but best in the world.

Sedona is satisfyingly diverse. It is a small town, filled with great restaurants, all levels of lodging, spa packages, and great outdoor malls to explore. The town is filled with shops to amble through, selling everything from fine art to desert themed key chains with your name on them. There are times when you realize you are in a tourist town and well, it is, and you are. At its heart though, Sedona is a city that caters to tourists, but also tries hard to maintain a sense of local community.

Within and surrounding the town of Sedona are its red rocks, each formation unique, each one with a name and no two alike. Some formations look like Snoopy, submarines, roosters, bells and even a warrior looking straight into the sky, to name just a handful. The citadels of rock in themselves are simply breathtaking, especially to hike in. Fortunately, with the vast number of trails to choose from, this is a paradise for hikers and mountain bikers alike. There are trails for everyone, from strolling along a creek path to more strenuous multiday hikes into the wilderness. You will need a Red Rock Pass to hike on many of the trails, see the inset for more information.

ALLOW

- Recommended – 1-4 days.
- Total Drive Time: 2 hours, 10 minutes
- Sedona: see below

You can get a taste of Sedona as a half day visit, typically done on the way out to the Phoenix Airport. A 2-3 day stopover is recommended if you have one week to travel, more if you have more travel time and enjoy hiking.

CAN BE COMBINED WITH

Side Trip 1 - "Ancient Lands," Side Trip 3 – "Historical Southwest," Side Trip 4 – "Phoenix on the Rise," and Side Trip 5 – "Petrified Forests."

Sedona Sunset

MYSTICAL SEDONA

GRAND CANYON NATIONAL PARK

GRAND CANYON VILLAGE

89

160

64

64

Grand Canyon South to Flagstaff
87.5 mi / 140.8 km / 1 hr 35 min

N

0   10 mi

0   10 km

180

89

64

40

89

40

FLAGSTAFF

Flagstaff to Slide Rock
22.6 mi / 36.4 km / 46 min

89A

17

SLIDE ROCK STATE PARK

Slide Rock to Sedona
6.9 mi / 11.1 km / 14 min

SEDONA

Sedona to Red Rock
9.4 mi / 15.1 km / 19 min

RED ROCK STATE PARK

Red Rock to Phoenix via Hwy 260 + Hwy 17
119 mi / 191.5 km / 2 hrs 3 min

260

© GONE BEYOND GUIDES 2017

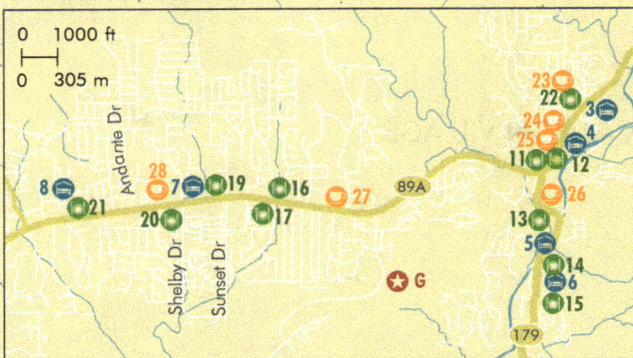

One of the many views of Cathedral Rock

SEDONA

Sedona is nestled at 4500 feet, so throw out the notions of Saguaro cactuses and desert bleakness, they grow in the lower and hotter elevations. Here, the red rock is covered with pinyon-juniper, giving off inviting scents and providing shade on hot days. Sedona sits in the transition zone of three ecosystems and is thus one of the most diverse areas for plants and birds in Arizona.

For many, Sedona is also a place of spirit and energy. In fact, the majority of those folks that are drawn to the area often say they are pulled from a deeper connection. Certain rock formations are focal areas, called vortexes. Some vortexes have strong masculine energy, others are softer and feminine, while others contain both. While not everyone feels the energy, many head to at least one vortex to see if they experience anything. There are a number of new age type stores that offer books, crystals, spirit tours, and tarot readings, should you feel inclined.

The drive to Sedona from the Grand Canyon takes you through Flagstaff, which is covered in detail in Side Trip 1 – "Ancient Lands." Once out of Flagstaff, head down Highway 89a through the stunningly picturesque Oak Creek Canyon. Rand McNally has named this canyon as one of the top 5 most scenic drives in Arizona. This journey starts just outside of Flagstaff at the top of the Mogollon Rim, and winds down hairpin turns through riparian woodland and high canyon walls, ending in Uptown Sedona. Be sure to visit Oak Creek Canyon Vista at the top, which is well marked and located just before dropping down. Seasonally one can find a wide array of Navajo jewelry and other handmade items.

SEDONA

Lodging

1	Junipine	A4
2	Oak Creek Terrace Resort	C5
3	Best Western Plus Arroyo Roble Hotel	B4
4	L'Auberge de Sedona	B4
5	Inn on Oak Creek	B4
6	Arabella Hotel Sedona	B4
7	Sedona Rouge	B2
8	Adobe Grand Villas	B1
9	Bell Rock Inn	G4
10	Enchantment Resort	C1

Restaurants

11	Wildflower Bread Company	B4
12	Cowboy Club	B4
13	Rene at Tlaquepaque	B4
14	The Hudson	B4
15	Elote Cafe	C4
16	Hiro's Sushi	B2
17	Picazzo's	B2
18	Miley's Cafe	H4
19	Coffee Pot Restaurant	B2
20	Dahl & Di Luca Ristorante	B2
21	Nick's Westside	B1
22	Oaxaca Restaurant	B4

Coffee and Sweets

23	Theia's	B4
24	Sedona Fudge Company	B4
25	Black Cow Cafe	B4
26	Creekside Coffee	B4
27	Sedona Bakery & Cafe	B3
28	Sedonuts	B2
29	DQ Oak Creek Canyon	C5

Things To Do

A	Palatki and Honanki Heritage Sites	C1
B	Doe Mountain Trail	C1
C	Fay Canyon Trail	C1
D	Boynton Canyon Trail	C1
E	Red Rock State Park	G2
F	Red Rock Crossing	F2
G	Airport Mesa Vortex	B3
H	Cathedral Rock Trail	F3
I	Soldier Pass Trail	D3
J	Little Horse Trail	F4
K	Brins Mesa Trail	D4
L	Uptown	D4
M	Tlaquepaque	E4
N	Chapel of the Holy Cross	F4
O	Bell Rock Loop Trail	G4
P	Slide Rock State Park	B4
Q	West Fork Oak Creek	A4

To sum up, Sedona is a fantastic place to experience the great outdoors and then come back to town to enjoy a delicious meal and relax in a nice room. The meals taste better, and the bed is more comfortable after a day among the red rocks. It is equally a place to just relax and do some shopping, get ice cream, go on a jeep tour, or sit by the creek and just watch the water go by.

THINGS TO DO IN SEDONA

HIKING

As mentioned, hiking is one of the top things to do in Sedona and there are the numerous hiking trails with something for everyone. Selected (and personal favorite) trails listed below.

BELL AND COURTHOUSE ROCK LOOP

Easy to Moderate – (4.2 mi / 6.4 km), round trip from trailhead, allow 2-2.5 hours, Red Rock Pass needed

Bell Rock and Courthouse Rock are two prominent formations found by heading south on Hwy 179 towards the Village of Oak Creek. The loop travels around these two locally famous features, offering splendid views along the entire path. The trail system here is well maintained, with wide trails and plenty of informative signs to help you along the way. This trail connects to Little Horse to the north and Big Park Loop to the south, giving the opportunity to combine into a longer hike.

Bell Rock is considered a vortex and many folks veer off the trail to venture on the formation itself. It is possible to climb to the top with a little courage and trust in the slick rock. Courthouse Rock is one massive and wide tower with sheer vertical walls on all sides. As you head south towards the trailhead, look at Courthouse and try to find the "Indian Warrior" looking straight up at the sky.

WEST FORK

Easy – (5.2 mi / 8.4 km), round trip from trailhead, allow 2-3 hours, $10-day use fee

West Fork Trail is a tributary of Oak Creek and is found by heading up Hwy 89A towards Flagstaff. This is a popular trail, especially in the summer and for good reason. The air temperature is cooler, well shaded and full of riparian flora set within grand red rock canyon walls. The trail is relatively flat with numerous creek crossings, 13 by the last count, making this a fun way to keep cool on a hot summers day. This is a trail to fall in love with any time of the year, with the golds and reds of fall foliage reflecting on still pools of clear stream water or a snowy playground in the winter.

Most call it quits at the end of the trail and turn around, but it is possible to hike to the end of the canyon. This 14-mile hike is as strenuous as it is a pure adventure, requiring an equal mix of boulder hopping, wading, and swimming in several deep pools as the creek itself becomes your trail. The off-trail trek is meant for experienced hikers equipped with survival skills and in good physical shape.

CATHEDRAL ROCK

Moderate to Strenuous – (1.5 mi / 2.4 km), round trip from trailhead, allow 1.5 hours, Red Rock Pass needed

This trail is found by taking Hwy 179 south to Back O' Beyond Road to the trailhead parking area. Cathedral Rock is considered to be the mother of all the formations in Sedona. This massive formation looks

For those that don't want to hike to the saddle but want a great view of Cathedral Rock, take a drive on Red Rock Loop, located just out of town on the way to Cottonwood on Highway 89A. Pull off at one of the parking areas before the road drops down to catch a great view of Cathedral, Bell Rock, Courthouse, and Seven Warriors. The views here are unique and spectacular.

as different as it does incredible from each angle you view it from. Cathedral sits on its own, seemingly in the middle of the red rocks, as a set of both formidable and delicate monolithic spires of rock. It is considered to be a vortex and is unique in that the red rock sandstone surrounds an intrusion of black volcanic basalt that can be seen as you look over the edge of the saddle towards Oak Creek.

Getting to the actual top of Cathedral Rock requires climbing gear, so when folks say, "the top" for this trail, don't worry, they mean the rather obvious saddle at the base of its tower walls. The trail is a short but continually steep and strenuous climb of 600 feet over 0.7 miles. There are some exposed areas, so if you are afraid of heights or just don't like climbing uphill, best to avoid this one. You are traveling on the slick rock itself for much of the hike, with numerous trail markers to lead the way.

The best way to experience Cathedral Rock is to go early or late in the day when you can have the saddle to yourself. From here, catch your breath from the climb and just sit. You will perhaps hear the wind through the pinyon-juniper forests below or catch the call of a raven echoing amongst the towers around you or maybe even hear the faint omnipresent murmur of Oak Creek. If you are looking for the "magic" of Sedona, it can be found here.

SOLDIERS PASS

Moderate – (4.8 mi / 7.7 km), round trip from trailhead, allow 2.5 hours, Red Rock Pass needed

Soldiers Pass is accessed from the trailhead parking area of the same name by going down Soldier Pass Road and following the signs through a residential neighborhood. Parking is limited, and it is difficult to find allowed parking in the surrounding area, so plan accordingly if you are in town during a peak time. The trail offers the usual above and beyond fantastic views, plus a few other attractions to check out. Just as you start, there is Devil's Kitchen, a large sinkhole worthy of veering over. A little farther on are the Seven Apache Pools, a set of naturally forming pools that typically contain standing water. Once deeper in and past the Jeep road that parallels the trail, you will also see a few arches to the

right that you can hike to on informal trails. The trail, as the name implies, climbs up to the top of Soldiers Pass, offering exceptional views from every angle. You can return back or combine with Brins Mesa Trail for a longer hike.

BRINS MESA

Moderate – (7.2 mi / 11.6 km), round trip from trailhead, allow 3.5 hours, Red Rock Pass needed

Brins Mesa, located in West Sedona off of the Jordan Trailhead is picked up from Jordan Road in Uptown Sedona or from the Soldiers Pass Trailhead. This trail is a longer hike offering wildflowers and ever-changing views as it climbs to the summit of the trail. The hike itself is very satisfying, but the true reward is the view from the top of Brins Mesa itself. The trail levels out at the top into a large clearing. There was a fire through this area in 2006, but the vegetation has grown back for the most part. You can return the way you came or combine this trail with Soldiers Pass.

LITTLE HORSE

Easy to Moderate – (3.5 mi / 5.6 km), round trip from trailhead, allow 1.5 hours, Red Rock Pass needed

Little Horse Trail is found by taking Hwy 179 south towards the Village of Oak Creek. Look for the parking area just off the road on the left at milepost 309.8. Beyond the fantastic views, the reason why Little Horse Trail made the cut for this "best of" selection is that it offers variety. You can hike the trail on its own as an out and back or connect to many other trails, including Broken Arrow, Bell Rock, Bryant Canyon, and Chapel Trail. There are many well-placed maps on these trails to show the way. Little Horse is also one of the best trails if it's raining when normally dry washes turn into gently flowing creeks and pleasant waterfalls. For that, Little Horse is a favorite wintertime hike. The trail has a few short moments of elevation gain, but for the most part, meanders up a creek bed before landing at Chicken Point. You'll know you've hit this nod to poultry when you reach a saddle that merges with the Broken Arrow 4WD road, which is popular with jeep tours. Chicken Point looks like a happy go lucky clucky on its back looking straight up.

Bell Rock and Courthouse Rock

FAY CANYON

Easy – (2.3 mi / 3.7 km), round trip from trailhead, allow 1.5 hours, Red Rock Pass needed

Fay is another box canyon on the northwestern edge of Sedona in the Boynton Canyon area. Fay is a great choice, offering plenty of scenic views in a short hike with little elevation gain. This is a favorite for anyone looking for true immersion without too much effort. In the canyon is Fay Arch, about 0.5 miles up the canyon on the right side. The natural arch is easy to miss. Also, while rarely a problem, this is bear country, so be mindful that you are in the wilderness.

Along Boynton Canyon Trail

48

BOYNTON CANYON

Moderate – (6.2 mi / 10 km), round trip from trailhead, allow 2.5 – 3 hours, Red Rock Pass needed

This is one of the best hikes in Sedona and though popular, is never too crowded. Boynton is a box canyon that is held sacred by the Yavapai and Hopi. Within it, one can see numerous ancestral ruins and burial sites along a path that climbs gently to the canyon's end. The trail passes along the perimeter to Enchantment Resort. If you are staying at the resort, you can bypass a mile of hiking. However, you will be gently directed back to trailhead parking lot if you aren't.

Boynton Canyon is a very satisfying hike. For the entire hike, one is surrounded by carved red rocks set in thick pinyon-juniper forests. The ascent is gradual for the most part, and the temperature gets cooler as you climb up the 500-foot elevation gain. One feels they are in true wilderness, in fact, brown bears have been spotted here. Boynton Canyon is also one of the vortex areas, and many folks do observe a peaceful feeling when hiking on this trail.

DOE MOUNTAIN

Moderate – (1.3 mi / 2.1 km), round trip from trailhead, allow 2 hours, Red Rock Pass needed

Doe Mountain is a small flat top mesa near the Boynton Canyon area. The trail climbs 459 feet over a short distance of 0.75 miles. Once at the top, one can explore the mesa top, which has only informal paths. Make sure you note where the trail is as this is how you will get back down. The views from the top are exceptional. This is a hike that offers a big reward for a relatively small uphill hike. If you love hiking and are looking for a bit of adventure, try this hike at night on a full moon. Ascending can be challenging, but once on top, the entire mesa and valley around you bask in the white glow of the moon.

JEEP TOURS

Outside of hiking, the Jeep tours are a ton of fun. Part adventure, part entertainment, the Jeep tours allow immersion into the red rocks without having to hike. Pink Jeep has been around since 1960 and has the best reputation. The other operators listed are recommended as well.

Pink Jeep Tours

204 N State Rte. 89A, Sedona, AZ 86336 Phone: (800) 873-3662

Red Rock Western Jeep Tours

301 N State Rte. 89A, Sedona, AZ 86336, Phone: (928) 282-6667

A Day in the West

252 AZ-89A, Sedona, AZ 86336, Phone: (928) 282-4320

CLIFF DWELLINGS

Several miles outside of town but still within the red rocks are the Palatki and Honanki Heritage Sites. Both are stunning examples of cliff dwellings of the Ancestral Puebloan people and are the largest in the Sedona area. Each ruin has restrictions on admission and are both accessed via a dirt road, so plan ahead before going.

Contact the Red Rock Ranger District at (928) 203-2900 for current information.

SHOPPING

There are several places to shop in Sedona. At the top of the list is the Tlaquepaque Arts & Crafts Village (336 AZ-179, Sedona, AZ 86336, tlaq.com), an outdoor mall with an equal eye for artistic quality and fun shops. Just across the bridge past the roundabout from Tlaquepaque are two must-see shops, Garlands Navajo Rugs (411 AZ-179, Sedona, AZ 86336, garlandsrugs.com) and Lanning Gallery of Fine Art (431 AZ-179, Sedona, AZ 86336, lanninggallery.com). Both have been a Sedona staple for decades and offer one of a kind items. Garland's is great to admire the quality of their rugs and Hopi Kachina doll collection. The Shops at Hyatt Pinon Pointe (179 AZ-89A, Sedona, AZ 86336) are newer and worth a look. Uptown Sedona has become a land for tourist souvenirs and offers a wide selection of items. While most of Uptown are shops selling T-shirts and mugs, the one exception is Clear Creek Trading Company (435 AZ-89A, Sedona, AZ 86336, clearcreektrading.com). They offer Native American merchandise from 30 tribes and is so unique that to tell you what they sell would almost give away the surprise of what you will find. You'll be amazed at what they offer for sale.

CHAPEL OF THE HOLY CROSS

This one of a kind church is a Roman Catholic chapel built into the rock itself and is worth visiting. The views are spectacular from inside. It can be tricky to find parking as it is a popular destination.

SCHNEBLY HILL ROAD

This high clearance dirt road ultimately goes to the top of the Mogollon Rim and to Flagstaff. This road has become a lot worse over the years and is only suitable for vehicles with high clearance designed for rough terrain. For those that do have such a vehicle, this road provides some of the best views down into Sedona.

AIRPORT MESA ROAD

Airport Mesa is popular for two reasons, it's one of the easiest ways to experience a vortex (as it's reputed to be one), and it is a commanding place to watch a sunset. If you want to go, make sure you plan enough time. Parking is notoriously difficult, and the town has started charging $3 a day to park in the area. If you are going to the vortex itself, allow about 30 minutes more than you would think to climb to the top. Also, bring a flashlight to help you back down.

RED ROCK CROSSING

Red Rock Crossing offers stunning views of Cathedral Rock with Oak Creek in the foreground, making it a favorite for photographers and creators of computer desktop backgrounds. This is one of the most photographed scenes in the world and is just amazing in person. The crossing can be accessed either from the north by taking Red Rock Loop Road to Blue Moon Picnic Site ($10-day use fee) or by taking Verde Valley School Road to reach its southern entrance. While the southern entrance is free, parking is limited and the drive is longer if staying in Sedona.

The swimming hole can change from year to year and is currently about a quarter mile upstream. There are paths on either side along the creek. In the summer, this is a popular and often crowded spot.

RED ROCK STATE PARK

Red Rock State Park is tucked outside of the city bustle off of Red Rock Loop Road. The park forms a subset of the trail system throughout Sedona. There are some modern historical sites to explore, and in general, the trails are easy to moderate, and most are less than 2 miles. This is a great way to take it easy and still get a sense of what Sedona has to offer.

The park is open year round. Summer hours are 8am - dusk, with last entry 30 minutes before dusk. Winter hours are from Labor Day to first weekend of May from 8am - 5pm. The visitor center is open 9am - 7:15pm in the summer. Entrance fees are $7 for adults, and $4 for children 7 -13, under 7 are free.

RATTLESNAKE RIDGE TRAIL

Easy – (1.3 mi / 2.1 km), round trip from visitor center, allow 1 hour

This is an easy trail giving great views of Red Rock State Park and Sedona. The trail connects to the Smoke Trail or the visitor center from the front picnic ramadas.

SMOKE TRAIL

Easy – (0.4 mi / 0.6 km), round trip from visitor center, allow 30 minutes

Typically done as a part of some loops within the park, the Smoke Trail ambles peacefully along Oak Creek. It is accessible for all users. Lots of riparian flora here along with ample bird watching possibilities. The great egret and blue heron have both been spotted on occasion along with woodpeckers and ravens.

KISVA TRAIL

Easy – (1.7 mi / 2.7 km), round trip from visitor center, allow 1 - 2 hours

This is a connector trail to Eagle's Nest Loop, Smoke and Yavapai Ridge Trail and the Apache Fire Loop. The trail follows along a branch of Oak Creek for the most part, climbing 112 feet as it connects with the other trails. Kisva is a Hopi word meaning "shady water," which describes this tranquil hike with near perfection.

Slide Rock State Park

EAGLE'S NEST LOOP

Moderate – (1.9 mi / 3.1 km), round trip from visitor center, allow 1 - 2 hours

The Eagle's Nest Loop is a great way to take in Sedona. It starts along Oak Creek before climbing to the top of a ridge, giving great views of Cathedral Rock, Seven Warriors, House Mountain, and West Sedona. The view also shows the ribbon of the Oak Creek riparian corridor as it weaves through the surrounding pinyon-juniper forests. The deciduous trees along Oak Creek

Cathedral Rock from Red Rock Crossing

PENDLEY HOMESTEAD TRAIL

Easy – (0.5 mi / 0.8 km), round trip, allow 30 minutes

Part of Slide Rock State Park, this is a paved trail that takes the visitor through a portion of the Pendley Homestead. The historical remnants seen along the trail includes the Pendley apple orchards and apple-packing barn along with magnificent views of the Oak Creek Canyon walls and watershed. This level trail is great for everyone and is still quite peaceful despite the crowds.

SLIDE ROCK ROUTE

Moderate – (0.6 mi / 1.0 km) round trip, allow 30 minutes

This trail is listed as moderate by the park but will seem easy to navigate for most. This is the primary route you take to get to the swimming area. Simply find parking and follow the hordes of people in front of you. Towards the creek, you'll need to step over sunbathers as the route becomes more like a public beach area with folks claiming base camp territories wherever they can. Look for a historic cabin on the west side of the creek that was used along with a Pelton wheel to generate electricity. Unless the creek is running high there is a footbridge to get to the other side.

Despite being crowded, the park is good fun. The water slide is capable of accommodating all, from kids to adults. It is very refreshing, and if you do it once, you will want to do it again, despite the line. Then there is the setting, which is magical. Filtered canyon sun against red and white cliff walls that bring forth emotions of a gentle strength. This is one of the top parks in the United States and for a good reason. During peak season, get there early to avoid the crowds.

Notes:

The Slide Rock area hit by a wildfire in 2014. The entire area was closed for a year to minimize erosion. Please help the area recover by staying on the trails in this area.

There are times when Oak Creek receives too much use resulting in high concentrations of E. coli bacteria. This can happen at any time but is especially prevalent during the summer when the population of visitors is up, and the water levels are down. The park does close as a result. Call the Oak Creek Water Quality Hotline at (602) 542-0202 before going. E. coli is definitely a thing at Slide Rock State Park. Despite multiple nonprofit agencies working to protect the Oak Creek watershed, the park and the creek are a victim of being "loved to death."

are quite dramatic in the fall as the changing color of the leaves meanders through the desert. Eagle's Nest can be combined with other trails and is accessed via the Smoke, Kisva, or Sentinel trails.

HOUSE OF APACHE FIRE LOOP

Moderate – (1.7 mi / 2.7 km), round trip from visitor center, allow 1 - 2 hours

Also shown as "Apache Fire Loop," this trail climbs about 100 feet to encircle the House of Apache Fire, a retreat home of Jack Frye, the president of Trans World Airlines. Jack and his wife Helen owned several hundred acres as a retreat from their east coast lives and built this house in 1947. The house was named from the campfires Yavapai Apache workers would make while building the house. The house was never completed.

The trail loops around the house giving signature views of the park and Sedona. Like most of the trails in this park, it can be combined with other trails for extended hiking.

SLIDE ROCK STATE PARK

Slide Rock is one of the most beloved outdoor spots in all of Arizona. The lure is simple, a clear flowing creek that is so smooth and slick in one spot that it creates a natural water slide. For this reason, the place is a zoo during peak season, with all manner of tourists looking for the choice sunny spots during the morning and the choice shady spots during the afternoon.

Beyond the water slide attraction, there are a handful of small trails. If you have kids, you have to go to Slide Rock State Park. It is for them one of the coolest places on earth. When you are done for the day, the Dairy Queen just below the park is another highlight for folks providing ice cream and snacks.

Slide Rock State Park charges an entrance fee of $20 on weekdays and $30 on weekends during the summer season of late May through Labor Day. The park is open 8am - 7pm in the summer.

LODGING

JUNIPINE RESORT

8351 N. Highway 89A, Sedona, AZ 86336, (928) 282-3375, junipine.com

Junipine Resort is one of several properties that are north of Sedona directly at Oak Creek Canyon. The experience here is different than staying in Sedona proper but just as magical. Oak Creek Canyon is absolutely beautiful, with towering red and white sandstone cliffs, the soothing waters, all nestled within mixed woodlands.

The resort offers a restaurant and full bar but lacks some of the amenities offered at other resort hotels. Where Junipine makes up for this is within the rooms themselves. The rooms are an ambiance of rustic and the grand southwest, with cobblestone fireplaces, spacious decks, well-appointed baths, and wood beamed ceilings as some of the features offered. Each room has distinctive features, the suites offer full kitchens and a large living area. If you are looking for the ability to take a glass of wine and head to your balcony to do nothing more than relax and listen to the creek, Junipine is an excellent choice.

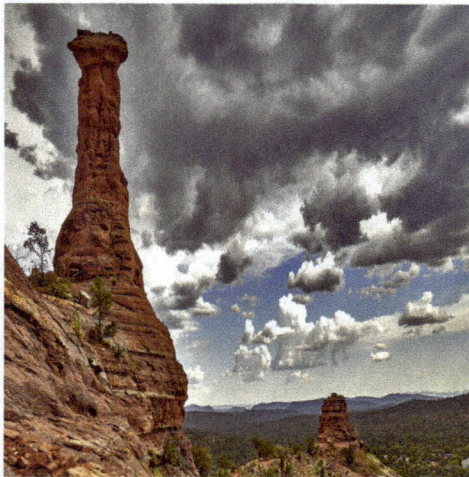

Kachina Woman near Enchantment Resort

OAK CREEK TERRACE RESORT

4548 N. Highway 89A, Sedona, AZ 86336, (928) 282-3562, oakcreekterrace.com

The Oak Creek Terrace is located up Oak Creek Canyon, offering a total of 23 cabins and bungalows along with basic and larger family rooms. The grounds along the Oak Creek are pleasant and peaceful. The rooms vary in features, but overall are rustic and comfortable. The Oak Creek Terrace is a little more low key than some of the other accommodations, making this a smart choice if you are looking for a cozy home away from home.

BEST WESTERN PLUS ARROYO ROBLE HOTEL & CREEKSIDE VILLAS

400 N State Route 89A, Sedona, AZ 86336-4214, (928) 282-4001, bestwesternsedona.com

This Best Western can be thought of as two properties. Located on the north end of Uptown Sedona, the street elevation hotel offers great service and clean rooms, plus free breakfast. The Arroyo Roble Resort is located down towards Oak Creek, where you can upgrade to creekside villas and cottages. The rooms here are larger and more private. The property also houses a clubhouse with indoor and outdoor pools, large fitness center, steam room and sauna, and a game room, including ping pong and arcade games.

The Best Western is a good choice, ripe with views from nearly every angle and close to both Oak Creek and Uptown. Being at the end of Uptown does have one drawback, it can get crowded, and this property is at the far end of all the craziness. Overall, high recommendations

L'AUBERGE DE SEDONA

301 L'Auberge Lane, Sedona, AZ 86336-4260, (800) 905-5745, lauberge.com

L'Auberge is the number one pick of this list. As a luxury class accommodation, staying here isn't cheap, but the staff, location, and overall ambiance make the stay work every penny. L'Auberge pampers their guests, but without being snooty. The experience is one of understated elegance. The staff doesn't take anything for granted. They treat you as if it has been a privilege to serve their guests and does not rest on their location alone. If you can afford it, L'Auberge is an unforgettable experience.

The resort is in Uptown but is down by the creek and away from the bustle of tourists. The property is 11 acres in total with 87 guest rooms and suites. They have a restaurant on premises along with an outdoor pool. They have a full spa menu, offering some of the best spa treatments in town. In the lobby of the spa is the L'Apothecary Blending Station, where you can make your own body rubs out of healing herbs and salts. This is a great family activity. They also have a fitness center, room service, and concierge, including a car and driver that will take you to wherever you want to go that is close by. The rooms are in harmony with the overall setting, filled with warmth and nice touches. The management has put in over $25 million to create one of the most tranquil atmospheres in Sedona.

THE INN ABOVE OAK CREEK

556 Highway 179, Sedona, AZ 86336-6145, (928) 282-7896, innaboveoakcreek.com

The Inn Above Oak Creek is one of the best overall hotels in Sedona. It's just a five-minute walk from Tlaquepaque and other great shops and is itself right on Oak Creek. The splendid views and the constant sounds of the water help to complete the picture of why folks come to Sedona. The hotel is unpretentious, relaxing, and just plain pleasant. They even offer free breakfast and Wi-Fi. If you are looking for a nice place to stay, think about upgrading to a creekside room. You'll get a terrace balcony along with great accommodations without breaking the bank.

51

ARABELLA HOTEL SEDONA

725 Highway 179, P.O. Box 180, Sedona, AZ 86336, (928) 282-7151, arabellahotelsedona.com

The Arabella offers great views along with great value. It's close to Tlaquepaque and other shops and dining experiences, including the Elote Café, which takes Mexican cuisine to an uncommonly elevated level. Breakfast is included, and they have a pool and gym. It is possible to see that this is a refurbished older hotel, but they've done a good job at remodeling the property. Arabella is a good choice for finding the right mix of quality and budget.

SEDONA ROUGE HOTEL AND SPA

2250 West Highway 89A, Sedona, AZ 86336, (928) 203-4111, sedonarouge.com

The Sedona Rouge is a boutique hotel that fires on some but not all marks. The ambiance is modern and hip, with bold colors and sometimes questionable style choices. Regardless, the hotel borders close to becoming a resort destination, offering its own restaurant, a full fitness center with red rock views, heated swimming pool and jacuzzi, outdoor fireplace seating, full day spa, and free breakfast for children under 12. Its location in West Sedona puts it in town without being in Uptown. Plus, it's close to the local favorite breakfast place, Coffee Pot Restaurant. The downside to Sedona Rouge is it seems to lean on its location as an excuse for a poorer showing in customer service. Given what the hotel is trying to achieve here, the expectations are higher, but there are times they aren't completely met, which is in part because the Sedona Rouge hasn't quite figured out what it wants to be. This is almost a true resort location and has the potential to be one if it was firing on all cylinders.

ADOBE GRAND VILLAS

35 Hozoni Drive, Sedona, AZ 86336-3765, (866) 900-7616, adobegrandvillas.com

The Adobe Grand Villas is an incredible boutique hotel. Every villa is so well appointed, and for the period of your stay, you will feel like a movie star. The rooms are that over the top, every piece of furniture is high end, and no detail is ignored. Each villa is decorated in its own unique styles, such as the Hacienda, Whispering Pine, or Tuscany Villas. Each villa is at least 900 square feet.

The service is as incredible. Adobe Grand Villas offers full concierge, one of the best free breakfasts in Sedona, plus a pool, hot tub, and day spa. Freshly baked bread is delivered daily to your room.

BELL ROCK INN

6246 State Route 179, Sedona, AZ 86351-8995, (928) 282-4161, diamondresortsandhotels.com

At one time, the Bell Rock Inn was the only hotel in the Village of Oak Creek. The hotel has continued to keep itself a relevant part of this southern section of the Sedona area. The location has been remodeled, offering clean rooms and great service. Amenities include pool, hot tub, and a fitness center. If you are looking for a solid choice on a budget, Bell Rock Inn is a good bet. Do keep in mind that the Village of Oak Creek is a 15-20 minute drive from central Sedona.

ENCHANTMENT RESORT

525 Boynton Canyon Rd., Sedona, AZ 86336-3042, (844) 244-9489, enchantmentresort.com

Enchantment Resort is located at the mouth of Boynton Canyon and is a 5-star rated luxury resort hotel. The location is simply incredible, with views of cliff dwellings in plain view, red rock spires all around and the smell of pinyon-juniper to warm the spirit with each breath. The Mii amo spa consistently receives high

Cathedral Rock at Red Rock Crossing

marks and is one of the best in Sedona, which is a nice plus. The resort has an outdoor pool with full service, restaurant, tennis courts, spa, and a small 3-hole golf course. Additionally, they offer children's programs for ages 4-12, curated guides experiences, and golfing at their sister property in Seven Canyons.

While the resort does check all the boxes for world-class luxury, the veneer is thin in places. With a premium price comes higher expectations and Enchantment doesn't always deliver to that high of a bar. The food is good, but not world class. The rooms are nice but are exceptional only if you upgrade, which relative to the rest of the hotels in this travel guide command the highest room rates of any of the hotels described.

There are a couple of other things to consider before going all in on Enchantment. It is a good 20 minutes from Sedona's center, which isn't bad as you are away from the bustle but does make you feel a bit trapped. The other thing to consider is the ethics of this resort. When it was approved to be built, there was a tremendous uproar from much of Northern Arizona, as the whole of Boynton Canyon is considered a sacred and deeply spiritual place by multiple tribes. To the resort management's credit, they have tried to iron out the controversy, in part by allowing a space on the premises for local tribes to use for ceremonies. Still, the whole concept of spiritual harmony walking hand in hand with profit seems a bit forced and doesn't fully add up for many.

If you are hiking up Boynton Canyon, staying at Enchantment allows you to cut a good mile off the journey, as you can start right from the resort rather than having to walk around it from the trailhead. The gate is at the end of the property, and while it does need a room key to unlock, this mechanism hasn't been working for some time and it doesn't seem to be monitored. Visitors not staying at the resort that want to have drinks or food can pull up to the security gate and will be let in, though officially you are not allowed to hike to Boynton from there.

RESTAURANTS

WILDFLOWER BREAD COMPANY

AMERICAN, $, 101 N Hwy 89A, Sedona, AZ 86336, (928) 204-2223, wildflowerbread.com, open weekdays 6am - 9pm, weekends 7am - 8pm, open to 9pm on Saturday

Wildflower is on here because it offers a suitable place to grab breakfast and/or lunch without breaking the bank. The place has fantastic views, the service is always fast and attentive, and the food is fresh. Pick up a baguette to go for snacking afterward. The Wildflower Bread Company is a chain within Arizona, each with similar menu items and service.

If you are just landing in Sedona, one recommendation is to fill up at Wildflower as your first stop and the Sedona Chamber of Commerce Visitor Center (331 Forest Rd, Sedona, AZ 86336) as the next thing you do. As mentioned earlier, the volunteers there are packed with knowledge on how to help you make the most of your time in the Sedona. You can also buy a red rock pass here.

Chapel of the Holy Cross

COWBOY CLUB GRILLE & SPIRITS

AMERICAN / STEAKHOUSE, $$, 241 N State Rte 89A, Sedona, AZ 86336, (928) 282-4200, club.barkingfrogsedona.com, open daily 11am - 9pm

Located in Uptown, Cowboy Club is the go-to place for the best steaks in Sedona. The Southwest atmosphere is upbeat and lively, with great service and the food is consistently top notch. They offer a wide selection to choose from but are most known for their beef ribeye and buffalo tenderloin. For appetizers, be sure to try the diamondback rattlesnake and cactus fries. True Southwest dining! Cowboy Club does not take reservations and does get filled up. Their sister restaurant, the Silver Saddle, is more upscale and does take reservations. Both offer similar menus, with Cowboy Club offering a wider selection.

RENE AT TLAQUEPAQUE

FRENCH/AMERICAN, $$, 336 State Rte. 179, Sedona, AZ 86336, (928) 282-9225, renerestaurantsedona.com, open daily 11:30am - 8:30pm, open till 9pm on Friday and Saturday

Rene's offers a mix of country French and American cuisine with touches of the Southwest in an elegant and refined ambiance. Rene's is a fine dining experience and is an excellent choice for special occasions or a vacation dinner splurge. From the roasted duck, rack of lamb, or filet mignon, everything is well prepared and presented. They take their service seriously to ensure you receive a wonderful experience, whether you go for lunch or dinner. Their wine selection is top notch as well.

THE HUDSON

AMERICAN, $$, 671 AZ-179 D, Sedona, AZ 86336, (928) 862-4099, thehudsonsedona.com, open daily 11:30am - 9pm

The Hudson is a newcomer to the Sedona scene and has hit the ground like a bolt of lightning, getting great reviews. They offer fresh farm to table fare. Each dish is hip and within the realm of slightly upscale comfort food, fresh and satisfying. The menu is varied and well thought out, with items ranging from chicken pot pie to Thai scallops to a nice white marble farm pork chop. Try the steamed mussels for starters.

ELOTE CAFÉ

MEXICAN, $, 771 State Rte. 179, Sedona, AZ 86336, (928) 203-0105, elotecafe.com, open Tuesday thru Saturday 5 - 9pm

Elote starts with the foundation of Mexican cuisine and elevates it. They've taken the traditional recipes, deconstructed them, and then rebuilt every dish from the ground up to take Mexican to a whole new level. From the corn crusted scallops to the buffalo mole poblano, the entrees are each uniquely wonderful. At least one person at the table orders elote, which is a fire roasted corn soup, but everyone should try it. The soup is quite excellent. If you do go, the coveted spots are outside when weather permits, where you dine with the views and if you time it right, a Sedona sunset. They don't take reservations and do get quite busy, but if you aren't famished by the time it's your turn, hold out for an outside table if the weather is good, it's worth the wait.

HIRO'S SUSHI & JAPANESE KITCHEN

SUSHI, $$, 1730 W State Rte. 89A, Sedona, AZ 86336, (928) 282-8906, hirosedona.com, open Tuesday thru Saturday for lunch 11:30am - 1:1:30pm and dinner 5-8pm, open Sunday for dinner only 5 - 8 pm, closed Monday

The first visit to Hiro's was filled with skepticism. How can one deliver great sushi in the middle of the desert? If you are wondering the same thing, be prepared to be pleasantly surprised. Having written now for almost the entire Southwest, let's go out on a limb here. Hiro's is one of the best sushi bars in the Southwest outside of the major cities. There, it's been said. The sushi is fresh, the rolls are well thought out, and the service is great. They offer lunch specials as well as a full dinner menu.

PICAZZO'S ORGANIC ITALIAN KITCHEN

PIZZA, $, 1855 W Hwy 89A, Sedona, AZ 86336, (928) 282-4140, picazzos.com, open daily 11am - 9pm, open until 10pm Friday and Saturday

Picazzo's is a boutique pizza restaurant. It is hopping most nights, with a lively and hip atmosphere. They do some great twists on the usual pizza, such as their hog and truffle and fig gorgonzola pizza pies. The ingredient combinations work together wonderfully, making it hard to pick a bad pizza. They also give you options to build your own. Be sure to combine the pizza with one their salads, you'll leave full and satisfied if you do. Picazzo's is one of the few pizza places to offer vegan and gluten-free options as well.

MILEY'S CAFÉ

MEXICAN/AMERICAN, $, 7000 AZ-179, Sedona, AZ 86351, (928) 284-4123, open daily 6:30am - 8pm, closes at 3pm Sunday - Wed

If you are just finishing a hike to Bell Rock or the surrounding area and are looking for a sit down meal at reasonable prices, Miley's is a local favorite. They offer a wide assortment of sandwiches, burgers and hot dogs along with an equally robust Mexican menu.

What makes Miley's a standout is that it still manages to maintain a quaint small town atmosphere. This isn't a typical stop for the tourist crowd, making this one of the last true diners in the Sedona area. Miley's doesn't try to be anything other than a great place serving good food.

Miley's is located in a small strip mall offering a number of food establishments, including Cucina Rustica a more upscale offering of Italian fare created by Chef Lisa Dahl and open for dinner only. If you go, make sure someone orders the Garganelli Don Quixote, a spicy mushroom pasta chicken dish that is simply out of this world.

COFFEE POT RESTAURANT

AMERICAN, $, 2050 W Hwy 89A, Sedona, AZ 86336, (928) 282-6626, coffeepotsedona.com, open daily 6am - 2pm

This is the oldest go to breakfast haunt of local Sedonans since the 1950's and is as much a part of Sedona as the surrounding red rocks. They offer a choice of 10 omelets, along with many other breakfast dishes (300 items in total), plus fresh brewed coffee. You can see pictures of all of the Hollywood stars that ate or visited here in its heyday when it was one of the few places to eat in town. Today, it continues to get accolades, including "Best Breakfast in Sedona." If the weather permits, they open up their outside patio, though it's shaded and covered, so no views.

DAHL & DILUCA RISTORANTE ITALIANO

ITALIAN, $$, 2321 W Hwy 89A, Sedona, AZ 86336, (928) 282-5219, cheflisadahl.com, open daily 5 - 9pm

Chef Lisa Dahl now has four restaurants in Sedona, but this is the one that started it all. Simply put, its consistently great Italian cuisine, served in a quiet and subdued atmosphere. Dahl & Diluca is a wonderful place for a romantic dinner, and in fact, while they tolerate kids, they don't exactly encourage them either. This is an adult restaurant, the service is on the fancier side, the meals are well prepared and presented, and the wines they serve have been carefully selected. While Chef Dahl has spread her wings to open other restaurants, the high quality of this restaurant continues. You won't be disappointed.

Surrounding Views at Slide Rock State Park

NICK'S ON THE WEST SIDE

AMERICAN, $, 2920 Hwy 89A, Sedona, AZ 86336, (928) 204-2088, nickswestside.com, open Monday thru Saturday 7am - 8:30pm, Sunday 8am - 2pm

Nick's offers a wide selection of dishes at reasonable prices. It's not the fanciest place in town, nor the best, but if you are looking for any meal, whether breakfast, lunch, or dinner, and you just want solid food, Nick's is an appropriate choice.

OAXACA RESTAURANT & CANTINA

MEXICAN, $, 321 N State Rte. 89A, Sedona, AZ 86336, (928) 282-4179, oaxacarestaurant.com, open daily 11am -9pm

Some of the locals intentionally mispronounce this place the "Why-Yuck-a." Is it even Mexican food, that is a question to ask, as it is unclear if they serve green and red dyed tortilla chips with salsa that tastes more like catsup anywhere in Mexico, but okay, let's say for the sake of argument that this is Mexican cuisine. The singular problem is that Oaxaca caters to the largest possible tourist audience and have thus dialed down all of the dishes so that they bear little resemblance to their true selves. It is also in an excellent location, which receives a constant influx of new tourists that keep the management busy and unaware that they could get repeat business if they increased the food quality. El Rincon Restaurante Mexicano in Tlaquepaque (336 State Route 179) or Javelina Cantina in Hillside (671 Hwy 179) are better choices for a traditional sit down Mexican food experience.

COFFEES AND SWEETS

THEIA'S

COFFEE, 361 Cedar St, Sedona, AZ 86336, (928) 282-8582, open daily 6am - 6pm

The first cool thing about Theia's is how it is in Uptown, but is tucked away from the main drag. When you find it and walk into its colorful interior, there's a feeling of having discovered something secret and special. Theia's offers hot and cold coffees and espresso drinks, as well as teas and smoothies. They also have a small section of baked items. If you find that you've had enough of the tourist circuit vibe of Uptown, search out the sanctuary of Theia.

THE SEDONA FUDGE COMPANY

FUDGE, 257 N Hwy 89A, Sedona, AZ 86336, (928) 282-1044, sedonafudge.com, open daily 10am - 9pm

Most every town that attracts tourists has a fudge store. It's a great place to get a free sample, but let's face it, for the most part, fudge is fudge. Or is it? The Sedona Fudge Company is pretty special as far as fudge goes. The fudge is made fresh daily and is a rich, creamy, melt in your mouth, can taste the difference confection that will delight all. Oh, and they make fresh cookies too.

BLACK COW CAFÉ

ICE CREAM, 229 N State Rte. 89A, Sedona, AZ 86336, (928) 203-9868, open daily 10:30am - 9pm

The Black Cow is right in the center of the Uptown action and gets a steady stream of traffic for its ice cream. They offer a fun selection of sundaes, including the Tin Roof, which has been on the menu since the 1960's when it was called the Sedona Ice Cream Parlor and sat next to a local grocery store (now a set of tourist shops). The Black Cow offers fast service, though seating is limited.

CREEKSIDE COFFEE AND BAKERY

COFFEE, 251 State Rte. 179, Sedona, AZ 86336, (928) 955-9888, creeksidecoffeesedona.com, open daily 6:30am - 5pm, until 6pm Friday and Saturday

Creekside Coffee is one of the few places to get a decent espresso drink in Sedona. For whatever reason, the town cannot hold on to a good espresso bar. What keeps Creekside on the map is that they also offer a selection of healthy comfort food, such as the smashed avocado toast with tomato and basil. The selection is small but complete in providing a nice meal, a warm loving made espresso drink, and an amazing view of red rocks.

55

SEDONA BAKERY & CAFE

BAGELS, 1350 AZ-89A Ste 22, Sedona, AZ 86336, (928) 204-1242, sedonabakery.com, open daily 6am - 3pm

Sedona Bakery & Cafe provides made from scratch cakes, cookies, cupcakes, pies, bagels, omelets, coffees, and other assorted goodies, making this a great place for a quick grab and go breakfast. They also carry a nice assortment of sandwiches and by the slice pizza for the lunch crowd. Their Reuben sandwich alone is worth a visit. The location offers something for everyone, with seating both inside and outside, offering views of Airport Mesa and surrounding area.

SEDONUTS

DONUTS, 2370 W State Route 89A, Sedona, AZ 86336, (928) 282-2013, open daily 6am - 12:30pm, closed Monday

Gotta have more donuts? Sedonuts has your answer. Look for them in West Sedona in the same shopping mall as Safeway and McDonalds. Note they close by lunchtime.

DAIRY QUEEN-OAK CREEK CANYON

ICE CREAM, 4551 N Hwy 89A, Sedona, AZ 86336, (928) 282-2789, dairyqueen.com, open daily 10am - 7pm, 8pm Saturday

This location is worthy of a stop, being tucked just off the road within the ever-peaceful Oak Creek Canyon. The real reason this made the guide book is there are several Navajo jewelry kiosks in the DQ parking lot that stand up shop each day during the warmer months. Here you can you get a cone of soft serve ice cream and browse Native American jewelry or just talk to the vendors. The Dairy Queen of Oak Creek more than just a greasy burger joint, it is a unique attraction and definitely worth checking out.

BEST FROM

South Rim of the Grand Canyon is the most direct way to take this side trip, add 3 hours if coming from the North Rim.

WHAT YOU'LL SEE

- Cottonwood, Arizona
- Tuzigoot National Monument
- Dead Horse Ranch State Park
- Jerome, Arizona
- Prescott, Arizona

56

WHY CHOOSE THIS SIDE TRIP

This side trip is all about relaxing, unwinding, doing some window shopping, eating well, and getting a little sightseeing in. The Historical Southwest Side Trip provides for a relaxing tour through some of the best towns in the state of Arizona. This includes Jerome, a living ghost mining town with lots of art galleries and other one of a kind shops and Prescott, a classic all-American town, with a tasteful offering of boutique stores and museums in a 1800's old west setting. As a compliment, you can take a tour of the ancestral Puebloan ruins of Tuzigoot or do some bird watching at Dead Horse Ranch.

ALLOW

- Recommended – 1-4 days
- Total Drive Time: 4 hours from Grand Canyon Village to Prescott, Arizona
- Cottonwood, Arizona: Use to stop for lunch or stay overnight, Tuzigoot National Monument and Dead Horse Ranch State Park are inside Cottonwood's city limits.
- Tuzigoot National Monument: Allow 30 - 45 minutes
- Dead Horse Ranch State Park: allow 2 hours to overnight if camping here.
- Jerome, Arizona: Jerome can be visited as a day trip or as an overnight visit. Allow 2-4 hours if going as a day trip.
- Prescott, Arizona: Prescott old town can be seen as a day trip, but recommend staying 1-2 nights here if looking to visit the Sharlot Hall Museum and boating on Watson Lake.

This trip can be completed in 2 -3 days with an overnight in either Prescott, Jerome, or Cottonwood. All the sites on this route can be easily done as day trips, allowing for a fair amount of flexibility in planning. If you want to extend the trip longer, there is more to see in Jerome and Prescott. Both are very unique towns, with Prescott having more options and Jerome offering a smaller and quiet setting.

CAN BE COMBINED WITH

Side Trip 1 – "Ancient Lands" and Side Trip 2 – "Mystical Sedona". If it's time to head home, Phoenix Sky Harbor International closest major airport.

COTTONWOOD AND SURROUNDING SITES

The first stop from the Grand Canyon is Cottonwood Arizona. The town has two parks that are easy to get to and visit and is also close to Jerome, a cute little mining town, as well as the red rocks of Sedona. This makes the town of Cottonwood a nice little hub for sightseeing.

Cottonwood isn't a typical tourist destination, but it is a great place to pick up any necessary amenities and hosts one of the few places in Arizona outside of Phoenix with a good selection of the big nationwide chain stores. Cottonwood is also a cheaper lodging destination for folks vacationing in the area and as such does offer a decent selection of no frill hotels coupled with surprisingly great restaurants.

THINGS TO DO IN COTTONWOOD

TUZIGOOT NATIONAL MONUMENT

Tuzigoot National Monument is a local treasure of the town of Cottonwood. The park's site sits on a small hilltop at the base of the Woodchute Wilderness and Mingus Mountain Wilderness. Within sight of the ruins, one can see the old mining town of Jerome, AZ, as well as the red rocks of Sedona in the far distance to the east.

The site contains a series of 2 -3 story ruins laid out in an elongated rectangle. There are some 110 rooms within the complex. The dwellings towards the center of the ancient complex stand higher than the other rooms and are thought to have been used for public activities.

Tuzigoot is a great way to spend an afternoon if you are visiting the area and makes a great side trip if you are heading to Jerome. It takes no more than 30 – 45 minutes to explore the site. You can also check out a small museum, visitor center, and bookstore on site.

HISTORICAL SOUTHWEST

GRAND CANYON NATIONAL PARK

N

○ **GRAND CANYON VILLAGE**

64

Grand Canyon South to Cottonwood
147 mi / 236.6 km / 2 hrs 24 min

64

160

64

180

89

40

40

TUZIGOOT
Tuzigoot to Jerome
6.1 mi / 9.8 km / 13 min

89

89A

DEAD HORSE RANCH
Dead Horse to Tuzigoot
3.6 mi / 5.8 km / 8 min

COTTONWOOD
Cottonwood to Dead Horse
1.6 mi / 2.6 km / 5 min

JEROME
Tuzigoot to Jerome
34.7 mi / 55.8 km / 54 min

○ **JEROME**   ○ E Cornville Rd

89A

260

17

Prescott to Phoenix via Hwy 17
101 mi / 162.5 km / 1 hr 48 min

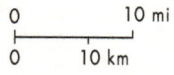

PRESCOTT ○

89

0   10 mi
0   10 km

© GONE BEYOND GUIDES 2017

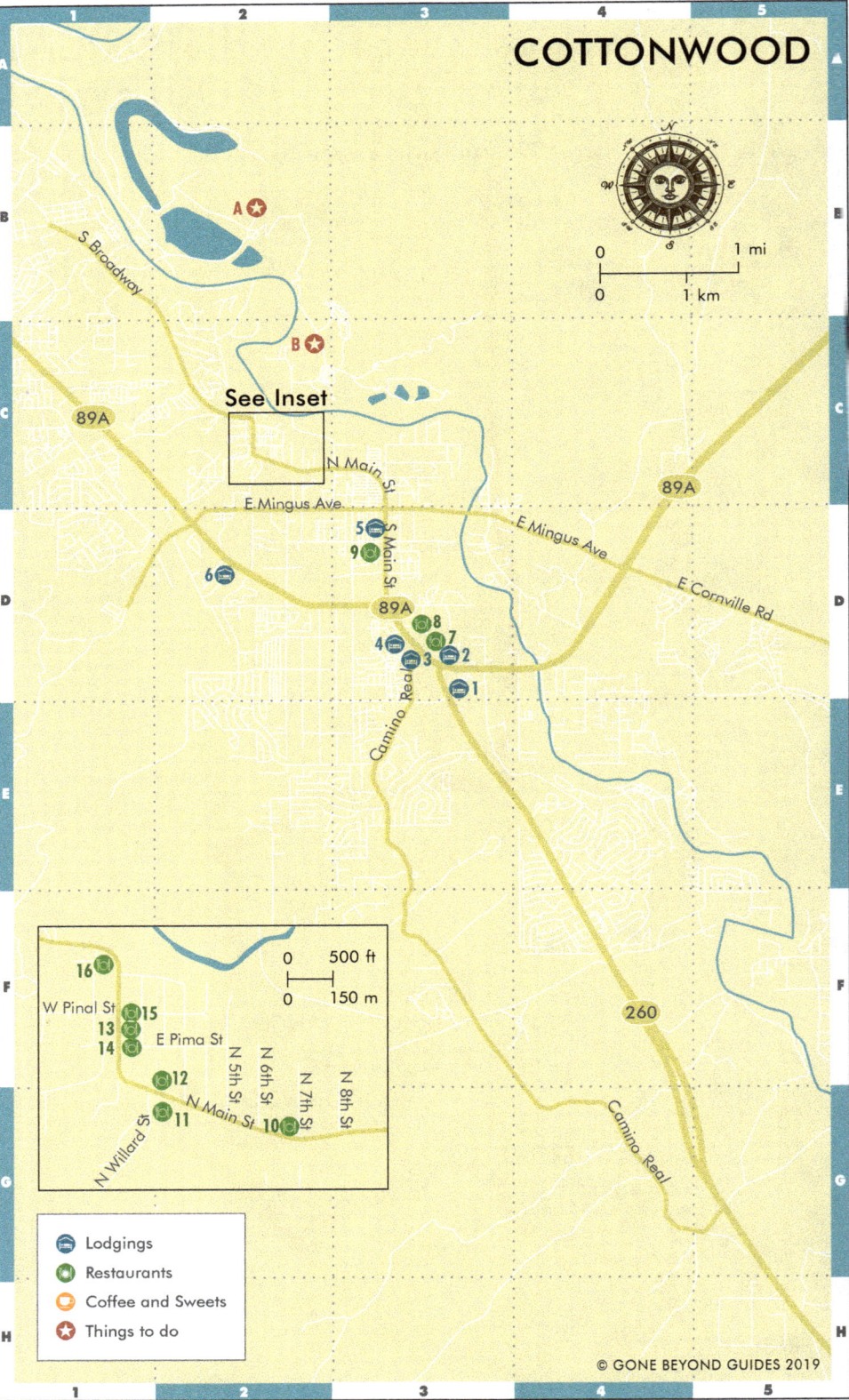

COTTONWOOD

S Broadway

89A

A ★

B ★

See Inset

N Main St

E Mingus Ave

S Main St

E Mingus Ave

89A

E Cornville Rd

5
9

6

89A

8
7
4
3 2

1

Camino Real

260

Camino Real

0   1 mi

0   1 km

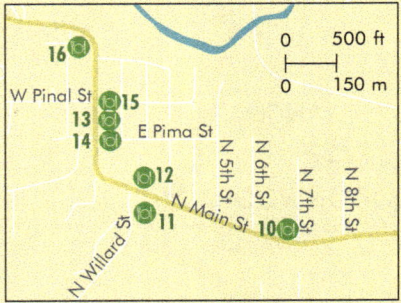

16

W Pinal St   15
13
14   E Pima St

12

N Willard St

N Main St

N 5th St

N 6th St

N 7th St

N 8th St

11   10

0   500 ft

0   150 m

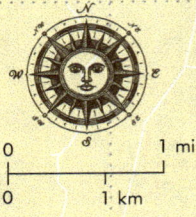

Lodgings

Restaurants

Coffee and Sweets

★ Things to do

© GONE BEYOND GUIDES 2019

Tuzigoot National Monument

The site is open daily from 8am – 5pm. There is an entrance fee of $10 for ages 16 and up. The good news is that this fee is good for both Tuzigoot and Montezuma Castle National Monuments for seven days. There are no campgrounds at Tuzigoot, but there are at the nearby Dead Horse Ranch State Park.

DEAD HORSE RANCH STATE PARK

Dead Horse Ranch State Park is a small park just outside the city center of Cottonwood that is a favorite of campers and anglers. There are stocked lagoons, picnic ramadas, cabins for rent, as well as numerous campsites to pitch a tent or park an RV. There are 106 RV/T sites in the park, plus 17 tent-only sites and 1 group site that holds 23 people. The campground contains ADA accessible restrooms, drinking water, showers, hookups, and a dump station.

Most of the hikes within the park are gentle walks. There is also a system of mountain bike trails that extend outside of the park. For information on the mountain biking trails, go to http://azstateparks.com/Parks/DEHO/downloads/DEHO_Trails_Map.pdf.

The park has a visitor center and a small gift shop along with restroom that is ADA compliant. Dead Horse is open daily from 8am – 10pm and charges $7 per vehicle or $3 per individual/bicyclist.

HIKING DEAD HORSE RANCH STATE PARK

CANOPY TRAIL

Easy – (0.25 mi / 0.4 km), round trip, allow 15 -30 minutes

This is a spur trail off Forest Loop and simply goes into the center of the loop. It is ADA accessible and once on the trail gives a good feeling of remoteness and nature under the blanket of Fremont's cottonwoods. The trail is a favorite of bird watchers.

FOREST LOOP

Easy – (0.5 mi / 0.8 km), round trip, allow 30 minutes

A short loop from the river day use area and nearby picnic area. Great for walking off a BBQ feast or simply exploring just for the fun of it. The trail is used for river access and as the name implies, runs through a forest of Fremont's cottonwoods. This is a tranquil hike.

MESA TRAIL

Easy – (1.0 mi / 1.6 km), one way, allow 30 minutes to 1 hour

The Mesa Trail is an interpretive loop that climbs to the top of a hill overlooking the Red Hawk Campground. From the top are good views of the Verde Valley, the towering Mingus Mountain and even the distant red rocks of Sedona. Along the way are kiosks pointing out various educational tidbits.

TAVASCI MARSH TRAIL

Easy – (2.0 mi / 3.2 km), round trip, allow 1 hour for the hike, more if visiting the ruins

Located at the end of Flycatcher Road at the north end of the park, Tavasci Marsh Trail is a very pleasant hike that ambles along a robust and healthy marshland ending at the entrance to Tuzigoot National Monument. This trail is like stepping back in time as you go from a campground environment into one of the best-preserved pueblo ruins of the Sinagua people. This is a great hike, but make sure you plan for time to explore the ruins. The marsh provides excellent birding opportunities.

59

COTTONWOOD

Things To Do

Lodging

Restaurants

Dead Horse Ranch State Park

QUAIL WASH TRAIL

Easy – (0.25 mi / 0.4 km), round trip, allow 15 - 30 minutes

This is a short and popular riparian trail near the River Day Use Area and intersects with the Hickey Ditch Trail. The trail is located at the south end of the West Lagoon parking lot.

HICKEY DITCH TRAIL

Easy – (0.5 mi / 0.8 km), round trip, allow 30 minutes

This trail walks under a canopy of Arizona Black Walnut and Willow trees along a historic irrigation ditch. A pleasant little hike that can be combined with Quail Wash.

CREOSOTE TRAIL

Easy – (0.5 mi / 0.8 km), round trip, allow 30 minutes

This trail is a spur from Hickey Ditch and Quail Wash that connects to the Lime Kiln Trail.

LIME KILN TRAIL

Moderate – (4.2 mi / 6.8 km), round trip, allow 2 - 3 hours

The described stretch of the Lime Kiln Trail is a 2.1-mile segment that is part of a larger 15-mile trail that connects Dead Horse Ranch State Park to Red Rock State Park in Sedona. The trail began as a road in the 1800's to transport lime from Cottonwood to Sedona. It was then forgotten until 2006 when it was reinstated as an official trail connecting the two parks.

The initial 2.1 miles of this trail heads outside of the park towards Sedona before intersecting with Thumper Trail. Limekiln ruins can be seen along the way. Once at the Thumper Trail, you can either head back the 2.1 miles or make a 5.2-mile extension by taking Thumper Trail (2.3 miles) to Lower Raptor Trail (2.9 miles), which returns Blackhawk Loop campsite at the northern end of the park. (See the mountain biking trail website listed above for more information on Thumper and Lower Raptor Trails).

VERDE RIVER GREENWAY

Easy – (2.0 mi / 3.2 km), round trip, allow 1 -2 hours

The Verde River Greenway winds through a forested canopy along the Verde River. This is a great place for seeing wildlife, especially for birds. Go for an early morning or dusk hike for optimal wildlife viewing. Can be made into a loop that follows along the lagoons.

COTTONWOOD LODGING

The lodging options in Cottonwood are pretty basic. There are several good clean choices in town that are easy on the wallet. If it is but a bed you need to lay your head down to slumber, Cottonwood makes for a central home base location for all of the sites on this route.

VERDE VALLEY INN

1089 S State Route 260, Cottonwood, AZ 86326, (928) 634-3678, verdevalleyinn.com

One of the long list of basic 2-star hotels in town, the Verde Valley Inn is one of the more modern and tasteful of the basic hotels. The lodging here is a great value for the money, though there is no free hotel breakfast or pool offered. They do offer free Wi-Fi and parking.

BEST WESTERN COTTONWOOD INN

993 S Main St, Cottonwood, AZ 86326, (928) 634-5575, bestwestern.com

This Best Western is one of the few 2.5-star hotels. Amenities include a tiny pool, free Wi-Fi, parking, and free breakfast. If you include the cost of breakfast, this lodging choice is a good value for the money.

AZ PINES MOTEL

920 Camino Real, Cottonwood, AZ 86326, (928) 634-9975, azpinesmotel.com

This is a 2-star hotel but is a terrific value for the money. Decent size outdoor pool, AC that works, free Wi-Fi, and rooms with kitchenettes available. They don't offer much in services, such as free breakfast, but for a place to stay, Pines Motel is a good choice.

SUPER 8 COTTONWOOD

800 S Main St, Cottonwood, AZ 86326, (928) 639-1888, wyndhamhotels.com

Unfortunately, upon entering your room at the Super 8 Cottonwood, you may think, "Egads, well, it's only one night." Some of the rooms range from run down to downright nasty. Avoid if possible.

LITTLE DAISY MOTEL

34 S Main St, Cottonwood, AZ 86326, (928) 634-7865, littledaisy.com

Another 2-star hotel, the Little Daisy is a bit tired out from all the guests it has seen over the years. Very little remodeling has been done recently other than a paint job, so don't expect much. An affordable, no-frills place to stay.

QUALITY INN – COTTONWOOD

301 W. Sr 89-A, Cottonwood, AZ 86326, (928) 634-4207, choicehotels.com

The Quality Inn Cottonwood delivers to expectation with free breakfast, Wi-Fi, and clean rooms. They state that they offer a restaurant and bar, but these facilities are only for events.

Cottonwood Restaurants

The dining options in Cottonwood have really grown in terms of quality over the years. Some of the restaurants listed are good if not better than those in Sedona. Cottonwood has a large local community combined with enough tourist traffic to allow restaurants to offer a consistently high quality of service. For a town with a local area reputation as being "where the nearest Target is located," the restaurants here are on a higher level.

RANDALL'S RESTAURANT

AMERICAN, meals for under $10, 891 S Main St, Cottonwood, AZ 86326, (928) 634-0043, blackknightproductions.net, open from 5:30am - 2pm most weekdays, opening at 7am on weekends

Randall's is a local grill and café, offering an assortment of omelets and hot coffee for breakfast and burgers and sandwiches for lunch. Nothing fancy, but they are open early if you want to grab breakfast before heading onwards on your journey.

CORK & CATCH

SEAFOOD, $$, 1750 E Villa Dr, Cottonwood, AZ 86326, (928) 649-2675, corkandcatch.com, open Tuesday - Saturday 11am - 8pm, closed Sunday and Monday

The Cork & Catch is refreshingly great food, offering fresh fish and steaks as well as huge salads and burgers. If you are looking for fresh food and large portions with a friendly staff, this is your place.

CONCHO'S MEXICAN FOOD

MEXICAN, meals for under $10, 206 S Main St, Cottonwood, AZ 86326, (928) 649-9680, open daily 10am - 8pm, Sunday until 7pm

Concho's is solid Mexican food, good chips, salsa, hearty plates, and low prices.

HOG WILD BBQ

BARBEQUE, $, 705 N Main St, Cottonwood, AZ 86326, (928) 639-3232, azhogwild.com, open Tuesday thru Saturday 11am - 8pm

Best BBQ in Cottonwood (and Sedona for that matter). This is fall off the bone goodness with huge portions and Texas toast as a side. They also offer Chicago style hot dogs and Italian beef sandwiches along with large cut fries.

ABBIE'S KITCHEN

AMERICAN, $$ 778 North Main St, Cottonwood, AZ 86326, (928) 634-3300, abbieskitchen.com, open Wednesday thru Saturday 5 - 9pm

Abbie's is homemade everything, where they offer a small but impeccably cooked, presented, and served options to choose from. The plates are a fusion of American and French, with offerings such as Duck Leg Confit with Fig Glaze, Scottish Salmon, and filet mignon. Abbie's Kitchen is a special occasion worthy venue from starters to deserts.

RIOT IN OLD TOWN

GASTROPUB, $ 777 N Main St, Cottonwood, AZ 86326, (928) 634-3777, hours vary, open most weekdays 4pm - 9pm, weekends 11am -11pm

Riot in Old Town is a cozy place with upscale dishes and a large beer selection. If you want to eat and drink well in a fun atmosphere, this place will do the trick.

CREMA CRAFT KITCHEN BAR

AMERICAN, $$, 917 N Main St, Cottonwood, AZ 86326, (928) 649-3533, www.cremacottonwood.com, open daily from 7am - 2pm

Crema Craft is one of the great places for breakfast in Cottonwood. Drop in for upscale omelettes and eggs benedicts, a casual atmosphere, and some tasty mimosas and espresso drinks. Their lunches are pretty awesome as well, with offerings such as Boston Lobster Roll and a Monte Cristo served with maple syrup.

OLD TOWN RED ROOSTER CAFÉ

AMERICAN, $, 901 N Main St, Cottonwood, AZ 86326, (928) 649-8100, oldtownredroostercafe.com, open daily 7:30am - 3:30pm, 2pm on Sunday

Red Rooster serves breakfast, lunch, and dinner meals that are large in portion and hearty in flavor. Great place for espresso coffees, omelets, or eggs benedict for breakfast. Their sandwiches are delicious as well.

NIC'S ITALIAN STEAK & CRAB HOUSE

ITALIAN, $$, 925 N Main St, Cottonwood, AZ 86326, (928) 634-9626, nicsaz.com, open daily 5 - 9pm

This is one of the best dining experiences in Cottonwood. The atmosphere is warm and the menu huge. Along with a good selection of pasta, seafood, ribs, and chicken dishes, Nic's also offers Tuscan style steaks, which are brushed with olive oil and Italian seasonings before being charbroiled to order. If you are spending a night in Cottonwood, give Nic's a visit, you will not be disappointed.

PIZZERIA BOCCE

PIZZA, $, 1060 N Main St, Cottonwood, AZ 86326, (928) 202-3597, pizzeriabocce.com, open Saturday 12pm - 11pm, Sunday 12pm - 4pm, weekdays 4pm - 10pm

Pizzeria Bocce has a hip and relaxed atmosphere with a full bar, outside seating and pizzas that are out of this world. Each slice has gobs of flavor, this isn't your usual greasy discs of pepperoni drowning in cheese and crust, these pies are masterpieces.

61

View into Cottonwood with Sedona in background

JEROME

Legend:
- 🛏 Lodgings
- 🍴 Restaurants
- ☕ Coffee and Sweets
- ⭐ Things to do

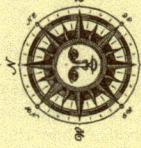

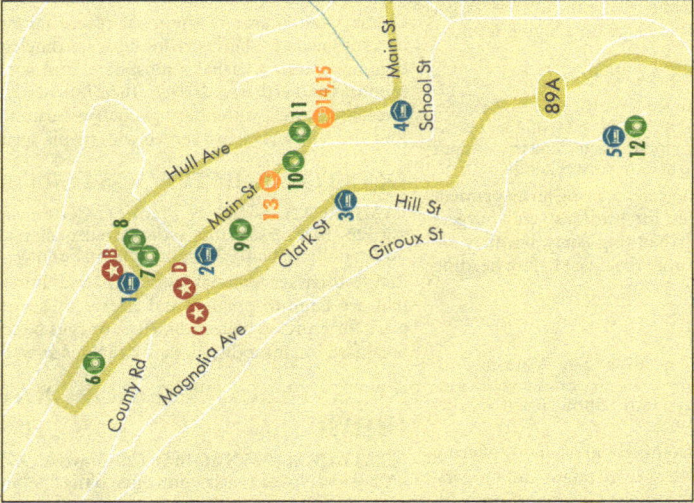

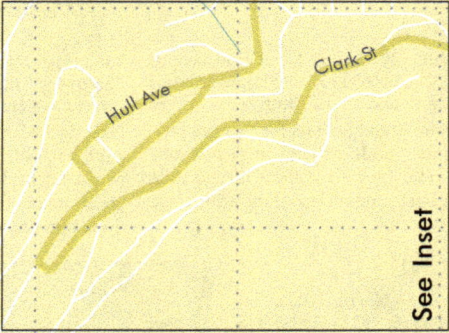

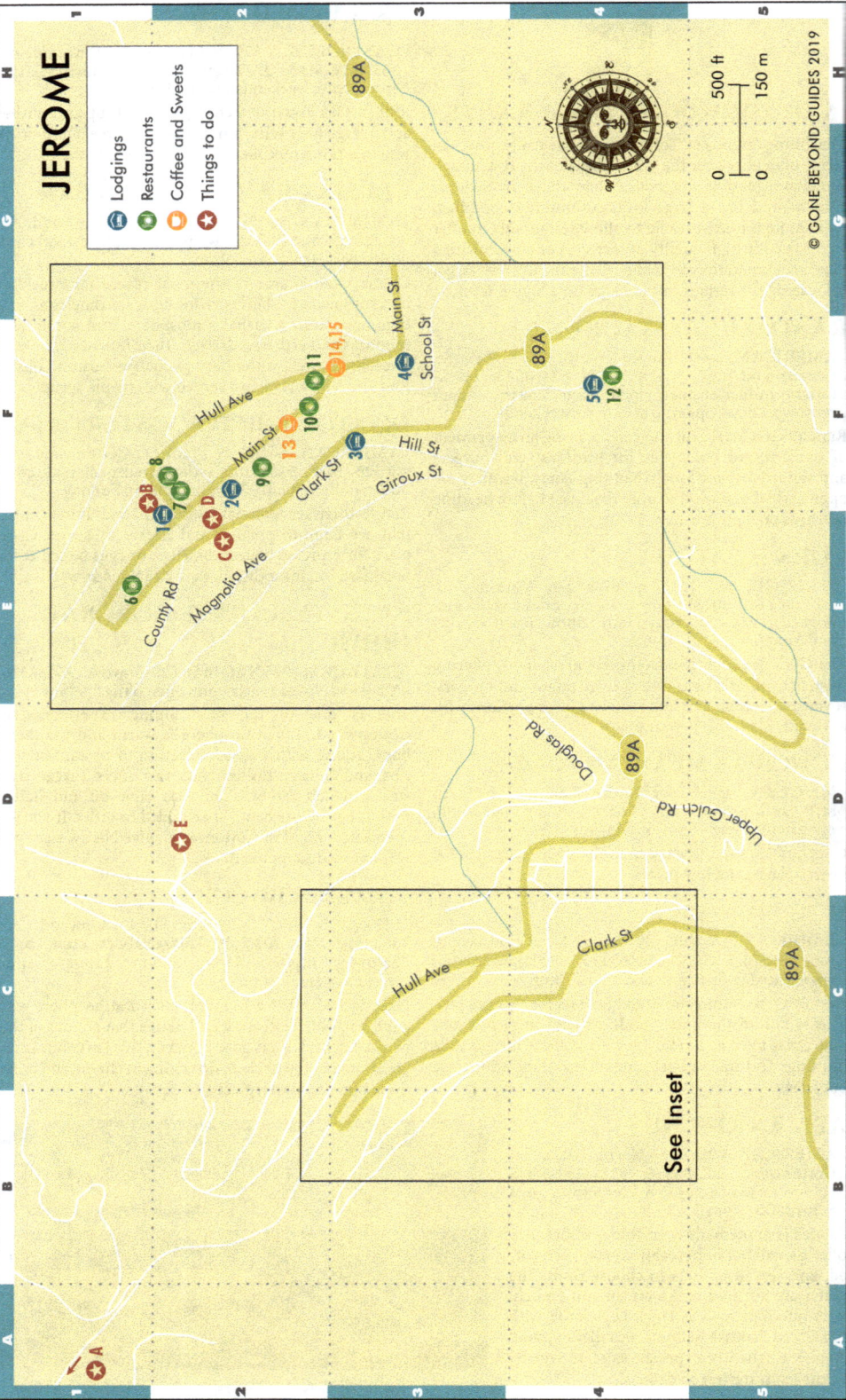

89A

Hull Ave

County Rd

Magnolia Ave

Main St

Clark St

Hill St

Giroux St

Main St

School St

89A

6

B
1
7
8

D
C
2
9
10
11
14,15

13

3

4

5
12

E

Douglas Rd

Upper Gulch Rd

89A

Hull Ave

Clark St

89A

See Inset

A

0   500 ft

0   150 m

© GONE BEYOND GUIDES 2019

62

JEROME

In its heyday, the bustling mining town of Jerome was proclaimed the "Wickedest Town in the West." This phrase wasn't given lightly. Jerome was once the fourth largest town in Arizona and held over 15,000 residents in the 1920's who lived, worked or provided services to support the mine. The copper mine that lay underneath the town was the largest in Arizona and is even estimated to be the largest in the world, producing over 3 million tons of copper ore every month.

With the Great Depression, four town fires, and lowering copper prices; the mine eventually closed in the 1950's. The population fell to just 50 residents and may have gone to a full ghost town had it not been for a few intrepid artists who saw Jerome's potential. The 1960's and 1970's saw a resurgence of Jerome as an artist community, where the creative minds of the time could live cheaply and create their arts. In 1967 the town leaders sought and obtained National Historic Landmark status for the town, which helped cement it into a new chapter as "The Largest Ghost Town in America."

Many of the historic buildings are still standing today, at least mostly standing. The town was built on a steep 30-degree slope, at an elevation of 5000 feet, and in some areas directly above the mine. This has led to some of the buildings to slide downhill over the years. The Sliding Jail is one of the most famous of these types of buildings, which has slid over 200 feet and is still viewable but unusable. It is important to not underestimate the steepness of walking around Jerome. It is definitely good exercise. You can drive around and pull over if needed though.

A great way to enjoy Jerome is too simply find parking along Main Street and walk among the shops, eateries, and historical buildings. Make sure to catch some of the most famous locations such as the Sliding Jail described above and what's left of the Cuban Queen Bordello. The Cuban Queen Bordello was once a house of ill repute with a modern attribution as being haunted. The house is also in ill repair and collapsed in 2017, but you can still see what's left of it. For a more immersive experience, start with the Jerome State Historic Park for some historical context, then take a ghost or history tour.

The mining town of Jerome

Don't feel you have to stay overnight. In fact, most folks that visit Jerome are content to window shop and talk with the often-colorful locals as a day visit.

JEROME STATE HISTORIC PARK

100 Douglas Road, Jerome, AZ 86331, (928) 634-5381, open daily 8:30am to 4:45pm

Housed in the Douglas Mansion built in 1916, Jerome State Historic Park is a smart way to introduce yourself to the town. One can watch a short video, pour over photographs and artifacts, and even see some mineral samples. Perhaps the best part of the museum is its large 3D model of both the above ground town of Jerome and the honeycomb of mine shafts underneath. The model is a faithful rendition of the magnitude of effort that went into the mining efforts in Jerome. Free for ages 0-6, $4 for ages 7-13, $7 for ages 14+

MINE MUSEUM

200 Main St, Jerome, AZ 86331, (928) 634-5477, open daily 9am – 6pm

The Mine Museum is centrally located and is operated by the Jerome Historical Society. This non-profit is responsible for helping restore and recover many of the historical buildings in Jerome and as the center of all of the town's history, is worth the nominal $2 charge for adults, ($1 for seniors, free for children under 12). The museum has been around since the 1950's. Here you can see lots of various mining equipment and other artifacts, including displays of how migrant and others worked and lived in Jerome. The Mine Museum also boasts a small curio-filled gift shop to wander through.

63

Jerome ruins

GHOST AND HISTORY TOURS

There are two main tour operators in Jerome, offering both historical and ghost tours. The tours are as entertaining as they are educational, and are well worth the time. You will see many buildings that may otherwise be overlooked, with a historical perspective to bring context to what you are seeing. The Jerome Historical Society does a fun ghost tour for between $15-$20. Check their website at https://jeromehistoricalsociety. com/event/ghostwalk-meeting-at-spook-hall/ as they offer this on an irregular basis. Ghost Town Tours (403 Clark St. Suite A-2, Jerome, AZ 86331, 928-634-6118) is the most popular, offering both walking and shuttle tours starting at $25. Allow 1-2 hours if taking a tour and best to book ahead. Tours of Jerome, (110 Main St, Suite 1, Jerome, AZ, +1 928-639-4361) is another operator that caters primarily to Sedona tourists, offering day trips to Jerome and back from Sedona. They also offer tours for folks in Jerome, including a 2-hour ghost tour in Jerome starting at dusk for $35.

GOLD KING MINE & GHOST TOWN

1000 Perkinsville Rd, Jerome, AZ 86331, open daily 10am – 5pm

This place offers gold panning and mining curious in an old west ghost town setting. The $5 entrance fee allows you to walk around this obviously staged place. It's something to do, but this is more of a roadside attraction and not a direct part of the history of Jerome.

JEROME LODGING

JEROME GRAND HOTEL

200 Hill St, Jerome, AZ 86331, (888) 817-6788, jeromegrandhotel.net

The Jerome Grand Hotel gets high marks for its ambiance. The hotel itself is huge and is the only town in the area to be registered as a National Historic Landmark Hotel. Even if you do not stay here, come into the lobby to take a look inside. The owners have gone to great lengths to restore the hotel to its original glory. Amenities include the recommended Asylum Restaurant and bar, free breakfast, free Wi-Fi, and suites available.

CONNOR HOTEL OF JEROME

160 Main St, Jerome, AZ 86331, (928) 634-5006, connorhotel.com

The Connor Hotel is another beautifully restored inn that is centrally located in downtown Jerome. The location makes it easy to tour the town during your stay. They don't offer a free breakfast but do have a bar and lounge for after hour alcoholic drinks.

SURGEON'S HOUSE BED AND BREAKFAST

100 Hill St, Jerome, AZ 86331, (928) 639-1452, surgeonshouse.com

The Surgeon's House is a wonderfully bright and positive home, 100 years old, and as much a part of the Jerome history as any of the buildings in town. This is a delightful bed and breakfast, with great personal touches, snacks all day long, and a buffet style breakfast served at 8:30am. The kitchen opens at 6:30am for guests looking for coffee or tea.

GHOST CITY INN

541 Main St, Jerome, AZ 86331, (928) 634-4678, ghostcityinn.com

The Ghost City Inn is another bed and breakfast worth considering. The building has been a boarding house almost its entire life and has been dutifully restored. Most rooms have nice views out towards Sedona along with private bathrooms and cable television. As an added bonus, the breakfasts here are worthy of praise.

MILE HIGH INN

309 Main St, Jerome, AZ 86331, (928) 634-5094, jeromemilehighinn.com

Conveniently located, the Mile High Inn and Grill offer very comfortable rooms and breakfast served daily from 8am -11am. The inn is on the second floor, so this is not an appropriate choice for those with disabilities. Mile High does offer free Wi-Fi, but no television.

Clark Street Elementary School - Jerome

Jerome Restaurants

ASYLUM RESTAURANT

AMERICAN, $, 200 Hill St, Jerome, AZ 86331, (928) 639-3197, asylumrestaurant.com, open daily for lunch 11am - 3:30pm, dinner 5-9pm

Dining at the Asylum is as much about the ambiance as it the food. Located inside the Jerome Grand Hotel, the restaurant gives a sense of what fine dining was like during the heyday of Jerome. The dining area is opulent without being overstated with views out towards Cottonwood and Sedona if the far distance. The food matches the rest of the experience, with a good list of dishes to choose from. Asylum is also excellent for lunch. Try the hot pastrami sandwich.

HAUNTED HAMBURGER

HAMBURGERS, $, 410 N Clark St, Jerome, AZ 86331, (928) 634-0554, thehauntedhamburger.com, open daily 11am -9pm

Hip, clean, and open ambiance with great views, full bar, and incredible hamburgers, fries and fixings make Haunted Hamburger the place to go when you need a burger fix in Jerome. Oh, and the restaurant's name? The owners swear the place is haunted. Nothing goes better with a frosty beer and tasty burger then the chilling whispers of a ghostly presence, though if those words are "tiiiip meeeee", that's likely your waiter.

BOBBY D'S BBQ

BBQ, $, 119 E Jerome Ave, Jerome, AZ 86331, (928) 634-6235, bobbydsbbqjerome.com, open daily 11am - 6pm, 8pm Friday and Saturday

Bobby D's is a cute local BBQ joint, serving classic ribs and burgers. The place has a cozy ambiance, with old booths and bar stools, along with folks to talk to as you wait for your order. The BBQ itself is good eating, with the ribs being a standout menu item.

GRAPES RESTAURANT

ITALIAN, $, 111 Main St, Jerome, AZ 86331, (928) 639-8477, grapesjerome.com, open daily 11am - 8pm

Grapes has incredible ambiance, very open, warm, and inviting. The menu is loaded with lots to choose from, and the food is nicely plated and well prepared, from their salads to the deserts. This is a birthday or special occasion worthy location. They also have a full bar and specialize in the Mule, which is a liquor of your choice, like rum or vodka, kicked into gear with ginger beer and lime.

THE BORDELLO OF JEROME

BURGERS, VEGETARIAN, $, 412 Main St, Jerome, AZ 86331, (928) 649-5855, open most days 11am-3pm, Sunday hours 11am-4pm, open until 8pm Thursday - Saturday

The Bordello is an excellent choice for vegetarians. They serve up an excellent veggie burger and have vegan options on their menu. The service is pleasant and positive with lots of local art to gaze at while eating.

VAQUEROS GRILL & CANTINA

MEXICAN, $, 363 Main St, Jerome, AZ 86331, (928) 649-9090, open daily 11am - 7pm, closes at 8pm on Friday and Saturday

A delightfully decorated restaurant, each chair has been hand painted and the entire place has been decorated in a "Dia de Los Muertos" theme. The food is as talented as the ambiance, serving hearty and fresh Mex food with quick, friendly service.

THE MINE CAFÉ

AMERICAN, $, 115 Jerome Ave, Jerome, AZ 86331, (928) 639-0123, minecafejerome.com, open daily 7am - 3pm, open for dinner Friday thru Sunday from 5-9pm

The Mine Café does make a hearty breakfast and open pretty early, but their lunches and dinners are really what put this place in the guidebook. The food here is phenomenal.

Coffee and Sweets

THE FLATIRON

COFFEE, 416 Main St, Jerome, AZ 86331, (928) 634-2733, theflatironjerome.com, open Thursday thru Monday 8:30am - 3:30pm

Their motto kind of says it all. "Art, Coffee, & Organic Food Served with a Side of Sarcasm." Fresh menu offerings for breakfast and lunch, plus coffee made with passion.

COPPER COUNTRY FUDGE

ICE CREAM/FUDGE, 337 Main St., Jerome, AZ 86331, (928) 634-4040, open daily 10am -6pm

If you are looking for a street treat while strolling along the haunted lanes of Jerome, Copper Country Fudge is a good bet. They serve ice cream, frozen yogurt, milkshakes, and as you may have already guessed, fudge.

RICKELDORIS CANDY & POPCORN CO

CANDY, 405 Hull Ave, Jerome, AZ 86331, (928) 639-1340, open daily 10am - 5:30pm

Note that Rickeldoris Candy & Popcorn will be closed for remodeling during the winter months of 2019. The token candy store of Jerome, with lots of hard to find candy to delight the child in all of us.

Downtown Jerome

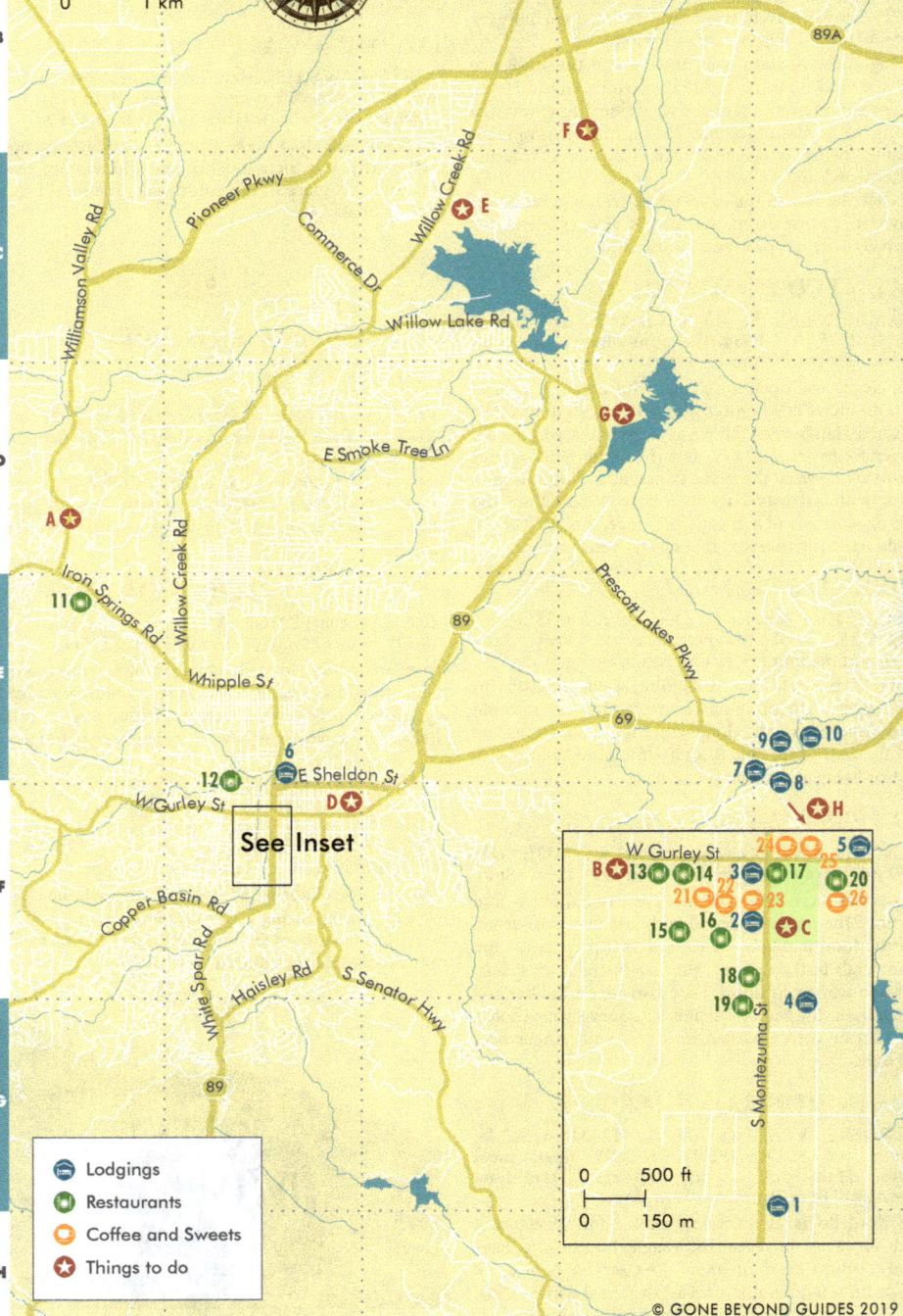

PRESCOTT

A

11

12

6 · E Sheldon St

W Gurley St

9

7

8

10

H

See Inset

D

B

Williamson Valley Rd

Pioneer Pkwy

Commerce Dr

Willow Creek Rd

E

F

G

Willow Lake Rd

E Smoke Tree Ln

Iron Springs Rd

Willow Creek Rd

Whipple St

W Gurley St

Copper Basin Rd

White Spar Rd

Haisley Rd

S Senator Hwy

Prescott Lakes Pkwy

89

89

89

89A

69

Inset

W Gurley St

B 13 14 3 17

21 22 23

15 16 2 C

18

19 4

1

24 5

25 20

26

S Montezuma St

0   500 ft

0   150 m

0   1 mi

0   1 km

Legend

🛏 Lodgings
🍴 Restaurants
☕ Coffee and Sweets
⭐ Things to do

© GONE BEYOND GUIDES 2019

PRESCOTT

Prescott is becoming quite the tourist destination of its own lately. The elements have always been there, a historical southwestern downtown, some of the best boutique shopping in Arizona, and with Prescott being at the intersection of three microclimates, there is a wide range of outdoor activities to choose from.

If there was a season that Prescott really shines, it's winter. They light the town up with festive Christmas cheer. It's crisp and cold, there's maybe some snow in view, the shops are all decorated, everyone's in a giving mood, and then at night, the downtown just transforms with trees and buildings all lit up. It's a winter wonderland that will warm the coldest hearts.

Don't feel you have to wait until summer though, Prescott has a lot to offer any time of the year. Around the 4th of July, they put on the Prescott Frontier Days, where you can see a real rodeo, locals in frontier attire and a full-on spectacular firework show. The event is also known as the "World's Oldest Rodeo." Tickets and schedule can be found at http://www.worldsoldestrodeo.com/.

Prescott Historic District

THINGS TO DO IN PRESCOTT, ARIZONA

DOWNTOWN HISTORIC AREA, INCLUDING WHISKY ROW AND THE YAVAPAI COUNTY COURTHOUSE SQUARE

135 S Granite St, Prescott, AZ 86303, (address is to a public parking garage that puts you close to the center of the Downtown Historic Area)

The Historic Area in the center of downtown is so quaint you might just get giddy with excitement. As you pull up to find parking, you feel like you are stepping back into the late 1800's. Prescott was the Territorial Capital in 1864 and 1877, and many of the buildings in the center of downtown remain into present day and have been restored to reflect the period. Whisky Row is at the heart of the shopping and is where you can walk into saloons once visited by Wyatt Earp and Doc Holliday. Here, you can have your own beer, though much of the bartending industry has been replaced by boutique shops. If you are looking for the saloons of lore, head into The Palace and Matt's Saloon. Across the street children play and couples stroll through the grassy square block surrounding the Yavapai Courthouse. The courthouse and surrounding area add to the charm and its sense of timelessness.

The downtown area also offers great shopping. In fact, it is arguable that Prescott has taken the lead in offering unique local shops and galleries. Prescott's galleries

PRESCOTT

Lodging

Restaurants

Coffee and Sweets

Things To Do

The granite dells of Watson Lake

are an honest and true reflection of American Southwest art, from native jewelry to local artists and artisan wares. Many of the large buildings have been divided into smaller shops, which adds to the fun. You go into a street-front shop and then find yourself exiting into an interior alleyway where there some more shops to discover. It makes for a terrific way to spend an afternoon.

SHARLOT HALL MUSEUM

415 W Gurley St, Prescott, AZ 86301-3691, 520-445-3122, www.sharlot.org, open Monday thru Saturday 10am – 4pm, Sunday 12 – 4pm.

The Sharlot Hall Museum is a collection of several historic buildings and grounds. Think of going to a ghost town that has been fully restored, including the housewares and other artifacts, whose buildings you can walk around in. There are knowledgeable volunteers that would be delighted to share what they know about the history of what you are looking at. This is one of the nicest southwest territory museums in Arizona and is within easy walking distance from the historic downtown section. Tickets are $9 for adults, Seniors (65 and older) are $8, children 13-17 are $5, under 13 are free. College students with ID get in for $6. You can also visit all three museums (Sharlot Hall, Smoki, and Pippen) at a reduced rate by getting a Culture Pass. Ask at any of the admission desks for these museums.

SMOKI MUSEUM

147 N Arizona Ave, Prescott, AZ 86301-3184, (928) 445-1230, www.smokimuseum.org, open daily 10am – 4pm, except Sunday 1-4pm

Smoki Museum is several blocks from historic downtown and is located in a unique stone building. Inside is a museum and trading post showcasing American Indian artifacts. The exhibits hold some remarkable examples of native artistry from all across the United States, including Apache and Midwestern tribes. There are truly few places that hold such a diverse collection. If you are an aficionado of native pottery and art, the museum is worth a visit.

Smoki Museum also has a trading post where you can purchase native pottery, basketry, rugs, and jewelry, primarily from the Navajo and Zuni tribes.

PHIPPEN MUSEUM

4701 AZ-89, Prescott, AZ 86301, (928) 778-1385, phippenartmuseum.org, open Tuesday thru Saturday 10am – 4pm, Sunday 1-4pm, closed Monday

The Phippen Museum is located on the way into downtown Prescott on Highway 89A. If you decide to visit, one option is to stop by as you come from Jerome, Arizona. The museum hosts a warm collection of Southwestern modern and traditional art. The paintings, drawings, etchings, and bronze sculptures range from the late 19th century to the present era. The exhibits have a way of drawing the viewer into the soulful and varied portrait of the American West.

WATSON LAKE

3101 Watson Lake Drive, Prescott, AZ 86301, 928-925-1410, open daily 7am – 10pm in the summer, 7am – sunset in winter

Watson Lake is one of two reservoirs located in the Granite Dells of Prescott. The reservoir is surrounded by gracefully eroded granitic outcroppings that nicely frame the blue waters of the lake. This is a recreational area, great for local fishing or renting a kayak or canoe. Boating Watson Lake is an incredible way to spend the afternoon. It is relaxing and peaceful, with lots of places to explore. Boat rentals are on a first come first served basis through Prescott Outdoors. They are located at the Watson Lake (and Goldwater Lake) boat ramps. You can rent by the hour for as little as $15 per hour. Make sure to bring a hat, sunscreen, and water for this outing!

HERITAGE PARK ZOOLOGICAL SANCTUARY

1403 Heritage Park Rd, Prescott, AZ 86301, (928) 778-4242, heritageparkzoo.org, open daily 9am -5pm in the summer, 10am – 4pm in winter (Nov – Apr)

The Heritage Park Zoo is a great place to take the kids, especially small ones. They have species a varied list of species, many of which have been taken in from other zoos. They care for tigers, wolves, bears, raptors, monkeys, javelinas, and many other animals that one can see.

The zoo has a couple of "must see" exhibits, including the Tarantula Grotto, which is one of the largest public displays of spiders in the world. They also hold the Reptile House, a large facility that houses species like the Gila monster, geckos, monitor lizards, and a 13-foot Burmese Python. Not all of the exhibits are meant to make your skin crawl, but both of these exhibits are quite unique and worth checking out.

HIGHLANDS CENTER FOR NATURAL HISTORY

1375 S. Walker Rd, Prescott, AZ 86303, (928) 776-9550, highlandscenter.org, open 9am - 4pm

The Highlands Center is located just inside the Prescott National Forest is a well-funded nonprofit naturalist experience aimed primarily at kids and families. The venue leases the land from the Forest Service to help enhance the education of nature. They offer a wide variety of programs and events, including the James Family Discovery Gardens and other educational programs. Highlands Center gets a lot of local volunteer love. It is a fantastic model of ecotourism and education within Prescott. To learn more on their charter of "Wonder – Explore – Discover," check out their website listed above.

COMMUNITY NATURE CENTER OPEN SPACE PRESERVE

1981 Williamson Valley Rd, Prescott, AZ 86305, prescott-az.gov, (928) 777-1121, open daily, 7am - sunset

Another local favorite, the Preserve offers 1.5 miles of hiking, birding, and nature study along with some history shows and log cabin It's a humble little place to get out and walk amongst nature without too much fuss.

69

PRESCOTT LODGING

THE MOTOR LODGE

503 S Montezuma St, Prescott, AZ 86303, (928) 717-0157, themotorlodge.com

The Motor Lodge offers solid rooms with a twist of fun. This refurbished set of cottages are each personal, nicely decorated, and comfortable. For this reason, there is a lot of repeat business with this establishment. On first look, you may see an older motel, but on a deeper look, the exterior is well kept up, and the interiors are also nicely appointed. The Motor Lodge is the surprise of Prescott for lodging. They offer free Wi-Fi but no breakfast.

GRAND HIGHLAND HOTEL

154 S Montezuma St, Prescott, AZ 86303, (928) 776-9963, grandhighlandhotel.com

The Grand Highland is the place to stay in Prescott if you are looking for convenience with a touch of grandeur. Situated on Whisky Row, it is dead center to all of the old town action. The rooms are clean and nicely decorated but may suffer from being old-fashioned for some, such as having a claw tub in some rooms with a curtain around it for bathing. Breakfast and free Wi-Fi are included.

HAMPTON INN PRESCOTT

3453 Ranch Dr, Prescott, AZ 86303, (928) 443-5500, hamptoninn3.hilton.com

There are some lodging options near the Prescott Gateway Mall about 5 minutes from the Downtown Historic Area. The area is a mix of hotels and shops for the Prescott locals, such as Trader Joes and Sears. This can be a good thing if you need a particular item on your vacation.

Now to the Hampton Inn. It is a 2.5-star hotel with clean rooms, a fitness center, breakfast, pool, and free Wi-Fi. They also have suites available.

SPRINGHILL SUITES PRESCOTT

200 E Sheldon St, Prescott, AZ 86301, (928) 776-0998, marriott.com

The SpringHill Suites Prescott is about an 8-minute walk to the Historic Downtown, making it a closer location than some of the chain hotel offerings. Like all SpringHill Suites, this is a clean and consistent 3-star hotel with free breakfast, pool, and suites available.

RESIDENCE INN PRESCOTT

3599 Lee Cir, Prescott, AZ 86301, (928) 775-2232, marriott.com

Another of the hotels near the Prescott Gateway Mall, the Residence Inns are great for families as each room comes with a full kitchen and free breakfast. The inn also has a small fitness center and nice outdoor pool.

HOTEL VENDOME

230 S Cortez St, Prescott, AZ 86303, (928) 776-0900, vendomehotel.com

The Hotel Vendome is super close to the Historic Downtown area and offers a quaint and comfortable bed. The 3-star hotel includes free breakfast, plus they have family rooms and a lounge with full bar. The hotel's ambiance is a mix of territorial western meets bed and breakfast. It's charming and old-fashioned.

HASSAYAMPA INN

122 E Gurley St, Prescott, AZ 86301, (928) 778-9434, assayampainn.com

The Hassayampa Inn is a completely renovated boutique hotel in the Historic Downtown. The hotel itself is grand, with an amazing hacienda-style lobby. The rooms are clean and well appointed. The Inn holds The Peacock Dining Room, which serves steaks and ribs, as well as their Glass Bar lounge for cocktails. They also offer room service.

HOTEL ST. MICHAEL

205 W Gurley St, Prescott, AZ 86301, (928) 776-1999, stmichaelhotel.com

The Hotel St. Michael is an upscale boutique hotel right on Whiskey Row in the Historic Downtown. The hotel is charming from its exterior to the rooms, offering convenient access to shopping and dining, including their own Bistro, which as described, is great food. The hotel offers suites, free Wi-Fi, and free breakfast. They also have a lounge area with bar.

THE FOREST VILLAS HOTEL

3645 Lee Cir, Prescott, AZ 86301, (928) 717-1200, forestvillas.com

The Forest Villas Hotel is another boutique lodging location close to the Prescott Gateway Mall. The setting is very tranquil and as you enter you feel as if you are going on a spa retreat, which is a pleasant surprise. The interiors are okay, but not as well appointed as you would imagine in seeing the outside. They offer room service, plus breakfast and Wi-Fi are included.

HOLIDAY INN EXPRESS PRESCOTT

3454 Ranch Dr, Prescott, AZ 86303, (928) 445-8900, ihg.com

The Holiday Inn Express is in the Prescott Gateway Mall area and has likely the nicest pool of the bunch in this location. They offer the usual amenities, including free breakfast, fitness center, free Wi-Fi, and suites available. The indoor pool and adjoining whirlpool are heated. There is a nice landscape mural that wraps around the walls of the pool area.

PRESCOTT RESTAURANTS

IRON SPRINGS CAFÉ

CAJUN/MEXICAN/AMERICAN, $, 1501 W Iron Springs Rd, Prescott, AZ 86305, (928) 443-8848, ironspringscafe.com, open Wed-Sat 11am -8pm, Sunday 9am -2pm, closed Monday and Tuesday

Iron Springs Café serves up a varied mixture of Cajun, Mexican, and American dishes. This makes the restaurant a good spot for groups that are looking for different things. The food is hearty and healthy, the service is fast and friendly. One of the local hotspots in Prescott.

LIMONCELLO PIZZERIA NAPOLITANA

ITALIAN, $, 220 W Goodwin St, Prescott, AZ 86303, (928) 237-4759, limoncelloitalianhomemadecompany.com, open daily 11am - 10pm

New to the Prescott scene, Limoncello's is already on the map as one of the best spots for fresh homemade pizzas, traditional Italian antipastas, soups and salads. There selection of pizzas is arguably the largest in Arizona, with 28 pies to choose from. Most everything is made from scratch, including the cheeses. Be sure to leave room for their Mousse al Cioccolato.

EL GATO AZUL

TAPAS BAR, $, 316 W Goodwin St, Prescott, AZ 86301, (928) 445-1070, elgatoazulprescott.com, open daily 11am - 8pm, till 9pm Th-Sat, Sunday 12-8pm

El Gato Azul (The Blue Cat) is brimming with a spunky and festive atmosphere. It's not a huge place, but it is fun. Their menu is filled with a wide variety to choose from, offering everything from crepes, paninis, carnitas, and a full range of tapas, just to highlight a few. This is one of those places where it is hard to decide what to get because it all sounds really good!

COPPERTOP ALEHOUSE

GERMAN, $, 220 S Montezuma St, Prescott, AZ 86303, (928) 351-7712, coppertopalehouse.com, open daily 11am -8pm, until 10pm Friday & Saturday

This is a family-friendly traditional alehouse, where you can get stouts, lagers, and ales all on tap. For food, they offer pub-style German bratwurst, Bavarian soft pretzels, Reuben sandwiches, and German potato salad are all offered as a compliment to Coppertop's craft beer selection. Their flagship Imperial Stout is good enough to brag about. It's excellent!

THE LOCAL

AMERICAN, $, 520 W Sheldon St, Prescott, AZ 86301, (928) 237-4724, open daily 7am - 2:30pm

This is a bit off the main tourist drag but is recommended for its simplicity. They offer good American dishes, serving both breakfast and lunch menu. If you are looking for your meal to come as expected, be served by friendly staff, be hot, delicious, and a mix of healthy and naughty, all at the same time, then The Local is the right choice.

ATMESFIR

FRENCH, $$, 520 W Sheldon St, Prescott, AZ 86301, (928) 445-1929, open Wed-Sat 5 - 9pm, Sun 4 - 8pm

Atmesfir is locally sourced, farm to table goodness. No frozen patties, no microwaves, just a low key, relaxed atmosphere, and simple menu. They serve a country French cuisine, including favorites such as French onion soup with homemade croutons and Scottish Salmon with herb aioli and potatoes croquette. The menu is rather limited, so make sure there's something for everyone before sitting down.

TARA FINE THAI CUISINE

THAI, $, 115 S Cortez St, Prescott, AZ 86303, (928) 772-3249, tarathaiprescott.com, open daily 11am - 8pm, closed Monday

If you are looking for a Thai fix, Tara Fine Thai offers some robust curry's, pad thai, and a rich Thai iced tea. The atmosphere is hip, warm with table and bar seating.

CASA ALVAREZ

MEXICAN, $, 321 W Gurley St, Prescott, AZ 86303, (928) 445-9888, open Wednesday thru Sunday 5-8:30pm, closed Monday and Tuesday

Of the Mexican restaurants near the Historic Downtown area, Casa Alvarez gets the vote. That said, for some reason, Prescott is hit or miss when it comes to the Mexican cuisine. It's not the food per se, which in the case of this restaurant is hearty Sonora style offerings, but the service has been known to be less than stellar here and at the other Mexican food places in town.

BISTRO ST. MICHAEL

AMERICAN, $, 205 W Gurley St, Prescott, AZ 86301, (928) 778-2500, stmichaelhotel.com, open Sunday thru Thursday 7am - 8:30pm, open until 10pm on Friday and Saturday

Located in the Hotel St. Michael, the bistro has a mix of bar and table seating within a warmly decorated ambiance of wood paneling and discrete lighting. They offer a wide variety of menu items for breakfast, lunch, and dinner. The menu is so good you may want to come for all three meals!

ROSA'S PIZZA

ITALIAN, $, 330 W Gurley St, Prescott, AZ 86301, (928) 445-7400, rosaspizzeriaprescott.com, open daily 11am - 9:30pm

Rosa's offers a full menu of Italian pasta, salads, entrees, and as is evident by the places name, pizzas. There is nothing fancy or over the top about Rosa's, you get what you expect, good Italian meals served hot and with a smile.

COFFEE AND SWEETS

FROZEN FRANNIE'S

FROZEN YOGURT, 104 W Gurley St, Prescott, AZ 86301, (928) 515-2316, frozenfrannies.com, open daily 7am - 8pm

Frannie's is the local place for frozen yogurt, with a decent selection to choose from. They are across the street from the Courthouse Square on Gurley Street.

MARINO'S MOB BURGERS AND ICE CREAM

ICE CREAM, 113 S Cortez St, Prescott, AZ 86303, (928) 515-1690, open daily 8am -9pm

Conveniently located in the heart of the Historic Downtown, Marino's has excellent service, great ice cream, and they serve a full lunch and dinner menu on top of all that sweetness. In fact, this could easily go in the restaurant section. They offer burgers, mac and cheese, Chicago dogs, and many other comfort food choices. This is a happy place.

WILD IRIS COFFEE HOUSE

COFFEE, 124 S Granite St, Prescott, AZ 86303, (928) 778-5155, wildiriscoffee.com, open daily 6am - 8pm

Wild Iris is one of those places were you innocently come in just for coffee and find that they have a full on homemade bakery section filled with yummy sweets, quiches, and other goodness. You look around to find that all the coffee drinks have latte art designs lovingly drawn into the foam. At this point, you decide to go "all in," ruining your dinner but leaving satiated with the snack choices you enjoyed. Conveniently close to the Historic Downtown District.

PRALINES OF PRESCOTT

CHOCOLATE, 130 W Gurley St, Prescott, AZ 86301, (928) 776-9880, pralinesofprescott.com, Open Monday thru Saturday 10am - 5:30pm, open Sunday 11am -5pm

Pralines is a family owned gift to Prescott filled with candies, fudge, toffees, pralines, buttercreams, brittles, and barks. The passion for confection definitely shows here. For starters, try the Amish Carmel. Pralines is located in the interior of Bashford Courts. Look for the building that says, "World's Oldest Rodeo" and enjoys the journey of this and over a dozen other shops inside.

TREAT CENTER ON COURTHOUSE SQUARE

ICE CREAM, 156 S Montezuma St, Prescott, AZ 86303, (928) 445-5377, treatcenter.com, open daily 9:30am - 7pm

At Treat Center, you can find ice cream sundaes, floats, cones, malts, and shakes made from your choice of over a dozen homemade flavors of ice cream. They also offer popcorns, candies, sodas, and a small gift shop. The one downside to Treat is it is a small space in one of the highest traffic areas in downtown.

BLACK BUTTERFLY ARTISAN CHOCOLATES

CHOCOLATE, 218 W Goodwin St, Prescott, AZ 86303, (928) 227-3274, open Tuesday thru Sunday 11am - 5pm, closed Monday

Each piece is a masterpiece in the art of chocolate creation. They are visually beautiful to look at, and the tastes range from dark and bold to a light sublime flavoring with hints of rose, violet, or lemon. Black Butterfly Artisan Chocolates is edible convection as art.

Side Trip 4 –
Phoenix on the Rise

Best From

South Rim is the most direct route to Phoenix, add 3 hours if coming from the North Rim Grand Canyon.

What You'll See

- Montezuma Castle
- Montezuma Well
- Aqua Fria National Monument
- Phoenix

Why Choose This Side Trip

This route is ideal for folks that need to get back home via the Phoenix airport but want to fit in one or two quick stops on the way down. Even if you are making a beeline back to the airport, there are a few cool stops along the way and are easy to visit time wisely.

The route is also ideal for those that want to check out what the Phoenix area has to offer. This side trip is loaded with stuff to do in Phoenix, Scottsdale, and Tempe.

Agua Fria National Monument is included but requires more time, a high clearance vehicle, and in the summer, ample preparedness (and tolerance) for omnipresent triple-digit heat.

Allow

- Recommended – 1-3 days
- Total Drive Time: 4 hours from Grand Canyon Village to Phoenix Sky Harbor Airport
- Montezuma Well: Allow 45 minutes to 1 hour
- Montezuma Castle: Allow 45 minutes to 1 hour
- Aqua Fria National Monument: allow 4 hours to overnight
- Phoenix: Depends on how much time you want to spend in Phoenix area.

Montezuma Well

Montezuma Castle and Montezuma Well are both day use sites that can be covered in less than an hour each. On visiting Phoenix, this depends on if you need to get to the airport or want to spend a few days. If you are flying home, be sure to allow an additional 30 minutes to return a rental car as the facility is about 1.5 – 2 miles away depending on which terminal you are flying out of. The other flying tip is to allow extra time for traffic. Each year the city pushes northward, causing more gridlock. The rush hour delays can be significant coming into Phoenix.

Aqua Fria National Monument is put on this side trip as an optional leg. It is completely undeveloped, with no paved roads, visitor center or other facilities. In the summer, it is also very hot. If you do go, allow a good half day or make it an overnight camping trip.

Can be combined with

Side Trip 1 – "Ancient Lands" and Side Trip 2 – "Mystical Sedona." If it's time to head home, Phoenix Sky Harbor International is the closest major airport.

MONTEZUMA WELL

The first stop is to Montezuma Well, which is eleven miles away from Montezuma Castle National Monument. This spot is amazing to visit and sacred to many Southwest cultures. The "well" is a limestone sinkhole with an underground spring. The spring itself is impressive, large enough to hold 15 million gallons of water and it pumps a consistent 1.5 million gallons of water out each day. The water's presence is due to a massive amount of groundwater from the Mogollon Rim traveling deep under the soil until it reaches a large underground volcanic basalt wall. The wall acts as a dam, causing the waters to rise up until it reaches the sinkhole.

There are some remnants of early Sinagua usage, including some cliff dwellings tightly integrated into the walls of the sinkhole. The Yavapai considers the area to be where their people emerged into this world.

Montezuma Well is free to visit and is open daily from 8am - 5pm.

Montezuma Well Trail

Easy – (0.5 mi / 0.8 km), round trip, allow 30 minutes

This trail is fun for many reasons. It's short and thus doable under most weather conditions. In the summer, the loop winds down to a shady grotto, with the outlet of the spring emptying into a tranquil canal set against a limestone cliff. Here there are ferns and cottonwoods helping to cool things down. Beaver Creek is nearby and accessible at this juncture as well.

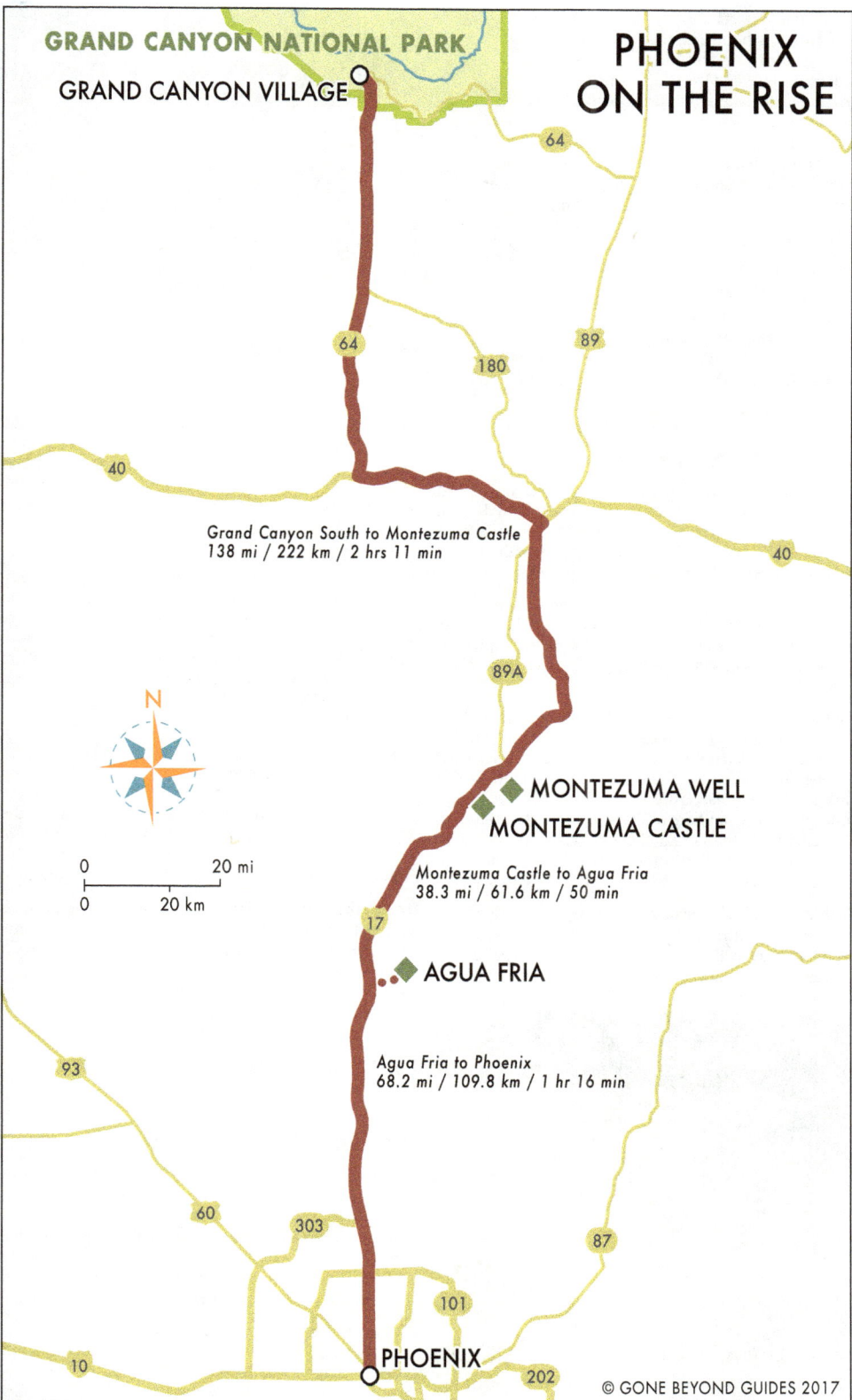

GRAND CANYON VILLAGE

PHOENIX ON THE RISE

64

64

180

89

40

Grand Canyon South to Montezuma Castle
138 mi / 222 km / 2 hrs 11 min

40

73

89A

N

◆ MONTEZUMA WELL

MONTEZUMA CASTLE

Montezuma Castle to Agua Fria
38.3 mi / 61.6 km / 50 min

0   20 mi
0   20 km

17

◆ AGUA FRIA

Agua Fria to Phoenix
68.2 mi / 109.8 km / 1 hr 16 min

93

60

303

87

101

10

PHOENIX

202

© GONE BEYOND GUIDES 2017

The trail starts at a small visitor information booth. If there is a ranger there, he or she will gladly give details about the area and the people who used it. After a short climb, the spring comes into view inside a rock bowl, with cliff dwelling ruins clinging to the sides. There is a short spur trail down to the bottom of the bowl which is worth taking to see another ruin site and some early graffiti. After coming back to the top of the spring, continue to wind down to its outlet described earlier and back to your car. There are interpretive signs along the way.

On the drive within the park, there are archeological remains of a pit house that is a short walk from the pullout. There are signs describing both the dig itself and what you are seeing.

MONTEZUMA CASTLE NATIONAL MONUMENT

Montezuma Castle is one in a long list of misnamed parks within the Grand Circle. It has nothing to do with Montezuma, the Aztec ruler killed by the Spanish conquests of Cortés. Nor is it a castle. It is actually one of the best-preserved cliff dwellings of the Sinagua People.

The ruins sit 90 feet up a sheer cliff within an alcove. Some of the walls have been reconstructed, complete with exterior plaster, which gives the visitor a splendid view of what the cliff dwelling would have looked like some 800 years ago.

The ruins are accessible to the eye only from a short one-third mile paved walkway amongst the fanning sounds of the surrounding Sycamore trees. This is what makes this park fun. There are no tours and no real hikes. Montezuma Castle is a quick side treat within one's journey from here to there. If you are traveling to Phoenix from the Grand Canyon or Sedona, the park makes a nice respite to stretch the legs and experience a bit of history.

The park trail and visitor center is open daily from 8am - 5pm. Entrance fee to the castle is $10, which is good for seven days at both Montezuma Castle and Tuzigoot National Monuments.

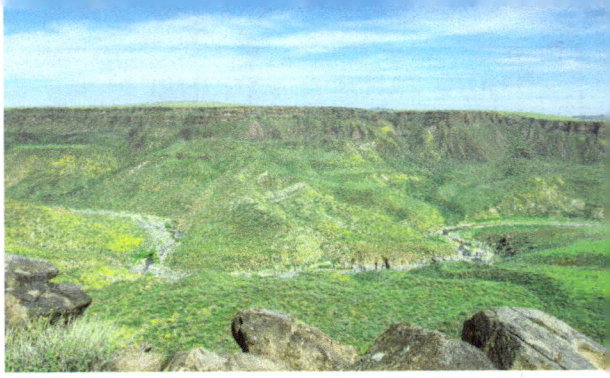

Agua Fria in springtime

AQUA FRIA NATIONAL MONUMENT

To get to Grand Canyon from Phoenix, one typically passes by Agua Fria National Monument, which is cut by Interstate 17. Three exits allow access to the park as you make your way north, but for the most part, the park doesn't get much attention.

Given that this park has been set aside to preserve 450 Ancestral Puebloan sites, the lack of publicity makes sense. Here there are no visitor centers, no lodges one official trail, and three dirt roads. The roads are primitive and not well maintained. High clearance vehicles recommended here. This isn't exactly a babymoon location nor a romantic getaway, well at least not for most anyway. It is a rugged land with no amenities. What the park does offer is the ability for off-trail hiking and some large unexcavated ruins to explore.

The land is inviting, composed primarily or basalt top layers with older Precambrian rock exposed by the Agua Fria at an elevation that at times holds both the Upper and Lower Sonoran flora and fauna. There are petroglyphs, multiple village sites, and many other minor ruins that make up the near 400 sites in the area.

The park does get very hot from mid-spring through summer and into the fall season. If you do go, come prepared for backcountry travel.

HIKING AGUA FRIA NATIONAL MONUMENT

PUEBLO LA PLATA RUINS

Easy – (0.5 mi / 0.8 km), round trip, allow 30 minutes
This ruin is 8.3 miles on Bloody Basin Road, which requires high clearance to cross the creek and in some rough patches, but is otherwise suitable for a 2WD car. The ruins of Pueblo la Plata were a large village of up to 100 rooms. The location of this site was by design as it sits on the defendable northwestern rim of Perry Mesa.

There are signs of looting at this site, which is the only site that is publicly listed by the BLM. Please do your part by staying off walls and watching your step as you walk. There are pottery shards and other artifact

Montezuma Castle National Monument

remnants on the premises. BLM's stance is its okay to touch and photograph your finds, but place them back where you found them. It is tempting to take an artifact home, but in the process, you will destroy scientific evidence that helps research. Beyond being illegal, most pottery shards end up collecting dust on a shelf and have no real value other than being a guilty memory of your trip. Take a picture and feel good that you aren't betraying the trust that the park system has placed on the visitor.

BADGER SPRINGS TRAIL

Easy – (1.5 mi / 2.4 km), round trip, allow 1 hour

This is a there and back trail that ends at some nice petroglyphs. The trail travels down a small dry wash to the Agua Fria River. The petroglyphs are at the end of the trail. It is possible to bushwhack upstream and down for another half to three-quarters of a mile. This trail is a bit sandy, but otherwise kid-friendly. You can get right up to the petroglyphs, but refrain from touching them as the cumulative oil from visitor's hands does have a negative effect on the rock art.

Saguaros at Sunset in Sonoran Desert near Phoenix

PHOENIX

From seeing one of the largest collections of cacti to the largest collection of musical instruments, there are a ton of things to do in the capital of Arizona. The city goes by the nickname of the Valley of the Sun, and it definitely lives up to it, being over 100°F for a minimum of 150 days out of any given year. In fact, it gets so hot here that plastic trashcans have melted and planes can't get enough lift to take off, but both of those are rare events.

For the most part, the city is built to handle the sun, with most folks traveling from air-conditioned cars to air-conditioned interior spaces, be it a museum or grocery store. While the town has grown tremendously over the last two decades, the sunsets haven't changed one bit, they are still world class.

THINGS TO DO IN THE PHOENIX AREA

JAPANESE FRIENDSHIP GARDEN

1125 N 3rd Ave, Phoenix, AZ 85003, (602) 274-8700, japanesefriendshipgarden.org, open October 1st - May 31st from 10am - 4pm

Come visit a serene and beautiful Japanese garden right in the middle of Phoenix! The gardens are truly tranquil, with waterfalls and a Zen-like mindfulness. A wonderful place to reset. Note that the gardens are only open to the public from October 1st to May 31st.

WELLS FARGO HISTORY MUSEUM

145 W Adams St, Phoenix, AZ 85003, (602) 378-1852, wellsfargohistory.com, open weekdays 9am - 5pm, closed weekends

The Wells Fargo History Museum is aimed at a younger audience and families, offering up an interactive telegraph device, a replica stagecoach you can sit in, as well as many other exhibits, a historic bank, and themed memorabilia to delight young imaginations. The museum sits inside the Wells Fargo building and is open during normal banking hours. Admission is free.

PHOENIX ART MUSEUM

1625 N Central Ave, Phoenix, AZ 85004, (602) 257-1222, open Tuesday, Thursday - Saturday 10am -5pm, closes at 9pm Wednesday, Sunday 12-5pm, Closed Monday

The Phoenix Art Museum is an awesome place to stroll amongst fine art from around the world right in downtown. This is the largest visual art museum in the Southwest, holding over 18,000 works within its vast 285,000 square foot facility. The museum focuses on modern and contemporary art from around the world. They also offer ever-changing exhibits that are exotic and surprisingly clever. On Wednesdays and other designated days, the museum is free (check their website for details). Otherwise, Adults are $18, Seniors $15, Children ages 6-17 are $9, under 6 are free.

HEARD MUSEUM

2301 N Central Ave, Phoenix, AZ 85004, (602) 252-8840, heard.org, open daily 9:30am - 5pm, except Sunday 11am - 5pm

This museum holds an amazing collection of American Indian art, both contemporary and traditional. This private, not for profit facility takes the curator role of native art seriously; the exhibits are compelling, with an eye for pieces that are timeless. Admission is free every first Friday, from 6pm - 10pm, except in March. General admission is $18 for adults, $13.50 for seniors, children ages 6-17 and college students with ID are $7.50, under 6 are free.

PHOENIX

Legend:
- 🛏 Lodgings
- 🍴 Restaurants
- ☕ Coffee and Sweets
- ⭐ Things to do

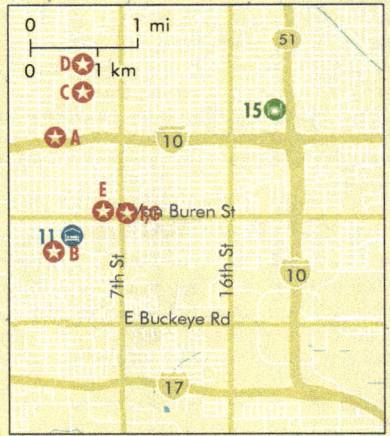

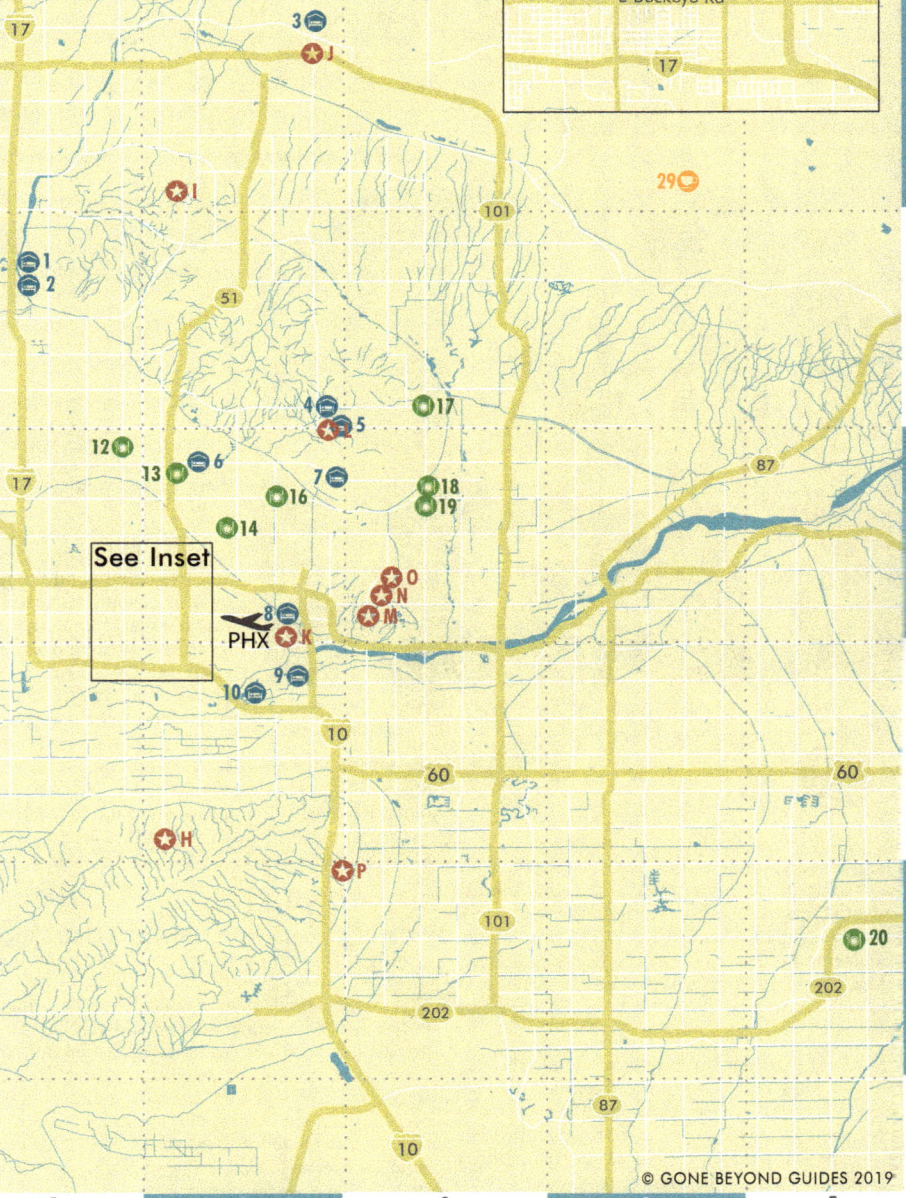

0 —— 1 mi
0 —— 1 km

Inset:
0 —— 1 mi
0 —— 1 km

D ⭐
C ⭐
A ⭐
15 🍴
51
10
E ⭐ Van Buren St
11 🛏 B
7th St
16th St
E Buckeye Rd
10
17

76

17
3 🛏
J ⭐
I ⭐
101
29 ☕
1 🛏
2 🛏
51
4 🛏
5 ⭐ 17 🍴
12 🍴
13 🍴 6 🛏
7 🛏
16 🍴
18 🍴
19 🍴
14 🍴
O ⭐
See Inset
N ⭐
M ⭐
8 🛏
PHX ✈ K ⭐
10 🛏 9 🛏
10
60
60
H ⭐
P ⭐
101
20 🍴
G
202
202
87
10

© GONE BEYOND GUIDES 2019

PHOENIX

Lodging

1 Candlewood Suites Phoenix.................D1
2 Hyatt Place Phoenix-North.................D1
3 Marriott's Canyon Villas.....................C2
4 Omni Scottsdale Resort & Spa...........D2
5 Sanctuary on Camelback Mountain.....E2
6 Courtyard by Marriott Phoenix...........E2
7 Royal Palms Resort and Spa..............E2
8 Crowne Plaza Phoenix Airport............E2
9 Hilton Phoenix Airport.......................F2
10 Drury Inn & Suites Phoenix Airport.......F2
11 Hyatt Regency Phoenix.......................B4

Restaurants

12 Mora Italian.....................................E1
13 Tratto...E2
14 Binkleys..E2
15 Tacos Chiwas...................................B5
16 UnderTow..E2
17 Fat Ox..D3
18 FnB..E3
19 Sel...E3
20 Barnone..G5

Things To Do

A Japanese Friendship Garden................B4
B Wells Fargo History Museum................B4
C Phoenix Art Museum..........................B4
D Heard Museum..................................A4
E St. Mary's Basilica............................B4
F Rosson House...................................B4
G Children's Museum of Phoenix.............B4
H Mystery Castle.................................F2
I Buddy Stubbs Harley-Davidson Museum......B2
J Musical Instrument Museum.................C2
K Pueblo Grande Museum.......................F2
L Camelback Mountain...........................E2
M Phoenix Zoo.....................................E3
N Hole in the Rock...............................E3
O Desert Botanical Garden.....................E3
P Main Event......................................G2

ST. MARY'S BASILICA

231 N 3rd St, Phoenix, AZ 85004, (602) 354-2100, hours vary, see website: http://saintmarysbasilica.org

Founded in 1881 and completed in 1914, this is not only one of the oldest buildings in Phoenix, but it also houses the largest stained-glass collections in the State. The church is a marvel to look at both inside and out with four domes spanning the length of the basilica. St Mary's Basilica continues to operate today, holding midnight Mass, vigils, and devotions. See their website for hours.

THE ROSSON HOUSE MUSEUM

113 N 6th St, Phoenix, AZ 85004, (602) 262-5070, heritagesquarephx.org, open 10am - 4pm Wednesday - Saturday, Sunday 12-4pm, closed Monday and Tuesday

The Rosson House Museum is an impeccably restored Queen Anne Victorian two-story home built in 1895. Tours are given daily that highlight what life was like for early Phoenicians when the land was but a territory. The tour is delightful and well worth carving out time to visit. Admission is $9 for adults, $4 for children, and $8 for seniors, military, and folks that have AAA.

CHILDREN'S MUSEUM OF PHOENIX

215 N 7th St, Phoenix, AZ 85034, (602) 253-0501, childrensmuseumofphoenix.org, open daily, 9am - 4pm, closed Monday

This world of wonder is aimed at babies, toddlers, and preschoolers, offering tons of things to do, see, touch, and craft. For a young one, this place is paradise. Tickets are $12 for adults and children, $11 for seniors, and children under 1 are free.

MYSTERY CASTLE

800 E Mineral Rd, Phoenix, AZ 85042, mymystery-castle.com, open Thursday - Sunday 11am -3:30pm

Tucked away in the foothills of South Mountain Park at the south edge of the city lies a monument and testimony to living out one's life however one chooses. In 1930, Boyce Luther Gulley moved from Seattle to Phoenix on hearing he had tuberculosis and built a castle of sorts from found and inexpensive materials. He built it for his daughter Lucy who moved in shortly after her father's death in 1945. She and her mom decided to offer tours of the place, which boasts a chapel and dungeon as part of the sprawling 18 room, three-story castle. Guided tours are $10 for adults, $5 for children ages 5-12.

BUDDY STUBBS HARLEY-DAVIDSON MOTORCYCLE MUSEUM

13850 N Cave Creek Rd, Phoenix, AZ 85022, (602) 971-3400, buddystubbshd.com, hours vary, summer hours, daily 9am -5pm

If you love motorcycles, you really need to visit Buddy Stubbs Museum. 3,000 square feet of two-wheeled history, with over 130 vintage machines of motorcycle power. Admission is free.

MUSICAL INSTRUMENT MUSEUM

4725 E Mayo Blvd, Phoenix, AZ 85050, (480) 478-6000, mim.org, open daily 9am - 5pm

The museum is on the edge of town and is a subject matter that may not be the first pick for some. That said, the collection of musical instruments along with their history is so robust and complete, this is one of the best museums in the area. They host musical instruments from around the world, including Africa, Asia, Europe, and the Americas. The displays are all well thought out and put together, making for an entertaining and satisfying visit and will reset what you thought you knew about the world of music!

Hole in the Rock

CAMELBACK MOUNTAIN

4925 E McDonald Dr, Phoenix, AZ 85018, (602) 261-8318

Camelback Mountain, named for its shape, is the prominent singular mountain feature northwest of Scottsdale. Two trails climb to the top of the 1,280-foot peak. Echo Canyon Trail starts at the address listed here and is 1.1 miles to the top. The other route is the 1.4-mile Cholla Trail. Echo is the more popular trail of the two given the rock formations seen along the way.

PUEBLO GRANDE MUSEUM

4619 E Washington St, Phoenix, AZ 85034, (602) 495-0901, pueblogrande.com, open most days 9am - 4:45pm, Sundays from 1pm - 4:45pm

The City of Phoenix Parks and Recreation Department run the Pueblo Grande Museum, holding exhibits of the Hohokam people inside an adobe block southwest style building. Completed in 1935, the museum has three galleries, plus an outdoor interpretative trail. Adults are $6, over 55 are $5, children ages 6-17 are $3 and under 6 are free.

MAIN EVENT

8545 S Emerald Dr, Tempe, AZ 85284, (480) 753-1200, https://www.mainevent.com/locations/tempe-az, open M-Th 11am -12am, to 2am on Fridays, opens at 9am on Saturdays

The Main Event is a fun place to chill out for both kids and adults. They offer laser tag, arcade games, bowling, full bar and more. There are three locations, the Tempe location is highlighted due to its overall central location to the airport. This choice is great if you have an hour or two to kill before heading to your plane home.

LODGING

OMNI SCOTTSDALE RESORT & SPA AT MONTELUCIA

4949 E Lincoln Dr, Paradise Valley, AZ 85253-4139, (800) 578-2900, omnihotels.com

The Omni Scottsdale is a 5-star hotel with the dramatic Camelback Mountains as a backdrop to its own spacious luxury. The resort offers the full-service Joya Spa and Salon, a nicely equipped fitness center, 6 dining options, and 3 pools bordered by 23 cabanas. A Spanish architectural theme permeates the design, both inside and out. The nearly 300 rooms are well appointed, timeless, and luxurious in the same moment. This is a great place for a romantic getaway or special occasion. Service here is top notch.

DESERT BOTANICAL GARDEN

1201 N Galvin Pkwy, Phoenix, AZ 85008, (480) 941-1225, dbg.org, open daily 7am - 8pm

The garden is wonderfully spread across 140 acres, hosting one of the best collections of desert fauna in the world. They have over 10,000 cacti species alone. There are special exhibits, such as the Australian, South American, and Baja plant collections. This is one of those places where the more you can slow yourself down, the more you will see and enjoy. Like the Phoenix Zoo, this place can get crowded, making early morning the best time to go. Adults are $24.95, children ages 3-17 are $12.95.

PHOENIX ZOO

455 N Galvin Pkwy, Phoenix, AZ 85008, (602) 286-3800, phoenixzoo.org, open seasonally at different times, check hours on website, typically open daily 9am - 4pm

The Phoenix Zoo offers a full day of fun with multiple animal sections, a water play area for small children, dining, and shopping. The zoo shelters animals from around the world, with a specific area dedicated to Arizona species. Ticket prices vary depending on the season, and there always seems to be a discount, check online and at local grocery stores. Standard rates are $25 for adults and $15 for children.

HOLE IN THE ROCK

625 N Galvin Pkwy, Phoenix, AZ 85008, (602) 495-5458, phoenix.gov, open daily 6am - 7pm

Hole in the Rock is part of Papago Park, near the Phoenix Zoo and the Desert Botanical Garden. The area offers multiple shaded picnic areas and good parking on most days. It is a short distance along a well-marked trail to the hole, which is a large opening in a larger rock formation that was once used by native people. This side trip is a quick and free way to see a little of the Phoenix desert, with views of the city from the hole's saddle. It can be crowded on weekends.

SANCTUARY CAMELBACK MOUNTAIN RESORT

5700 E McDonald Dr, Paradise Valley, AZ 85253-5218, (855) 245-2051, sanctuaryoncamelback.com

Paradise Valley is essentially where you will find all the luxury resort class hotels and the Sanctuary is one of the best of the best in this area. The 5-star hotel checks all the usual boxes for a resort, with stylish grounds and interiors, pool, Asian inspired spa, tennis courts and several restaurants. What sets the Sanctuary apart is in its service and dining experience. The service is simply impeccable. The dining is equally sublime, setting a world-class standard for quality and table service. Cannot say enough about Sanctuary Camelback Mountain Resort, it's the favorite of the bunch listed here and was voted the #1 resort in Arizona by Conde Nest Traveler.

MARRIOTT'S CANYON VILLAS

5220 E Marriott Dr, Phoenix, AZ 85054-6150, (480) 629-3200, marriott.com

The Marriott Canyon Villas are a sister property to the JW Marriott and Golf Resort. The 3.5-star hotel offers many of the amenities of its nearby resort property without the resort fees. Each villa is a full studio, with fully stocked kitchen, washer and dryer and separate living and sleeping areas. This is a good choice if you like to do your own cooking or are looking for a home away from home, but with more service and amenities. The hotel offers its own heated pool as well as access to JW's spa, pools, and 18-hole golf course.

CANDLEWOOD SUITES PHOENIX

11411 N Black Canyon Hwy, Phoenix, AZ 85029-3448, (602) 861-4900, ihg.com

Candlewood is one of the best values for a hotel in the 2.5-star category. It is reasonably priced, but with a lot of amenities, including a full kitchen, outdoor heated pool, fitness center, and free parking. The one item not offered here is a free breakfast, though they do have a snack store inside the hotel if you've lost all hope of finding a meal in the area.

HYATT PLACE PHOENIX – NORTH

10838 N 25th Ave, Phoenix, AZ 85029-4746, (602) 997-8800, phoenixnorth.place.hyatt.com

Hyatt Place Phoenix - North makes the grade for those looking for good value for their money. The 3-star hotel offers everything it should for lodging in this class, including free parking and breakfast, and an outdoor pool.

ROYAL PALMS RESORT AND SPA

5200 East Camelback Road, Phoenix, AZ 85018-3020, (602) 283-1234, royalpalms.hyatt.com

Granada style tiled roofs, Mediterranean inspired dining, and frequent entertainment is just some of the features of this luxury 5-star resort. As with all of the luxury class hotels, the bar is already high, so the focus is on what differentiates one from the other. For the Royal Palms, it is three things. First is the Alvadora Spa, that offers spa treatments, yoga, meditation, and even fitness classes, making this spa one of the best in the area. The rooms are also well appointed, nearly over the top, yet featuring timeless touches that help to keep to an understatedly elegant tone. Finally, this boutique resort hotel wraps its entire Spanish/Mediterranean theme up nicely with little touches that take the entire theme to a higher level. As a boutique, it is a complete package, from the service to the grounds to the dining and architecture.

CROWNE PLAZA PHOENIX AIRPORT

4300 E Washington St, Phoenix, AZ 85034-1818, (682) 273-7778, crowneplazaphx.com

This 4-star hotel offers modern architectural themes, great service, and as the name implies, close proximity to the airport. If are in need for one last moment of luxury but have an early flight, this is a good choice.

COURTYARD PHOENIX CAMELBACK

2101 East Camelback Road, Phoenix, AZ 85016-4712, (602) 955-5200, marriott.com

The Courtyard Camelback is a consistent choice and in the same category for the best value for the money. The Starbucks menu, pool, service, rooms, it's the same at every Courtyard and no different here. That is a fine option for those looking for good service and value without high resort prices.

HILTON PHOENIX AIRPORT

2435 S 47th St, Phoenix, AZ 85034-6410, (480) 894-1600, hilton.com

The Hilton Phoenix Airport is another solid choice for those looking for good service and no surprises in a hotel close to their flight out the next morning. The management recently completed a full renovation of the property, and it certainly does look and feel like a new hotel. The place is clean, well lit, and modern, with nice touches, like origami towels in the rooms. They offer a breakfast buffet, free parking, on-site restaurant, and an outdoor pool.

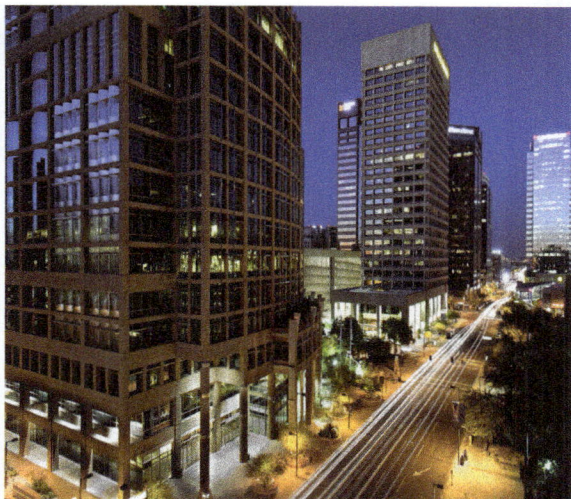

Downtown Phoenix

79

HYATT REGENCY PHOENIX

122 N 2nd St, Phoenix, AZ 85004-2379, (602) 252-1234, phoenix.regency.hyatt.com

The Hyatt Regency is right in the center of downtown Phoenix, with modern interiors and views of the city from about every room. The hotel offers an on-site restaurant, outdoor pool, 24-hour gym and easy access to the city.

DRURY INN & SUITES PHOENIX AIRPORT

3333 E University Dr, Phoenix, AZ 85034-7215, (888) 324-1835, druryhotels.com

Free breakfast, parking, and Wi-Fi, plus being close to the airport makes this another in the list of fair value for money hotels. The Drury also offers the 5:30 Kickback, where you can pig out on free hot food and cold beverages, served till 7pm each day. Overall, the Drury Inn is a great choice.

RESTAURANTS

BARNONE

AMERICAN, $, 3000 E Ray Rd, Gilbert, AZ 85296, (480) 988-1238, barnoneaz.com, open daily 10am - 9pm, except Thursday thru Saturday open until 11pm, closed Monday

Barnone is not one restaurant, but a collective of eateries, plus a winery and brewmaster housed in a converted and very modern looking barn. You can get wood-fired pizza at the Fire & Brimstone or farm to table fare at the Uprooted Kitchen. Round out the experience with a beer at 12 West Brewing or Garage-East for wine. Barnone is a community of makers beyond food, including Lettercraft which makes custom laser and woodcut gifts. Also, check out Johnston Arms which restores firearms to an art form like quality.

FAT OX

ITALIAN, $$$, 6316 N Scottsdale Rd, Scottsdale, AZ 85253, (480) 307-6900, ilovefatox.com, open daily 4:30 - 9:30pm, open until 10:30pm Friday and Sat

The ambiance is swanky and spirited, the food is as if the chef had been taught to cook under the tutelage of his old school Italian mother and had just left home, allowing him a new freedom to put modern interpretations on the dishes from which he was originally trained. Try the tableside caesar salad for a starter or the steamed mussels. For mains, chef Matt Carter casts a wide net, including rigatoni lamb verde and rabbit with white wine, along with a monster 40-ounce porterhouse and other steak and seafood selections.

FNB RESTAURANT

AMERICAN, $, 7125 E 5th Ave Ste 31, Scottsdale, AZ 85251, (480) 264-4777, fnbrestaurant.com, open Tuesday - Sunday 3 - 10pm, closed Monday

FnB is a small venue that serves inventively designed farm to table fare in Old Town Scottsdale. Their menu is small and changes seasonally, leaning heavily on vegetarian items, making this a top selection for those that don't eat meat. Their wine knowledge is impressive, be sure to ask what to pair your meal with. The small venue makes this a good recommendation for couples and small parties but is not a good choice for large groups.

SEL

AMERICAN, $$$$ 7044 E Main St, Scottsdale, AZ 85251, (480) 949-6296, selrestaurant.com, open Tuesday thru Saturday 5:30 - 9pm, closed Sunday and Monday

Sel is another boutique restaurant offering in Old Town Scottsdale. The restaurant offers a tasting menu with limited options, but from what they do offer the preparation and plating are exceptional. There is a true mastery in the art of culinary delight here. The ingredient combinations are impressive and at times surprising. The ambiance is small and elegant, making this a great place to impress a date. Try the seared Hudson Valley foie gras and the BBQ grilled octopus. An evening at Sel is not cheap, bring the plastic.

Sunset over Phoenix Sky Harbor Airport

The Saguaro cacti don't say anything, they just wave

UNDERTOW

COCKTAIL BAR, $, 3620 E Indian School Rd, Phoenix, AZ 85018, undertowphx.com, open Monday thru Saturday 4pm - 12am, open until 2am Friday and Saturday, Sunday 2 - 10pm

Well, not only is the first and only cocktail bar listed in this guide but the first tiki-themed cocktail bar at that. UnderTow offers a wide selection of incredibly well-balanced rum drinks within the décor of the hull of a 19th-century clipper ship. Space is small, and reservations are recommended. You will not find an experience in mixology quite this in the entire Southwest. If you are looking to impress your friends, try the Smoking Cannon, with infused smoke. Just watching the bartender make the drink is an experience.

BINKLEY'S

AMERICAN, $$$$, 2320 E Osborn Rd, Phoenix, AZ 85016, (602) 388-4874, binkleysrestaurant.com, open Thursday thru Sunday 6:30 - 10pm

Chef Kevin Binkley is well known in the sport of culinary excellence and has been a James Beard finalist for Best Chef several years in a row. Binkley's allows for his mastery to be experienced by mere mortals, offering seating for 24 total Thursday thru Sunday. The offering is a tasting menu of the chef's choice, allow 3.5 hours for the dining experience. Reservations are required. This is dining within the alchemical aethers of gastronomic perfection, you will not be disappointed.

TRATTO

ITALIAN, $$, 4743 N 20th St, Phoenix, AZ 85016, (602) 296-7761, trattophx.com, open Monday thru Saturday 5 - 9pm, open until 10pm Friday and Saturday, closed Monday

Award-winning chef Chris Bianco serves up the best Italian in the Phoenix area. The place is small and understated with just 35 seats and is next door the chef's other restaurant experience, Pizzeria Bianco. If you have but one night to enjoy Phoenician food, Tratto's is an excellent choice.

MORA ITALIAN

ITALIAN, $$, 5651 N 7th St, Phoenix, AZ 85014, (602) 795-9943, moraitalian.com, open daily 4 - 9pm, open until 10pm Friday and Saturday

Chopped chef star Scott Conant offers a fresh, vibrant selection of Italian favorites and signature dishes. Pastas are homemade, and the pizzas are absolutely out of this world. Located in north Phoenix.

TACOS CHIWAS

MEXICAN, $, 1923 E McDowell Rd, Phoenix, AZ 85006, (602) 358-8830, tacoschiwas. com, open Tuesday to Saturday 10am - 9pm, Sunday 10am - 4pm

The ambiance is Clark Kent, as in it is a completely unassuming taqueria, not unlike the other thousands within the Southwest. The food, however, is pure Superman. Tacos Chiwas is the pinnacle of homemade Mexican cuisine. The corn tortillas are cooked to order, the meats are savory and boldly flavorful, and they offer a full bar of homemade salsas. This was a secret, now it's not. If you want authentic out of this world Chihuahua Mexican, seek out Tacos Chiwas.

Camelback Mountain

Side Trip 5 –
Petrified Forests

BEST FROM

South Rim on this one, add three hours if coming from the North Rim

WHAT YOU'LL SEE

- Meteor Crater
- Winslow, Arizona
- Holbrook, Arizona
- Petrified Forest National Park

WHY CHOOSE THIS SIDE TRIP

A vacation to Grand Canyon National Park coupled with a stop at Petrified Forest National Park is as classic Americana as two scoops of ice cream on a sugar cone. The trip is one where you can count out-of-state license plates, sing songs in the car together, or stare out into the scenic vastness of Arizona. The side trip offers a chance to walk amongst giant petrified logs, peer over an impressive meteor crater, and visit Holbrook, AZ, a town that never left the 1950's and home to one of the last teepee motels in the US. You can even put some miles on Route 66, the mythic highway of epic vacations since the dawn of road trips.

ALLOW

- Recommended 2-3 days
- Total Drive Time: Allow 3.5 hours
- Meteor Crater: Allow about 45 minutes
- Petrified Forest National Park: Best if done as a day trip with an overnight in Holbrook. Can be seen in a couple of hours if you have little time or extended with a night in the park's backcountry.

CAN BE COMBINED WITH

Side Trip 1 – "Ancient Lands" and Side Trip 2 – "Mystical Sedona."

METEOR CRATER

Your first stop to consider is a roadside attraction called Meteor Crater. When Meteor Crater was first discovered, folks weren't even certain that the huge hole in the ground was in fact created by a meteor. Daniel Barringer originally bought the land around Meteor Crater as a mining operation. He was convinced the impact crater was due to a meteorite, something still in debate in 1903. He mined the area on the belief that a 10-million-ton iron ore meteor lay hidden at the bottom. The mining operation nearly bankrupted him, but he did prove that the impact was due to a meteorite. Today, the scientific community calls the formation the Barringer Crater and the Barringer family still own the land in and around the impact site, offering it up as an attraction for passing visitors.

The details of this crater are impressive. When it hit the earth about 50,000 years ago, it was going at a speed of 34,000 mph and landed with an energy of about 4.5 megatons, which is another way of saying "with the force of 4.5 million tons of TNT". As a comparison, the Fat Man bomb dropped on Nagasaki during WWII had the energy of about 20 kilotons or 20,000 tons of TNT. The rolling grasslands of the impact area turned from pasture land for wooly mammoths into a crater three-quarters of a mile across and 560 feet deep, with a circumference of 2.4 miles. Note that some of these figures come from a study NASA did back in 1979 and are still impressive but somehow smaller than the figures posted by the Meteor Crater owners.

Fast forward to the present, Meteor Crater, the attraction, offers an RV park and visitor center along with a 20-minute movie on the formation. Visiting isn't cheap. Adults are $18, over 60 are $17, ages 6-17 are $9, and under 6 are free. The price brings up a fair amount of debate on the question, "but is it worth it?" You can't walk to the bottom, so the experience is limited to peering over the edge and imagining what it must have been like when the meteorite fell to earth, plus the video, and let's not discount the quality time in a gift shop. For some, this is a must-see, but honestly, many vacationers pass, so don't feel you must do this one. It depends on whether you see this attraction as a big hole in the ground or visual evidence of what 4.5million tons of TNT could do.

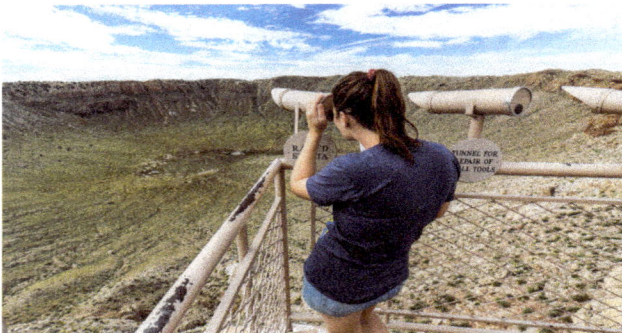

Checking out the other side of Meteor Crater

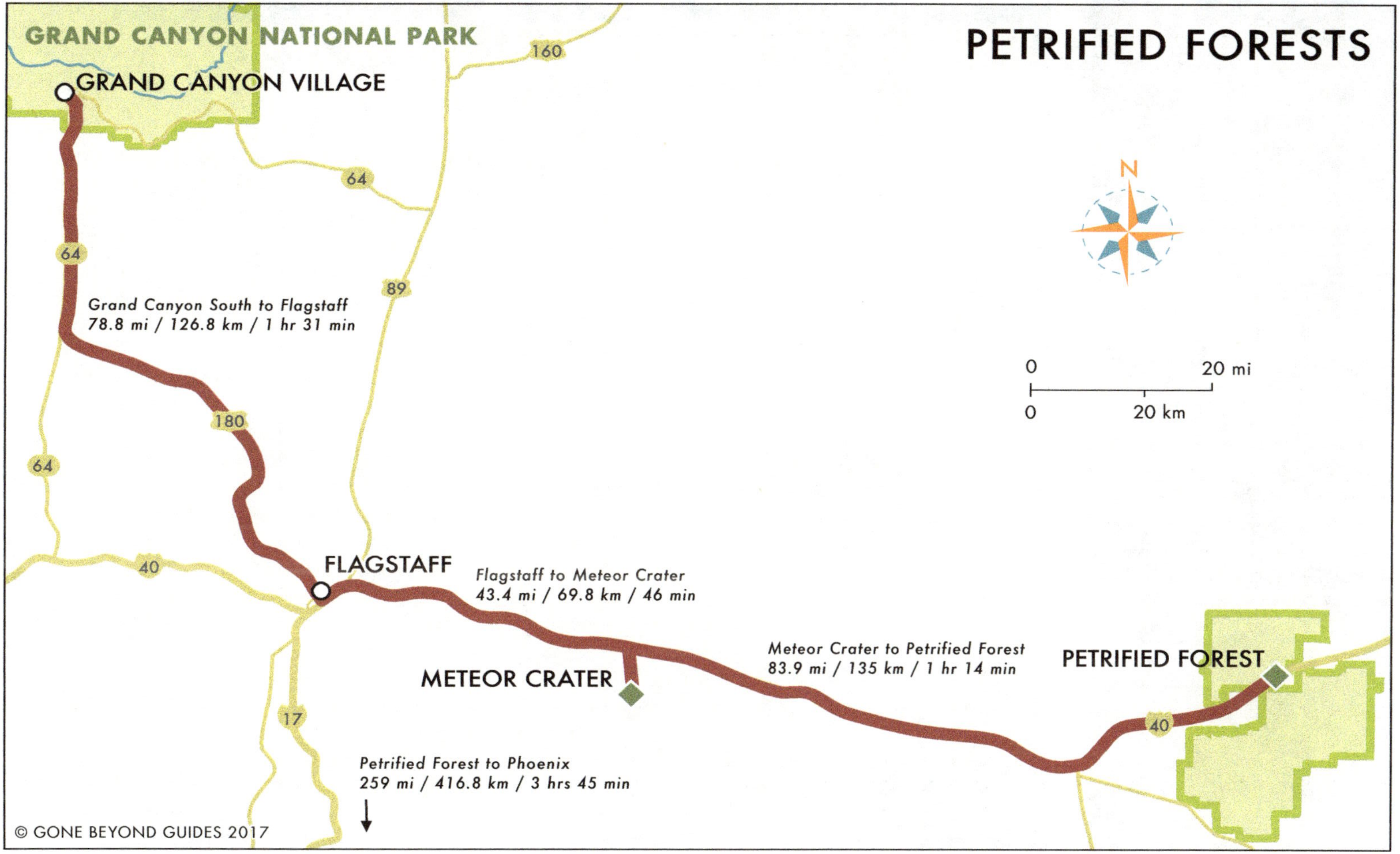

PETRIFIED FORESTS
GRAND CANYON NATIONAL PARK
GRAND CANYON VILLAGE
160
64
64
89
Grand Canyon South to Flagstaff
78.8 mi / 126.8 km / 1 hr 31 min
180
64
40
FLAGSTAFF
Flagstaff to Meteor Crater
43.4 mi / 69.8 km / 46 min
METEOR CRATER
17
Petrified Forest to Phoenix
259 mi / 416.8 km / 3 hrs 45 min
Meteor Crater to Petrified Forest
83.9 mi / 135 km / 1 hr 14 min
PETRIFIED FOREST
40
N
0
20 mi
0
20 km
© GONE BEYOND GUIDES 2017

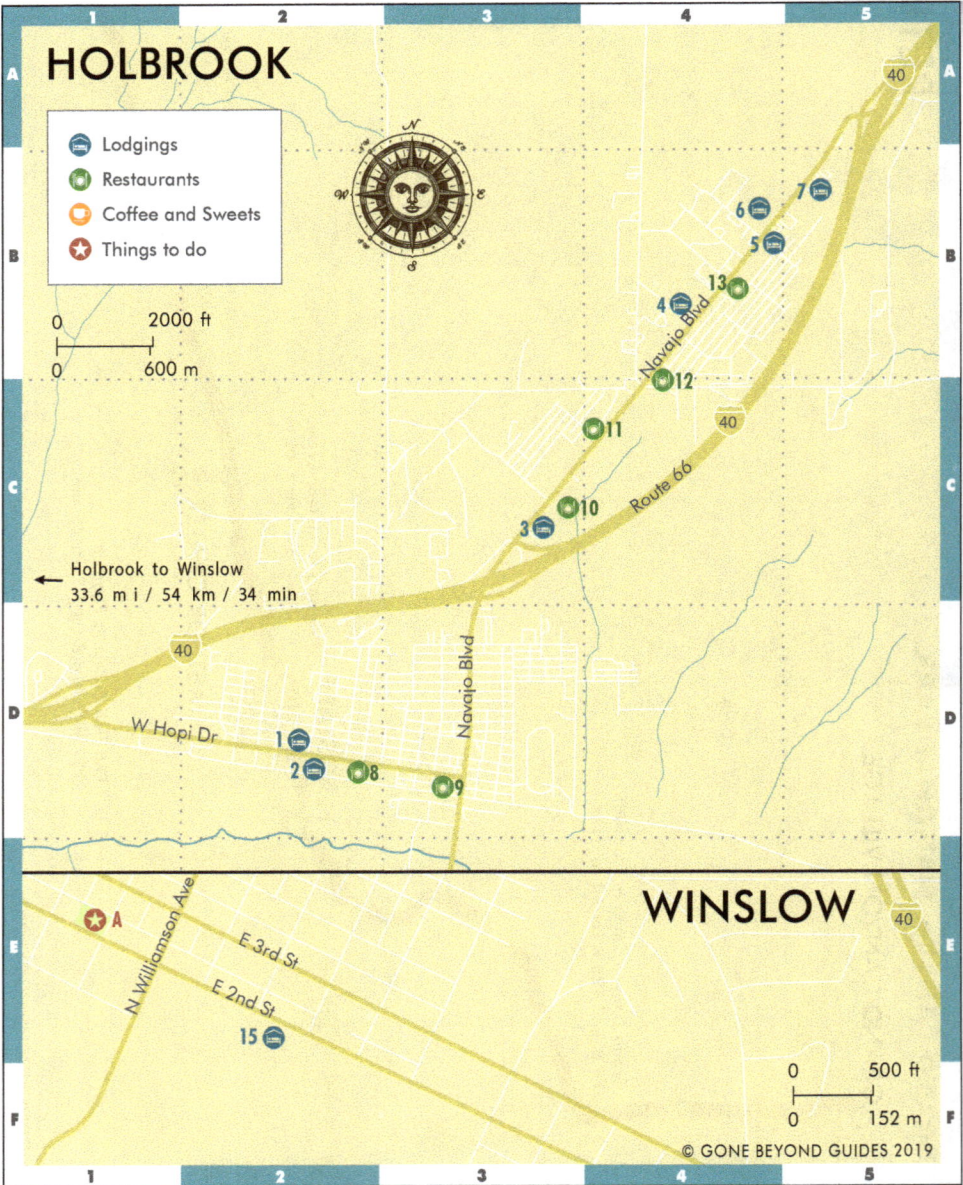

HOLBROOK

- 🛏️ Lodgings
- 🍽️ Restaurants
- ☕ Coffee and Sweets
- ⭐ Things to do

0	2000 ft
0	600 m

Navajo Blvd

Route 66

40

← Holbrook to Winslow
33.6 mi / 54 km / 34 min

W Hopi Dr

Navajo Blvd

6
7
5
13
4
12
11
3
10

1
2 8
9

WINSLOW

40

⭐ A

N Williamson Ave

E 3rd St

E 2nd St

15

0	500 ft
0	152 m

© GONE BEYOND GUIDES 2019

Petrified Forest National Park

WINSLOW, ARIZONA

There really isn't much to say about Winslow, Arizona. It's a town of fewer than 10,000 folks, offers little regarding services and things to do, with the exception of two notable standouts.

The first is about musicians Jackson Browne and the Eagles. In 1972, Jackson Brown wrote "Take it Easy" along with Eagles band member, Glenn Frey. It was in fact, the Eagles first single. Jackson Browne later recorded the same song and put it on his early career album "For Everyman." Now, the song really has nothing to do with Arizona at all, except for one line, *"Well, I'm a standing on a corner in Winslow, Arizona and such a fine sight to see."*

This line was enough for the little town of Winslow to go from nothing to something, forever putting them on the map for local small town admiration. Winslow council members voted to erect a statue of Jackson Browne, create the "Standin' on the Corner Park," commission a two-story mural, and even hold a yearly street festival around this one liner claim to fame at the end of each September. If you like Jackson Browne, the Eagles, or just statues of guys with guitars, then definitely check this out.

The other must-see site in Winslow is also a place to stay, La Posada Hotel (303 E 2nd St, Winslow, AZ 86047, laposada.org, (928) 289-4366). La Posada is magical, historical, beautiful, and certainly a shining star within Winslow. The hotel was architected by Mary Jane Coulter, who also designed many of the buildings in the Grand Canyon, including the Desert View Watchtower, Hopi House, and the Phantom Ranch Canteen. La Posada was originally built for travelers coming to the Southwest by train and was part of a depot/hotel complex built by the Santa Fe Railway in 1930.

The hotel declined out of favor along with the railway that served it and was shuttered in 1957. It was then purchased and completely renovated in 1997. Today, it is simply a beacon of fine architecture, exceptional dining, comfortable lodging, and includes a sculpture garden, orchard, and some of the finest artwork galleries in Arizona created by some the Southwest's most notable artists. The Turquoise Room & Martini Lounge serves up breakfast from 7am and dinner until 9pm. The restaurant offers an award-winning selection of American fare with some clever Southwest twists.

If you are looking for a beautiful place to stay, a place that seamlessly incorporates the romance period of travel along with the modern amenities, look into "takin' it easy" at La Posada.

HOLBROOK

Lodging

Restaurants

WINSLOW

Lodging and Things to Do

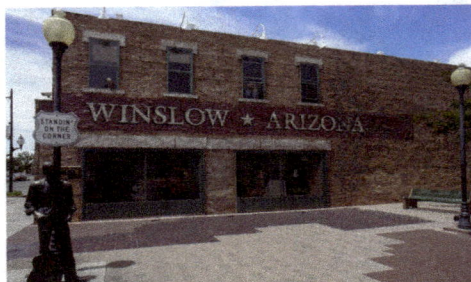

Standin' on the Corner Park, Winslow, AZ

HOLBROOK, ARIZONA

The closest town to Petrified Forest NP is Holbrook, Arizona, which is about a 20-minute drive away. Holbrook is a small town with only about 5000 residents, but it makes up for it in old-school Route 66 charm. It is certainly worth a stop, with dinosaur statue-laden rock shops, hand-painted signs of the west, and, well, let's just say it seems that about every piece of American kitsch along Route 66 has ended up here in Holbrook. Traveling here is like going back in time.

LODGING IN HOLBROOK

For the weary traveler, there are plenty of motels in Holbrook. Among the many lodging chains, two motels stand out amongst the others. Both are near each other and within walking distance of several restaurants. These are both recommended because they offer an experience greater than just staying in a room with a bed and pillows. They are the Globetrotter Lodge and the Wigwam Village Motel, which is at the top of the list below.

GLOBETROTTER LODGE

902 West Hopi Dr., Holbrook, AZ 86025, (928)-297-0158, http://hotelsholbrookaz.com

Small and retro, at first this place may seem too outdated from the outside to be worthy of a family stay, but the rooms inside are refreshingly updated and very clean. Each room has a slightly different theme and is decorated tastefully. That said, this isn't a luxury class, five-star hotel; this is a trip back in time to the heyday of Route 66. Each room has air conditioning and a flat-screen TV. Plus, there is a small outdoor pool that is, well, you have to see it for yourself. The owners have really done a fantastic job of taking an old hotel with good bones and breathing new life into it. Don't be fooled by the retro architecture; this is a wonderful place to stay.

WIGWAM VILLAGE MOTEL #6

811 W Hopi Dr., Holbrook, AZ 86025, Phone: (928)-524-3048, www.sleepinawigwam.com

This is one of the original motels that continue to offer guests the opportunity to "Sleep in a Wigwam!" That's right; this is one of the last three places along Route 66 where you can spend the night in a teepee. The rooms look just like large white and red teepees on the outside but once inside, they look and feel like normal motel rooms. Each teepee has its own bathroom with a toilet and a shower. There is even a TV and air conditioning.

There are 1950s-style cars out front and plenty of other retro features that help with the overall quirky, fun vibe. The place is on the National Register of Historic Places and includes a small museum that holds an assortment of historical artifacts collected by the original owner, Chester E. Lewis. There are 15 concrete and steel teepees arranged in a semicircle around the main office.

LEXINGTON INN - HOLBROOK, AZ

1308 Navajo Boulevard, Holbrook, AZ 86025, (928) 524-1466, www.redlion.com/lexington-holbrook

Indoor pool, free breakfast, Wi-Fi, free parking, air conditioning, suites available.

ECONO LODGE

2211 Navajo Boulevard, Holbrook, AZ 86025, (928) 297-0292, www.choicehotels.com

Clean 2-star hotel, breakfast available, free Wi-Fi, free parking, air conditioning, family rooms, good value for money.

BEST WESTERN ARIZONIAN INN

2508 Navajo Boulevard, Holbrook, AZ 86025, (928) 524-2611, www.bestwestern.com

Outdoor pool, free breakfast, Wi-Fi, free parking, air conditioning.

DAYS INN HOLBROOK

2601 Navajo Boulevard, Holbrook, AZ 86025, (928) 297-0630, www.wyndhamhotels.com

Indoor pool, free breakfast, Wi-Fi, free parking, air conditioning, room service.

QUALITY INN

2602 E. Navajo Boulevard., Holbrook, AZ 86025, (928)-524-6131, www.choicehotels.com

Outdoor pool, free breakfast, Wi-Fi, free parking, air conditioning, restaurant.

Wigwam Village Motel, Holbrook, AZ

DINING IN HOLBROOK

Holbrook's dining options are a limited. If you are looking for an American diner or Sonora style Mexican food, you should do pretty good as that's pretty much all that's offered in this small town besides the usual fast food chains.

BUTTERFIELD STAGE CO STEAK HOUSE

STEAKHOUSE, $$, 609 W Hopi Dr, Holbrook, AZ 86025, (928) 524-3447, open daily 4pm - 9pm

If on your trip you are hoping to get a great steak meal, don't look to find it here. The décor is a plus, with average food. Butterfield Stage Co gets a fair amount of traffic from the Wigwam Motel, more so than from locals.

ROMO'S CAFÉ

MEXICAN, $$, 121 W Hopi Dr, Holbrook, AZ 86025, (928) 524-2153, open daily 10am - 8pm, closed Sunday

Romo's serves up huge plates brimming with everything you are looking for in a Mexican restaurant.

ALIBERTO'S MEXICAN FOOD

MEXICAN, $, 1440 Navajo Blvd, Holbrook, AZ 86025, (928) 524-7899, open daily 7am - 10pm

Local Mexican fast food, great for food on the go.

TOM & SUZIE'S DINER

AMERICAN, $$, 2001 Navajo Blvd, Holbrook, AZ 86025, (928) 524-9700, open daily 7am - 9pm

Taking up in an old Pizza Hut, the red-roofed diner is hard to miss. The food is hearty and the service quick and friendly. Hard to go wrong here.

CHAMELEON CAFÉ

AMERICAN/MEXICAN, $$, 2102 Navajo Blvd, Holbrook, AZ 86025, (928) 524-2446, open daily 6am - 9pm, 6am - 1pm Sundays

So named because they serve both American and Mexican dishes, don't let the wishy-washy name confound you. They serve up a rib-sticking chicken fried steak side by side with hearty enchiladas. There is something for everyone here.

MESA ITALIANA RESTAURANT

ITALIAN, $$, 2318 Navajo Blvd, Holbrook, AZ 86025, (928) 524-6697, open weekdays 11am - 2pm, 4pm - 9pm, weekends 4pm - 9pm

Remember, you are in Holbrook, which is not exactly the culinary hotspot of the world. It's okay Italian, not the best nor the worst. The service is friendly and quick.

87

The vastness of sunset colors upon ancient forests

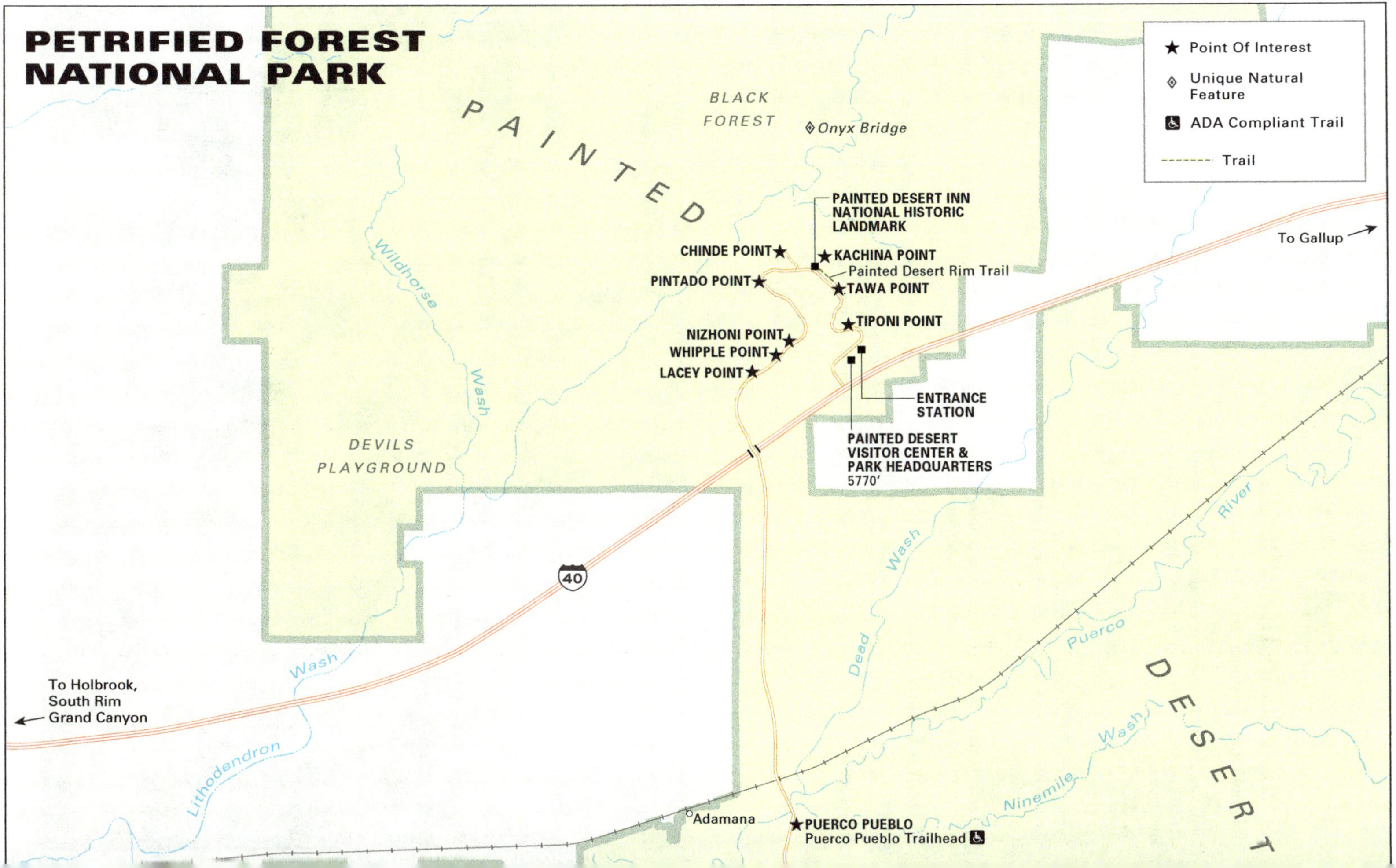

PETRIFIED FOREST
NATIONAL PARK

To Gallup →

DESERT

PAINTED

BLACK FOREST

◈ Onyx Bridge

PAINTED DESERT INN NATIONAL HISTORIC LANDMARK
★ **KACHINA POINT**
Painted Desert Rim Trail
★ **TAWA POINT**
★ **TIPONI POINT**

CHINDE POINT ★

PINTADO POINT ★

NIZHONI POINT ★
WHIPPLE POINT ★
LACEY POINT ★

ENTRANCE STATION

PAINTED DESERT VISITOR CENTER & PARK HEADQUARTERS
5770'

Puerco River

Nintaile Wash

Dead Wash

○ Adamana

★ **PUERCO PUEBLO**
Puerco Pueblo Trailhead 🦽

40

Wash

Wildhorse Wash

DEVILS PLAYGROUND

Lithodendron Wash

To Holbrook,
South Rim
Grand Canyon

Legend

★ Point Of Interest

◈ Unique Natural Feature

🦽 ADA Compliant Trail

-------- Trail

PETRIFIED FOREST NATIONAL PARK

BLACK KNOLL

BLUE FOREST
★ BLUE FOREST
Blue Forest Trail
★ BLUE MESA
Blue Mesa Trailhead
◈ Billings Gap

Dry Wash

★ AGATE BRIDGE

★ JASPER FOREST
Jasper Forest Road Trailhead

Crystal Forest Trail
★ CRYSTAL FOREST

PUERCO RIDGE

TWIN BUTTES

THE FLATTOPS

◈ Marthas Butte

RAINBOW FOREST MUSEUM
Giant Logs, Long Logs, and Agate House Trailheads
5476 ■
★ GIANT LOGS

★ LONG LOGS
★ AGATE HOUSE

FOREST

RAINBOW

Jim Camp Wash

Cottonwood Wash

ENTRANCE STATION ■

180

To St. Johns

To Holbrook, South Rim Grand Canyon

N

5 mi
5 km
0   0

© GONE BEYOND GUIDES 2015-2016

89

The Old Ones

PETRIFIED FOREST NATIONAL PARK

There was once a supercontinent called Pangaea, which contained most of the land mass that makes up Earth as we know it today. Before it split into the several continents, the area currently known as Arizona sat closer to the equator some 225 million years ago.

During this time, the land was a robust forest of plants, trees, and shrubs, most of which are now extinct, including every species of tree found in Petrified Forest National Park. Standing in the park is to stand in an ancient river channel that not only acted as a collection mechanism for the fallen trees but also helped slow their decay. The river channel likely meandered, forming a U shape that was pinched off at some point. Alternatively, perhaps the river simply dried up over time.

The river channel and its collection of logs were slowly covered with sediment such as volcanic ash. The silica within the ash gradually permeated the wood cells and replaced it with minerals. Once silica is allowed to crystallize, it can take on many forms, including agate, opal, chalcedony, and jasper. Other minerals such as iron oxide and manganese oxide help to produce the variety of color within the petrified wood. Then, over time, the softer sediment eroded away, leaving the logs. It is fascinating to walk among them and wonder what the world must have been like over 200 million years ago.

The park has two visitor centers and charges and entrance fee of $20 for a seven day pass. The Painted Desert Visitor Center is open from 7am – 7pm from June 4 to September 2 and Rainbow Forest Museum & Visitor Center is open from 8am - 7pm during this same period. Both visitor centers close an hour earlier from September 3 to October 28. The park itself is open year-round during daylight hours. While there are no camping facilities inside the park, it is possible to get a backcountry permit to camp in the park's wilderness. To stay overnight, you will need to get a free permit and hike at least a mile into the wilderness before setting up camp. Also, you'll need to bring your own water, which is about a gallon per person per day. Camp stoves only. No wood fires, and, of course, no collecting allowed. Most hikers start out from the northern access trail and head into the Painted Desert Wilderness Area. Less used is a pullout off the main park road that gives access to the southern Wilderness Area.

HIKING IN THE PETRIFIED FOREST NATIONAL PARK

GIANT LOGS

Easy – (0.4 mi / 0.6 km), round trip, allow 30 minutes, elev. Δ: 41 ft / 12 m, trailhead behind Rainbow Forest Museum

This trail walks amongst some of the largest most accessible logs in the park. There is one petrified log named "Old Faithful" that is nearly ten feet wide at the base. There is a trail guide available at the Rainbow Forest Museum.

LONG LOGS

Easy – (1.6 mi / 2.6 km), round trip, allow 1 hour, elev. Δ:50 ft / 15 m, trailhead at Rainbow Forest Museum parking area

Along with the Blue Mesa and Agate House, Long Logs Trail is something more of a true trail. Don't let the fact the first half of it is well paved fool you, it doesn't stay paved for the entire length. The trail allows one the ability to fully take in the views of the surrounding grasslands. This area is hard to fully describe, the land carries a forgotten loneliness to it, while at the same time sends an invitation to just walk off towards the horizon in just about any direction. It is a place that is easy to lose oneself and yet hard to get lost.

As the trail becomes dirt, the collection of petrified logs increase, both in size and quantity. This is, in fact, the largest concentration of petrified wood in the park. There are wonderful examples here that allow the hiker to get up close and personal with some ancient and rather larger trees.

The trail can be combined with the Agate House trail. The total round trip distance for both is 2.6 miles (4.2 km).

AGATE HOUSE

Easy – (2.0 mi / 3.2 km), round trip, allow 1 – 2 hours, elev. Δ: 41 ft / 12 m, trailhead at Rainbow Forest Museum parking area

As the name suggests, this is a very cool eight-room pueblo made entirely out of agate blocks. It is believed to have been built some 700 years ago. The ruins of this

Car Relic as part of Route 66

pueblo were rebuilt in 1933-34 by the Civilian Conservation Corps (CCC). They rebuilt parts of the pueblo and completely rebuilt "room 7", including a roof.

The inhabitants entered in through the ceiling. The Agate House today is for viewing only. Please don't climb or sit on what is now a piece of history.

CRYSTAL FOREST

Easy – (0.75 mi / 1.2 km), round trip, allow 30 minutes, elev. Δ: 121 ft / 37 m, trailhead at Crystal Forest parking area

One of the trails that contain the petrified wood you came for; the trail is named for the many amazing crystals that are found in the logs.

This is a chance to take a close look at the colorful crystal formations within the petrified logs. Please refrain from the temptation to take even small pieces.

JASPER FOREST ROAD

Easy – (2.5 mi / 4.0 km), round trip, allow 2 hours, elev. Δ: negligible, trailhead at Jasper Forest Road parking area

There is an eroded forgotten road built in the 1930's by the CCC that makes for a wonderful hike today. Originally, a wagon path for rock hounds coming in by train, it was later transformed into a proper road with the advent of the automobile. The path allows for a great hike today amongst a large display of petrified wood that has rolled down with erosion from the bluffs above the road. Given this isn't one of the main trails; it's a great find for those that want to feel they have the park to themselves.

BLUE MESA

Easy with short steep incline– (1.0 mi / 1.6 km), round trip, allow 30 -45 minutes, elev. Δ: 97 ft / 30 m, trailhead at Blue Mesa parking area

The Blue Mesa is one of the most unique areas within the Grand Circle. First off, it's not expected. You came

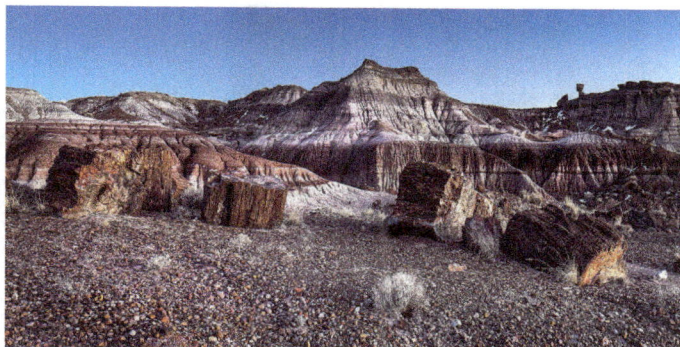
Jasper Forest - Petrified Forest National Park

for the petrified wood and anticipate seeing a red rock or two. The Blue Mesa Trail takes one into bentonite badland hills that have alternate stripes of white and blue clay. It really must be seen to be believed and is certainly a photographer's paradise. As an added bonus, there are several fossils, including the famous namesake petrified trees.

PUERCO PUEBLO

Easy – (0.3 mi / 0.5 km), round trip, allow 30 minutes, elev. Δ: 41 ft / 12 m, trailhead at Puerco Pueblo parking area

A paved and accessible trail with petroglyphs near the southern segment. This trail passes by the foundational remains of a hundred ancestral Puebloan site, dating back some 600 years. Aside from the ruins, there are some good views of the grasslands that are the signature of the prairies in this part of Arizona.

PAINTED DESERT RIM TRAIL

Easy – (1.0 mi / 1.6 km), round trip, allow 30 minutes, elev. Δ: 14 ft / 4 m, trailhead at Tawa Point and Kachina Point

The Painted Desert Rim Trail sits near the park visitor center and gives expansive views of the Painted Desert badlands. This area is comprised mainly of bentonite clay formed from volcanic ash and silt deposits. The entire area is a multicolored palette of red, pink, and white hillsides that are all the more striking due to the lack of vegetation due to the poor soils. While this isn't the trail for petrified wood, it is worth seeing.

The open wonder of Petrified Forest National Park

Side Trip 6 –
Rim to Rim and Beyond

Best From

You'll see both sides of the Grand Canyon, so it's best from either rim.

What You'll See

- Antelope Canyon
- Vermilion Cliffs National Monument
- Both the south and north rims of Grand Canyon National Park

Why Choose this Side Trip

For some, going from one rim to the other is the only way to truly experience the Grand Canyon. With some planning and good physical fitness, it is possible to walk from one rim to the other and take a shuttle to complete the loop. Some attempt this monster of a hike in one day, but most camp overnight at the river. It is long, strenuous, and for those that love to hike, a very rewarding journey.

This side trip also goes from rim to rim, but it describes a different journey. It's about going to the busy and bustling South Rim, that despite being crowded offers up one of a kind stops, including the El Tovar Hotel, which was built in 1905 and remains a part of the grand mythic quality of the Grand Canyon. At the South Rim, there is also the Kolb Studio, the Desert View Watchtower, and of course some of the most popular trails in the park. Once done, the side trip then heads by car to the North Rim, which is higher in elevation, cooler in temperature, less populated, and more tranquil. The North Rim consistently receives just 5% of the total visitor population, making it a very different experience.

In between, this route offers up a short jeep tour to Antelope Canyon, one of the most admired slot canyons of the Southwest and a place where one can take photographs worthy of any desert landscape calendar. The journey also takes you past Vermilion Cliffs National Monument, which hosts some of the best wilderness backcountry hiking in Arizona. Even if you do nothing more than the drive by the Vermilion Cliffs; it is a journey that is vast, lonely, scenic, and hauntingly beautiful, with big skies and ever-changing desert views.

Allow

- Recommended – 5 to 7 days
- Total Drive Time: 5 hours
- South Rim: 1-3 Days
- Drive to Antelope Canyon: about 2 hours, 30 minutes
- Antelope Canyon tour: Allow 4 hours for the tour itself. Stay in Page or continue to Vermilion Cliffs National Monument or North Rim. Allow 1-3 days for this segment
- Vermilion Cliffs National Monument: It is possible to gander at the park as you drive by it. For the adventurous with the right gear, allow 2-3 days for a more immersive experience.
- North Rim: 1-3 Days

This side trip is really about a full immersion of the Grand Canyon and could take up an entire 7-9-day vacation. Just driving from one rim to another is a 5-hour trip. For Antelope Canyon, it takes about a half day, including time to find the tour office and check-in. Vermilion Cliffs is a bit more of a wildcard regarding time to allow because it depends on the gear you bring. If you have a 4WD vehicle with high clearance and a decent supply of backcountry camping gear, you could easily spend days in this park. For those of us with a mid-size rental and a suitcase, carve out a half day in your planning to do one of the day hikes listed or simply enjoy the drive along the borders of this remote park as you make your way to the North Rim.

Can be combined with

Side Trip 7 - "Monument Valley" and Side Trip 8 - "Into Zion and Utah."

Vermilion Cliffs Panorama

RIM TO RIM AND BEYOND

89

89

UTAH
ARIZONA

VERMILION CLIFFS

ANTELOPE
CANYON

North Rim to Zion
111 mi / 178.6 km / 2 hrs 15 min

89A

89

98

89A

Vermilion Cliffs to North Rim
84.4 mi / 135.8 km / 1 hr 44 min

Antelope Canyon to Vermilion Cliffs
44.8 mi / 72.1 km / 52 min

67

89

N

0   10 mi

0   10 km

NORTH RIM GRAND CANYON

GRAND CANYON
NATIONAL PARK

Grand Canyon South
to Antelope Canyon
137 mi / 220.4 km / 2 hrs 32 min

160

GRAND CANYON VILLAGE

64

Grand Canyon South to Phoenix
229 mi / 220.4 km / 3 hrs 30 min

64

89

© GONE BEYOND GUIDES 2017

GRAND CANYON SOUTH AND NORTH RIMS

See the main Grand Canyon section for planning both rims. This side trip starts at the South Rim, making Antelope Canyon the first stop.

ANTELOPE CANYON

Antelope Slot Canyon is, on the surface, one of the most incredible and beautiful sights one can see on a trip to the Southwest. If you are fortunate enough to book a high noon tour, when the beams of sunlight shine down onto the sands of the canyon floor, the experience is transcendent. Antelope Slot Canyon is a delight to the eye, with narrow water-carved walls of multihued sandstone, towering high above into an infinitely blue sky. The contrast of light combined with shadow play brings out an experience that is certainly worth the trip and is often a highlight of any vacation to the western deserts of the United States.

This is despite the downsides of the slot canyon. Once an unknown secret canyon occasionally revealed by photographers in desert themed coffee table books, the canyon is now wide open to the public via tours given by the Navajo. Herein lies the flipside of this heavenly experience. The narrow canyon is packed with tourists. Look up, and the views are stunningly divine. Look at eye level, and it's like being in Times Square on New Year's Eve. Adding to this is the equally dichotomous Navajo sentiment towards the site; a people torn between guarding a place held sacred and exploiting this "outdoor church" for money.

This is not in any way meant to discourage one from going; the trip is definitely worth it. Also, what is described above is reflective of peak season traffic. If you go in the off-season, the experience can be more intimate.

There are almost as many tour groups going to the slot canyon as there are layers of sandstone in the canyon. Some are recommended below. There are also two major sections to visit, the upper and lower slot canyons. Most tours go to the upper canyon due to access and popularity. The lower canyon can be more intimate though it is getting more crowded with each passing year.

The best time to go for photography and lighting effect is during the high noon tour. There is direct sunlight into the canyon at this time, and the guides will toss sand high up which brings out filtered streams of light, which make for incredible photos. (Wait until the dust settles a bit for the best photos). The canyon is so narrow the sun penetrates like beams from heaven, bright and with crisply defined lines. Keep in mind that this is peak time, so expect to take your shot quickly before being herded along. If you don't like crowds, your best bet is to take one of the early morning or evening tours.

Logistically, each tour group gets into the back of an open-air truck that has been retrofitted to carry people. The driver heads into a sandy wash at a decent speed until the entrance of the canyon is reached. One tour driver pretended to be stuck in the sand, presumably to invoke the thrill of adventure. Keep your hats on your lap or tightly on your head as there is no stopping. Once out of the vehicle, the tour guide does his or her genuine best to make the trip as enjoyable as possible for his group. The biggest advice is to stay with your tour leader. Getting left behind has happened, but more typically, your late return to the vehicle will be met with glib looks from the fellow tour group members. Some tours feature a hoop dance back at the tour guide headquarters.

Tours typically depart from 8:45am - 4pm MST. Tour operators typically open at 8am.

Looking up to the sky in Antelope Canyon

Antelope Slot Canyon Tours

Adventurous Antelope Canyon Photo Tours

Highway 98, Page, AZ 86040, Phone: (928) 380-1874, www.navajoantelopecanyon.com

Antelope Slot Canyon Tours by Chief Tsosie

55 S Lake Powell Blvd, Page AZ 86040, Phone: (928) 645-5594, www.antelopeslotcanyon.com

Ken's Guided Tour of Lower Antelope Canyon

Indian Route 222, Page, AZ 86040, Phone: (928) 606-2168, lowerantelope.com

Dixie Ellis' Lower Antelope Canyon Tours

Indian Route 222, Page, AZ 86040, Phone: (928) 640-1761, antelopelowercanyon.com

VERMILION CLIFF NATIONAL MONUMENT

Vermilion Cliffs National Monument is certainly a candidate for one of the top Southwestern park destinations. Nearly as large as all of the three sections of the Canyonlands and yet relatively new and unheard of, this is one of the most unspoiled parks to be found. It is also one of the most remote. The park is located north of Grand Canyon and east of the Navajo lands, touching the border of Utah, an area referred to as the Arizona Strip. This park has no visitor center, few roads, little previous development, and only a scattered handful of trails. The Vermilion Cliffs are true desert wilderness. It is untouched, insufferable, rugged, and pure. There are places within it where it feels as if no person has ever stepped foot.

It was only made into a national monument in 2000, though the land had been protected under other measures prior. Much of the 280,000 acres protect the Paria Plateau, a significant mesa that spans over 20 miles and is roughly square in shape. The plateau itself is a vast desert island oasis, invoking feelings of freedom and of being on top of the world. However, it is the areas along the edges of the plateau that offers some of the most amazing sections of the park. One highlight is The Wave, a striated section of carved sandstone that has to be seen to be believed. Then there is Buckskin Gulch, a tributary of the Paria River and at a length of 20 miles is considered the longest slot canyon in the world.

Vermilion Cliffs National Monument is well protected, and much of the land is accessed by permit only. While day use permits are more readily available, overnight permits are limited and can be obtained by going to the URL below and following the online instructions: www.blm.gov/az/st/en/arolrsmain.html. Also, keep in mind that this land can be extremely challenging. Flash floods, venomous reptiles and insects, sun exposure, and remoteness make this park much different than say, taking the shuttle from the Zion Lodge and taking a hike. This area is ideally suited for experienced hikers and desert backpackers.

A quick note on the permitting system. One consistent theme within all of these parks is finding a balance between preservation of the land and the ability to share it for the enjoyment and recreation of others. Vermilion Cliffs NM pushes this balance more on the preservation side. There is a capacity to the number of visitors allowed to use the park each day, and while it may be frustrating if you are the unfortunate soul that didn't get a permit, you have to re-spect the process. The desert is fragile and takes a very long time to recover. Some parks, especially the national parks, are pushing the balance more towards recreation and the wear on them does show. Having explored all of these parks since the 1980's, the impact over just 35 years is quite evident and not in a good way. Vermilion Cliffs National Monument continues to retain that pristine hallowed ground of desert experience because of the permit process. Not everyone will get to go, especially for those permitted areas only available by lottery, but those that do will experience the difference.

For those that have read this far and are thinking Vermilion Cliffs is a place to fully explore, there are some hikes listed below to help you plan your own adventure. The side trip route drives past the eastern edge of the national monument only, so factor in a lot more driving, primarily on high clearance 4WD roads, to get to nearly all of the hikes listed. For those that want to stick to the route outlined and are just looking for a day hike, hike up the Buckskin Gulch Trail in Paria Canyon or try the Soap Creek Trail or Stone House in the Marble Canyon Section.

While most camping at Vermilion Cliffs is backcountry style, there are two small campgrounds at the park. Stateline has 4 tent sites, and White House has 5 tent-only sites. Both of these have pit toilet restrooms, no water and are open year-round on a first come-first served basis.

The Wave - Vermilion Cliffs

Before Heading Out

Here are some tips to ensure a safe and successful trip:

- First, get a permit. Overnight access to Buckskin Gulch is limited to 20 folks per day. The online process is listed in the web URL above.

- Speak to the BLM rangers. The rangers are the best versed in current conditions, what to expect and general guidance on how to prepare and execute this hike. Kanab Field Office – 318 North 100 East, Kanab, UT 84741 – Phone: (435) 644-4600 Fax: (435) 644-4620 or by email: utknmail@blm.gov

- Use a shuttle or two cars. These are long distances, so if you are short on time, this is best way to do this hike. Try Paria Outfitters (www.paria.com) for shuttle

services. At the very least, check out their site for the cool pics of the areas they serve.

- Check the weather forecast. Backpacker Magazine puts this as one of the 10 most dangerous hikes, primarily due to flash flood risks. As they put it, "Should thunderstorm-bloated flood waters come charging down the tunnel, you're no better than a bug in a firehose."

- Bring water shoes, plenty of drinking water, and multiple layers of clothing. There are points where the watercourse is the trail so bring some decent water shoes. While there are seeps, pools and water, it can be downright murky, so best to bring in what you need.

- Finally, fires are not permitted in the area, so make sure you have layer coverage for the temperature range of the trip.

HIKING VERMILION CLIFFS NATIONAL MONUMENT

PARIA CANYON TRAILS
BUCKSKIN GULCH TRAIL

Moderate – (5.7 mi / 9.2 km), one way to Wire Pass Trailhead, allow 3 hours

Strenuous – (23 mi / 37 km), one way, to White House Trailhead, full day hike or 2-day backpacking trip

Strenuous – (47 mi / 76 km), one way, to Lee's Ferry Trailhead, 3-5-day backpacking trip

Buckskin Gulch is the longest and deepest slot canyon in the Grand Circle. The narrows extend nearly 15 miles, with some sections being but 10 feet in width. The terrain and views are as inspiring as they are varied, making this a popular hike. The slot canyon leaves for very few exits during a flash flood and rain as far as Bryce Canyon 50 miles away can drain into Buckskin. The gulch is also known for muck pools, in the middle of summer you may find yourself with no other choice but to wade through residual pools that become foul smelling mud pots. They are normally no more than 3 feet deep, but some folks have noted being chest deep in one pool. Additionally, expect to do a fair amount of scrambling and even rappelling. In many spots, there is a rope left behind as a gesture of courtesy to rappel down the 15-foot drops, but you'll want to bring rope just in case.

There are many entry points into Buckskin Gulch. There is the Buckskin Gulch Trailhead or Wire Pass Trailhead to the east, heading downstream to a juncture where you can either head north to White House Trailhead or southeast through Paria

Canyon down to Lee's Ferry. The most popular hike is from Wire Pass Trailhead to White House Trailhead. This section describes the route starting from Buckskin Gulch Trailhead. Use this route if you want to say you hiked the full extent of Buckskin Gulch.

Take Highway 89 east from Kanab, UT 38 miles or west from Page, AZ for 34 miles and turn onto House Valley Road. This will be a right if coming from Kanab. The Buckskin Trailhead is 4.5 miles down a dirt road and is suitable for 2WD vehicles. That said, the clay-based soils are super sticky in some areas and like driving on ice in others when wet. It is not recommended, even in a 4WD vehicle, to drive this road when wet.

There is no established campground here, but camping is allowed at the trailhead. The trail is obvious and dry for most of the year to the junction to Wire Pass Trailhead, starting off fairly wide relative to the narrows later on. From the junction to Wire Pass, the canyon begins its journey as the longest narrows in the Southwest.

Cliff Dwellers Village - Vermilion Cliffs

VERMILION CLIFFS NATIONAL MONUMENT

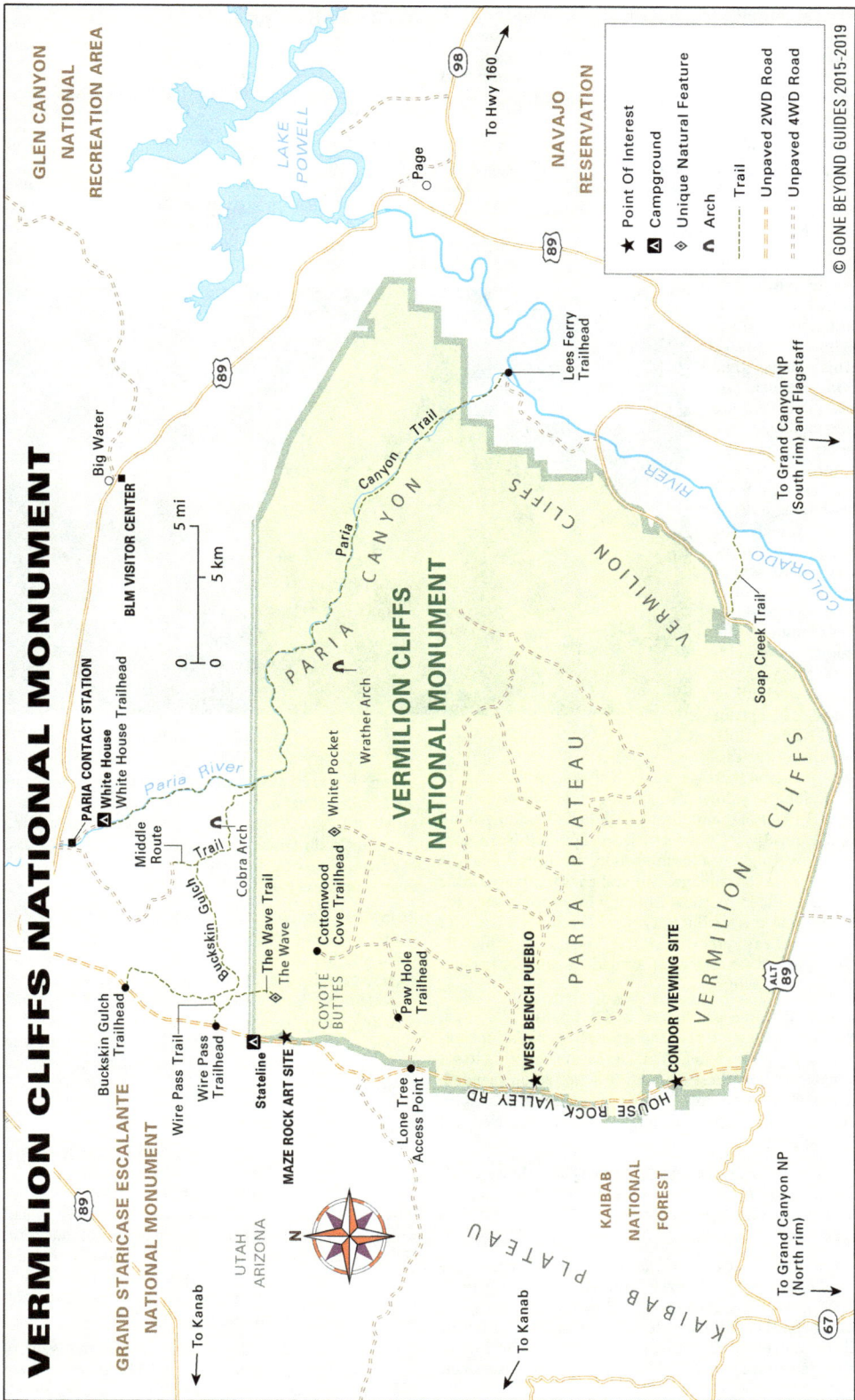

GLEN CANYON NATIONAL RECREATION AREA

LAKE POWELL

To Hwy 160

NAVAJO RESERVATION

Page

98

89

Point Of Interest
Campground
Unique Natural Feature
Arch
Trail
Unpaved 2WD Road
Unpaved 4WD Road

© GONE BEYOND GUIDES 2015-2019

97

Lees Ferry Trailhead

To Grand Canyon NP (South rim) and Flagstaff

COLORADO RIVER

VERMILION CLIFFS

Soap Creek Trail

89

Big Water

BLM VISITOR CENTER

5 mi

5 km

0

0

Paria River

Paria Canyon Trail

PARIA CANYON

VERMILION CLIFFS NATIONAL MONUMENT

PARIA CONTACT STATION

White House
White House Trailhead

Middle Route

Buckskin Gulch Trail

Cobra Arch

Wrather Arch

White Pocket

PARIA PLATEAU

GRAND STARICASE ESCALANTE NATIONAL MONUMENT

89

Buckskin Gulch Trailhead

Wire Pass Trail

Wire Pass Trailhead

Stateline

MAZE ROCK ART SITE

The Wave Trail
The Wave

COYOTE BUTTES

Cottonwood Cove Trailhead

Paw Hole Trailhead

WEST BENCH PUEBLO

CONDOR VIEWING SITE

VERMILION CLIFFS

ALT 89

Lone Tree Access Point

HOUSE ROCK VALLEY RD

N

UTAH
ARIZONA

To Kanab

To Kanab

KAIBAB NATIONAL FOREST

KAIBAB PLATEAU

To Grand Canyon NP (North rim)

67

The next big milestone is Buckskin Gulch Junction (1.8 miles, 1 hour). Here, (and beyond), the narrows are quite spectacular. Every turn is a different "wow!" moment. Along this section are The Cesspools, a stretch of murky, muddy, god-awful water that you have to wade through to continue.

The trek through this section of the narrows is 6.5 miles long, with the next milestone being Middle Route. Allow 4 hours for this part. Middle Route is yet another passage into Buckskin over a 4WD drive road and is described later in the book.

From Middle Route to Rock Fall (aka Rock Jam) is another 3 miles (allow 2 hours). This area has some rock problem areas that require scrambling. In spots, it can get quite dark, though not enough for a flashlight. Rock Fall presents the toughest of the areas where scrambling is needed. The scramble is easy enough, with some footholds into the rock for the downclimb or hikers can opt for the Rabbit Hole, which is the eas-

98

iest of methods to get through this scramble of rock (look for a way down through the rocks rather than up over the face of them). From Rock Fall the campground and Paria River Confluence is in sight and is the spot for an overnight rest for most folks. The distance here is 1.3 miles to the campground and another quarter mile to the confluence. Allow 1 hour. It is not recommended to camp at the confluence due to the potential risk of "going to Lee's Ferry prematurely" due to flooding. The campground sits higher up providing some protection from rising waters.

The hike to the confluence is dry for the most part, aside from the mud pots and stronger seeps and springs providing some runoff. While it may be tempting to get the water from these sources, it is not recommended. You will need 1.5 to 2 gallons of water for this leg in the summer, more depending on distance traveled and time spent.

If you are continuing upstream to White House Trailhead, you have another 4 hours and 7.5 miles ahead of you. This route is possible to do as a day trip, but it is a full day.

Heading downstream will take you to Lee's Ferry. The total distance to Lee's Ferry from Buckskin Gulch Trailhead is 47 miles. Plan on a 3 - 5-day backpacking trip and definitely use a shuttle. Along with Paria Outpost listed above, Circle Tours, (888) 854-7862 and End of the Trail Shuttles, (928) 355-2252 offer shuttle services.

WIRE PASS TRAIL

Moderate – (5.7 mi / 9.2 km), one way to Buckskin Gulch Trailhead, allow 3 hours

Strenuous – (21 mi / 34 km), one way, to White House Trailhead, full day hike or 2-day backpacking trip

Strenuous – (44 mi / 71 km), one way, to Lee's Ferry Trailhead, 3-5-day backpacking trip

Wire Pass Trail offers an alternate entrance into Buckskin Gulch through Wire Pass Gulch. Wire Pass Trailhead is often chosen over entering directly from the Buckskin Gulch Trailhead because it is shorter and

White Pocket- Vermilion Cliffs

the gulch is itself a very nice set of narrows. It only cuts off 2 miles from any destination but does offer help satisfy the "slot canyon" fix a little faster than starting from Buckskin Gulch Trailhead. This trailhead is also used as the starting destination for a popular sandstone formation known as The Wave, described later on.

To get here, just follow the directions above to Buckskin Gulch Trailhead and continue on House Rock Valley Road another 3.8 miles (8.3 miles from Highway 89). Again, permits are needed as is reading all the tips provided in the Buckskin Gulch Trail description. Stateline Campground is one mile south of the Wire Pass Trailhead, and camping is allowed at the trailhead if the campground is full. There are restrooms here, but no water.

MIDDLE ROUTE

Strenuous – (1.4 mi / 2.3 km), one way to Buckskin Gulch, allow 1 - 2 hours

The Middle Route is a viable alternative if you are looking to bypass many of the cold, stagnant pools of water as you wind through the narrows of Buckskin Gulch. It also saves a day of hiking. It is a short easy route to navigate into the gulch via a long, sandy, unsigned, and at times impassable 4WD road with multiple forks to consider.

About midway through Buckskin Gulch, the walls of the canyon lower down to about 100 feet. Here there is a very steep crack that is possible to scramble up if one needs an early exit out of the gulch or as a means to downclimb into the slot canyon. This is Middle Route. This crack is definitely for the experienced canyoneer and bringing a 50-foot rope is highly recommended for lowering packs. The crack contains steep drop-offs and climbing down slickrock. Exposure aside, this is a Class 3 - 4 scramble and doesn't require any technical climbing per se.

Getting to Middle Route is not straightforward as hinted at above. It's best to consult with the Paria Contact Station for directions, road conditions and even a video of Middle Route.

WHITE HOUSE TRAIL

Strenuous – (23 mi / 37 km), one way to Buckskin Gulch Trailhead, full day hike or 2-day backpacking trip

Strenuous – (21 mi / 34 km), one way, to Wire Pass Trailhead, full day hike or 2-day backpacking trip

Strenuous – (38 mi / 61 km), one way, to Lee's Ferry Trailhead, 3-5-day backpacking trip

Continuing in our extensive list of trails that lead to Buckskin Gulch, let's add White House Trail.

Following the directions in the Buckskin Gulch Trail description, take the dirt road towards the Paria Contact Station and turn onto the obvious dirt road just before it. Follow this 2WD road for 2 miles to the trailhead.

White House trail is a popular exit route for Buckskin because of the possibility to utilize a shuttle or second car. It is also adjacent to the White House Campground. There is no water here, but there are restrooms. The trail

The Wave

follows the Paria River downstream as it heads towards Lee's Ferry and the Colorado River. It is 7.5 miles to Buckskin Gulch. This section does require some wading at times, with the occasional spot of quicksand. Wrap gear and wear water shoes for this section. See the Buckskin Gulch Trail for more information.

COYOTE BUTTES NORTH
THE WAVE

Strenuous – (5.6 mi / 9.0 km), round trip, from Wire Pass Trailhead, allow 3 – 4 hours

If ever there was a destination that could compete with Buckskin Gulch, the longest slot canyon in the Southwest and perhaps even the world, it a little place called The Wave. In the Grand Circle there is a lot of red rock, so much in fact, that after a few weeks of it, one starts dreaming of fantastic mashups of slickrock canyons and formations that don't actually exist. The Wave is a place that is so fantastic; it is as if it came from one of these dreams. Seeing an image of The Wave is to reset the art of the possible within the realm of red rock. To see it in person can be surreal as if it shouldn't exist, yet it does. As an added bonus, the whole terrain getting to it and around it is cool to explore. This area is part of the Coyote Buttes North. This whole area is day use only and requires a permit. Permits are limited to 20 people a day with 10 folks chosen through a walk in lottery process the day before and 10 folks obtaining the permit via an online process via (www.blm.gov/az/paria/obtainpermits.cfm?usearea=CB).

For the online process, the lottery opens up 4 months before the use date. Generally, online permits for the Coyote Buttes North are hard to obtain. The cost to apply is $5 per group, and you can select up to three dates. See the lottery schedule below for exact dates, but in general, the process works like this. For a permit in say the month of May, one would apply at any time four months earlier, from January 1-31, in this case. On February 1, at 1:05pm MST, the permits holders are chosen. If you are successful, you will be notified via email and will then need to pay $7 per individual.

There is no established trail to The Wave. There are two routes, however. The most readily accessible method is to start from Wire Pass Trailhead. The drive is easy enough and more straightforward of a hike than the other method known as The Notch. The route from Wire Pass Trailhead will be described here.

Start by following the instructions to Wire Pass Trailhead listed above. Enter Wire Pass Gulch across the road and travel down the wash for about half a mile. Take the juncture to the right, marked Coyote Buttes, where you will find an obvious trail. The trail climbs up a hill and across a desert field ending at a wash. The total distance of the trail is approximately 0.65 miles.

From here on out the trail becomes route and the area is by permit only. On the other side of the wash is a slickrock incline that is typically marked with cairns. Climb this saddle and head towards the BLM marker ahead of you. This saddle is a great point to mark if you have a GPS, as it will greatly aid in finding the trail on the return.

Continue to follow the BLM markers south, heading towards and staying to the left of a landmark known as Twin Buttes. Once you pass by this landmark, you are about 0.6 miles from the Utah – Arizona border and 1.0 mile from the Wave. The next landmark to aim for is a narrow crack like gully in the cliffs as you continue south. As you get closer to the gully look for a small sand dune left of the gully. Climb the sand dune, then the slickrock to arrive at The Wave. There are many other features to check out in the area, including The Second Wave, The Alcove, and some petroglyphs and dinosaur tracks. See the below website for a list of all of them.

One exceptional site dedicated to The Wave feature is a site called "thewave." It covers everything outlined here and has a virtual tour of the hike itself, sunset/sunrise calculator, weather, and other details. Go here: www.thewave.info/CoyoteButtesNorthCode/Map.html

Maze Rock Art Site

Just beyond Wire Pass Trailhead and State Line Campground is a trailhead to a rich petroglyph site. There are numerous examples of Ancestral Puebloan art, including the namesake, a petroglyph that looks like a maze. Head south from State Line Campground on House Valley Road for about a mile to find the trailhead.

Coyote Buttes South

The Coyote Buttes South region of Vermilion Cliffs NM is, like its northern counterpart, accessed by permit only. The good news is the permits are much easier to obtain for this region. Just go online and follow the instructions.

https://www.blm.gov/az/paria/obtainpermits.cfm?usearea=CB

All of the hiking here is for the experienced. Beyond needing a permit, you'll need a 4WD vehicle and topo maps. Per the BLM, these are both mandatory. As the BLM site indicates these aren't really trailheads, they are access points. After driving through deep sands and rough terrain, after figuring out on numerous occasions which junction you should take at the many spur roads on the way, you find yourself parking at the beginning of your own adventure.

For all of the below access points listed below, there are no trails, no markers, direction signs, or navigational information once you leave the road that got you there. In places like these, there is this advice. You will find at least one piece of trash, typically a Budweiser can, and you will wonder how it got there. You will have the opportunity to step where no human has stepped, and see things that no one has seen in quite the same way. You will hopefully take solace in knowing that the closest Starbucks to your tent is a good 3 hours away and that when the sun sets, you will likely see one of the darkest skies you have ever seen. This is the middle of nowhere. It is desert nirvana, BFE, God's country. Whatever you call it, the place will leave its mark on the soul as days remembered for the rest of your life.

Cottonwood Cove Trailhead

This access point leads to the Cottonwood Teepees, a series of cone-shaped sandstone formations. In general, the red rock is twisted and deformed, resembling something more reminiscent of a Salvador Dali landscape.

The rocks at times look like huge spine fossils of some large monster, eroded away by time until only the backbone remains curved out on a pedestal of rock. There is also one teepee formation called the Queen, looking like a typical cone-shaped formation but with the smallest of capstones on top.

Getting to Cottonwood Cove Trailhead starts by taking House Rock Road, the same road taken for Buckskin Gulch and Wire Pass Trailheads. Head south past Wire Pass for 20.2 miles and turn left on BLM 1017, (Pine Tree Road). If coming from the south, the distance on House Rock Road will be 9.4 miles to this intersection.

Mark the trip meter and take Pine Tree Road for 3.1 miles and then turn left on Red Pockets Road and begin heading in a northwest bearing. At 6.0 miles, you should see a cattle gate (leave as you found it, whether open or closed). At 8.3 miles, bear to the right and

The desert wilderness of Vermilion Cliffs National Monument

at 8.7 miles turn left onto Upper Pawhole Road. This area, called Poverty Flat has several outbuildings worth checking out. At 9.0 miles keep to the right until you reach a closed gate with a sign that says Coyote Buttes Fee Area. End of the road worth driving on is at 11.4 miles. Park on your left, the Cottonwood Teepees are to the west.

Paw Hole Trailhead

Paw Hole is close to Cottonwood Cove, offering slightly different topography. Doing both in one trip is possible. Paw Hole has some interesting, often delicate striations in the sandstone. Paw Hole is a small water hole that looks like, (wait for it), a paw. One recommended route is to stay at Cottonwood Cove the first night and then Paw Hole the next. This method allows for a loop back to House Valley Road.

Coming from Cottonwood Cove, double back to BLM 1079 and take it to the signs showing Paw Hole. To head out, continue on BLM 1079 to connect back to House Valley Road. It is not recommended to take this road to Paw Hole directly from House Valley as it is uphill and is too steep for many vehicles.

Lone Tree Access Point

This is an access point to Paw Hole and the Coyote Buttes South for folks that have a 2WD vehicle only. Take House Valley Road south to BLM 1079 and turn left. Drive on 1079 for 0.2 miles and park the car near the obvious lone tree. Continue hiking east to Paw Hole along BLM 1079 from here. It is approximately 2.4 miles to Paw Hole from the tree.

Marble Canyon
Stone House

A woman by the name of Blanche Russell was driving through the area, and her car broke down. She took it as fate and built a house where her car stopped in 1930. The ruins, called Stone House, as well as oddly eroded and balanced rocks, can be found here. Stone House is 8.4 miles south of Marble Canyon, AZ and about 0.3 miles north of the Cliff Dwellers Lodge.

Soap Creek Trail

Strenuous – (8.0 mi / 12.9 km), round trip, allow 2 - 3 hours

Soap Canyon is a feeder canyon to the Colorado River. The trail passes much of its time within the Grand Canyon National Park, which protects either side of the river north to Glen Canyon NRA. The trail is found by driving south on Highway 89A approximately 9 miles from Marble Canyon, AZ. Look for mile marker 548 and after that a latched gate. Turn left onto this dirt road, pass some abandoned buildings, and drive about 0.6 miles to the trailhead.

Soap Canyon allows for quick access to the Colorado River and is popular with anglers as a result. It does have two dry falls that must be navigated. If you find yourself wondering how you are going to get down the first 10-foot one, then you might want to turn back as the second one is 25 feet high. The gradient is easy going at first, and the canyon becomes narrower and steeper on its way to the river. Both dryfalls have alternate routes to allow access to them. The tributary opens up shortly after the second dryfall at the inspiring Soap Creek Rapids. If you plan to stay overnight, you will need to obtain a permit from Grand Canyon NP.

GRAND CANYON SOUTH AND NORTH RIMS

See the main Grand Canyon section.

Side Trip 7 – Monument Valley

BEST FROM

This side trip can be started from either the North or South Rims of the Grand Canyon.

WHAT YOU'LL SEE

- Antelope Canyon
- Navajo National Monument
- Monument Valley Tribal Park
- Four Corners

WHY CHOOSE THIS SIDE TRIP

The side trip is ideal for those that are passing either up into the north-eastern Utah parks of Arches and Canyonlands, across to Colorado or down into New Mexico. The scenic views of the drive alone are remarkable. This is classic Southwest, with miles of untouched land that is starkly powerful in its beauty. It's a land that seems to stretch forever in its vastness, helping to reset perspective and align the traveler to the land.

Then there are the sites themselves. Antelope Canyon was introduced in the previous side trip but again, it's a scenic must see. Monument Valley is an altogether different landscape, strong, reverent, and majestic. It is easy to see why the area has become the iconic image of the west in so many movies.

While not as large as Mesa Verde, Navajo National Monument offers a better-preserved example of Ancestral Puebloan cliff dwellings. Finally, this leg takes the intrepid vacationer to the Four Corners, with its equal combination of touristy kitsch and one of a kind uniqueness.

ALLOW

- Recommended – 2 to 5 days
- Total drive time: About 7 hours
- Antelope Canyon: Allow 4 hours for this tour, start to finish
- Navajo National Monument: Allow 1-2 hours if not taking a tour. If taking a tour, as they start in the morning and last up to 5 hours, plan to camp at the park overnight.
- Monument Valley: While it is possible to drive through Monument Valley, it is highly recommended to stay at least one night here. Camping, lodging, and dining are available.
- Four Corners: 30 minutes to 1 hour

CAN BE COMBINED WITH

Side Trip 6 - "Rim to Rim and Beyond" and Side Trip 5 – "Petrified Forests."

ANTELOPE CANYON

Antelope Canyon is an incredibly picturesque slot canyon, where the rock dances upwards from the canyon floor to the thin slit of the sky above. Please refer to Side Trip 6 – "Rim to Rim and Beyond," for details on taking a tour of this Southwest wonder.

NAVAJO NATIONAL MONUMENT

Navajo National Monument is made up of three well-preserved cliff dwellings of the Ancestral Puebloans. While there had been a fair amount of plunder at Mesa Verde before its protection, the Navajo NM ruins were put under protection in a more intact state. Keet Seel is considered by some archaeologists to be the best-preserved cliff dwelling in the Southwest and Betatakin wasn't even found until after the park was created in 1909.

Besides the cliff dwellings, the redrock canyon setting and even the alcoves themselves are worth the visit. These alcoves are giant grand arcs of rock, with the centerpiece within being the ruins themselves. The first glimpse of them is breathtaking.

There are free ranger-led tours of the Keet Seel and Betatakin sites. The third site, Inscription House, is currently closed to the public. There is also a short 1-mile walk to an overlook of Betatakin ruins. Amenities include two small campgrounds, picnic area, visitor center, and museum.

Navajo National Monument offers two campgrounds. Sunset View Campground is the largest with 33 tent/RV sites, drinking water, restrooms, no hookups, and some pull thru sites. This campground is a no-fee site and is offered on a first come-first served basis.

Canyon View Campground has 14 tent only sites, compost toilets, no water, and is also offered for free on a first come-first served basis.

There is a visitor center open to the public from 8am – 5:30am in the summer (late May – September) and 9am – 5pm in the winter season (October – late May, before Memorial Day). There is neither a fee to enter this park or for the ranger led tours.

MONUMENT VALLEY

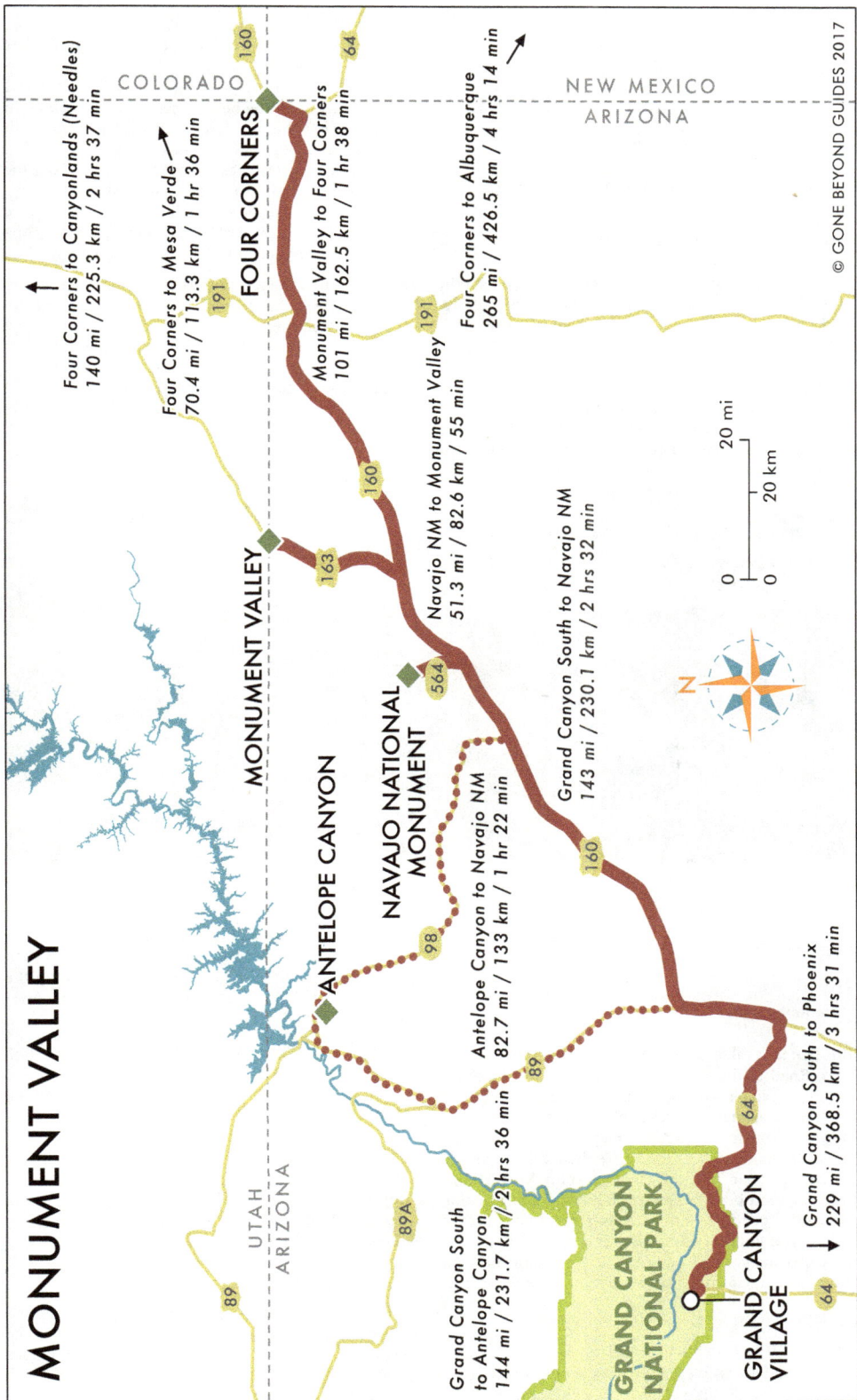

COLORADO

NEW MEXICO
ARIZONA

FOUR CORNERS

Four Corners to Canyonlands (Needles)
140 mi / 225.3 km / 2 hrs 37 min

Four Corners to Mesa Verde
70.4 mi / 113.3 km / 1 hr 36 min

Monument Valley to Four Corners
101 mi / 162.5 km / 1 hr 38 min

Four Corners to Albuquerque
265 mi / 426.5 km / 4 hrs 14 min

© GONE BEYOND GUIDES 2017

160

64

191

191

160

MONUMENT VALLEY

163

Navajo NM to Monument Valley
51.3 mi / 82.6 km / 55 min

ANTELOPE CANYON

NAVAJO NATIONAL MONUMENT

564

98

Grand Canyon South to Navajo NM
143 mi / 230.1 km / 2 hrs 32 min

Antelope Canyon to Navajo NM
82.7 mi / 133 km / 1 hr 22 min

89

160

20 mi

20 km

0

0

103

N

UTAH
ARIZONA

89

89A

64

64

Grand Canyon South to Antelope Canyon
144 mi / 231.7 km / 2 hrs 36 min

Grand Canyon South to Phoenix
229 mi / 368.5 km / 3 hrs 31 min

GRAND CANYON NATIONAL PARK

GRAND CANYON VILLAGE

Hiking Navajo National Monument

Shorter Betatakin Guided Site Tour

Strenuous – (3.0 mi / 4.8 km), round trip, allow 3 – 4 hours

This is a free ranger-led hiking tour to the Betatakin Ruins. The tour follows Sandal and Aspen Trails down to the bottom of the canyon. With an elevation loss of 700 feet, the hike is strenuous. The tour is offered seasonally, so check with the visitor center first on exact times. The tour starts at 10 AM. Folks meet for a briefing with the ranger behind the visitor center and then follow the ranger as he/she describes the people and their culture, as well as flora, fauna, and geography. Visitors are welcome to walk back at their own pace. The ranger will be the last person out.

Keet Seel

Strenuous – (17.0 mi / 27.4 km), round trip, full day or overnight backpacking trip

Visiting the ruins of Keet Seel is possible. Some consider this to be the best-preserved cliff dwelling in the Southwest. The ruins are laden with artifacts, both in volume and variety. These include pieces of jewelry, arrowheads, and corncobs. Many of the rooms have the original ceiling beams and exterior plaster still intact. There is a ranger on site who will lead you around once you arrive. For visitors that feel 17 miles is too long for a day hike, there is a primitive campground nearby.

The park limits the number of visitors to Keet Seel to 20 per day. Advanced reservation and a backcountry permit are required. Before receiving a permit, one must listen to orientation, which is held daily at 8:15am and 3:00pm. Keep the permit with you at all times as you hike. Fortunately, it is not difficult to obtain a permit due to the monument's location and the trail's distance.

The route starts similarly as the "Longer Betatakin Guided Site Tour." A permitted visitor takes Tsegi Road

Betakin Ruins and Navajo National Monument

Longer Betatakin Guided Site Tour

Strenuous – (5.0 mi / 8.0 km), round trip, allow 3 – 5hours

This free tour takes a different path, using the old Tsegi Point Road to the Betatakin Ruins. As with the other tour, it is ranger-led and quite informative. The tour is offered seasonally. To take this tour, start in front of the visitor center at 8:15 AM for a preliminary briefing. Then, the group will need to take their vehicle to end of the navigable portion of Tsegi Point Road. From here, the road becomes a trail, following along a wide peninsular portion of the canyon's rim, with alcoves and canyon floor on both sides. This part of the hike is quite spectacular. The road ends at Tsegi Point and then climbs steeply down to the canyon floor and the ruins.

Sandal Trail

Easy – (1.0 mi / 1.6 km), round trip, allow 30 minutes

A paved and accessible trail that leads to an overlook of Betatakin cliff dwelling and surrounding canyon.

to Tsegi Trail down to the canyon floor. From there, look for signs indicating the side canyon for Keet Seel. This primitive trail heads up the canyon, crossing the stream multiple times and passes a 100-foot, awe-inspiring waterfall.

Keet Seel is not open in the winter and early spring. Also, during the summer monsoon season, the park may cancel reservations due to potential flash flooding in the park.

Aspen Trail

Moderate – (0.8 mi / 1.3 km), round trip, allow 30 minutes

A spur trail off Sandal Trail that heads lower into the canyon and an old growth grove of Aspen trees.

Canyon View Trail

Easy – (0.4 mi / 0.6 km), round trip, allow 30 minutes

This is an easy walk along the rim, leading from the visitor center and campground to the historic ranger station

NAVAJO NATIONAL MONUMENT

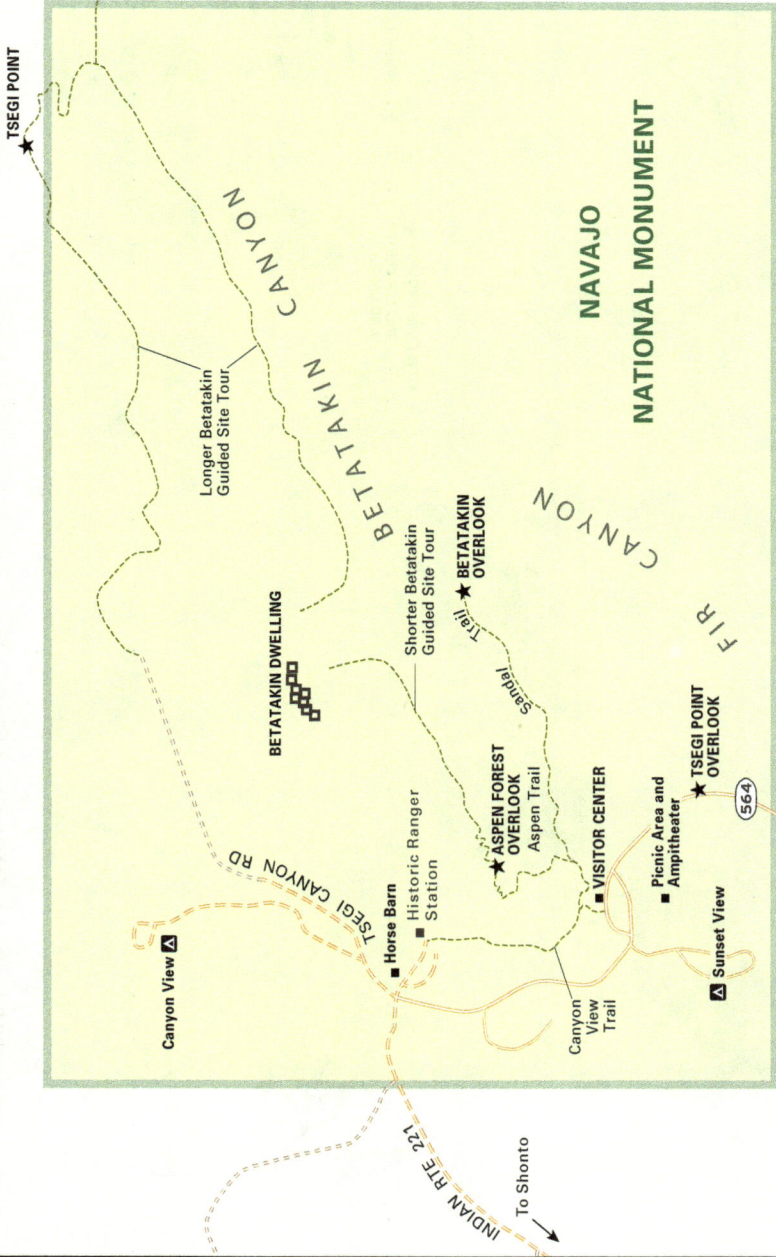

Legend:
- ★ Point Of Interest
- ⚠ Campground
- ▫ Native American Building
- ■ Historical Site
- - - - Trail
- - - - Unpaved 2WD Road
- - - - Unpaved 4WD Road

N

0   0.5 mi
0   0.5 km

★ TSEGI POINT

LONG CANYON

Keet Seel Trail

BETATAKIN CANYON

Longer Betatakin Guided Site Tour

Shorter Betatakin Guided Site Tour

BETATAKIN DWELLING

★ BETATAKIN OVERLOOK

FIR CANYON

Sandal Trail

Aspen Trail

★ ASPEN FOREST OVERLOOK

■ Historic Ranger Station

TSEGI CANYON RD

■ Horse Barn

⚠ Canyon View

Canyon View Trail

ᵢ VISITOR CENTER

■ Picnic Area and Ampitheater

★ TSEGI POINT OVERLOOK

⚠ Sunset View

564

To Hwy 160

INDIAN RTE 221

To Shonto

NAVAJO NATIONAL MONUMENT

105

MONUMENT VALLEY NAVAJO TRIBAL PARK

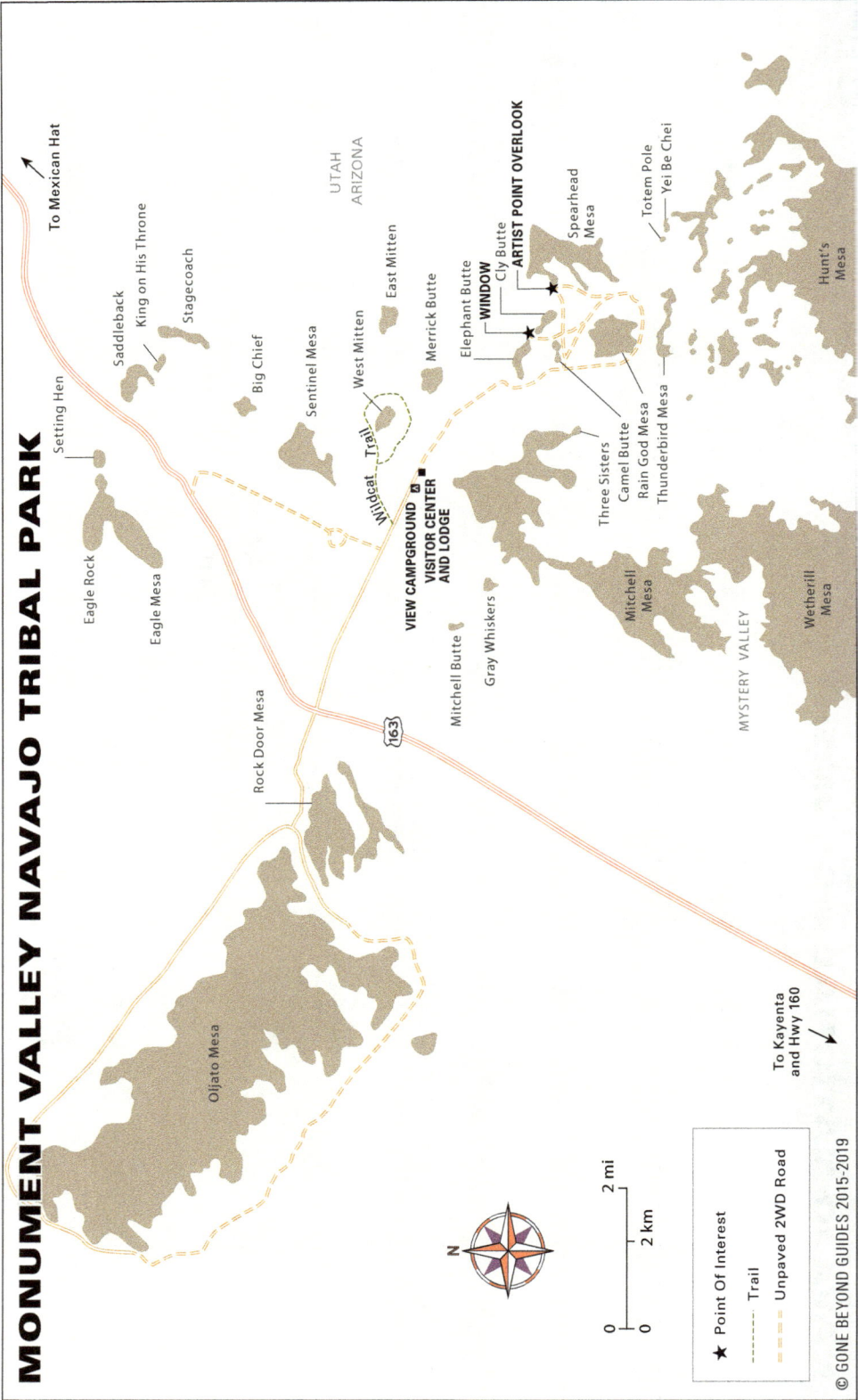

To Mexican Hat

UTAH
ARIZONA

ARTIST POINT OVERLOOK
WINDOW
Cly Butte
Spearhead Mesa
Totem Pole
Yei Be Chei
Hunt's Mesa

Setting Hen
Saddleback
King on His Throne
Stagecoach
Big Chief
Sentinel Mesa
West Mitten
East Mitten
Merrick Butte
Elephant Butte

Eagle Rock
Eagle Mesa

Wildcat Trail

VIEW CAMPGROUND
VISITOR CENTER
AND LODGE

Three Sisters
Camel Butte
Rain God Mesa
Thunderbird Mesa

Rock Door Mesa

163

Mitchell Butte
Gray Whiskers

Mitchell Mesa

MYSTERY VALLEY

Wetherill Mesa

Oljato Mesa

To Kayenta
and Hwy 160

N

0
0
2 mi
2 km

★ Point Of Interest
Trail
Unpaved 2WD Road

© GONE BEYOND GUIDES 2015-2019

MONUMENT VALLEY TRIBAL PARK

If you have ever watched the classic movie Stagecoach, one of the top westerns of all time, you will notice one thing. No matter where that stagecoach is heading, they are always passing through Monument Valley. The movie was John Wayne's breakthrough role and put Monument Valley on the map for America. From 1939, when the movie was made, to present, Monument Valley has become THE definitive icon of the Southwest.

The problem with any icon is it tends to become larger than reality itself, and we are let down when we finally meet it. The good news with Monument Valley is it will not disappoint in this way. It is as sweeping and epic in real life as it is on film. It is a place where time seems to slow down and watching the late afternoon sun slowly slip off the monuments is a memory that will stick with you for life.

Monument Valley is easy to drive through, but to capture the impact of this area, it is recommended to stay overnight. The campground set up by the Navajo Tribal Park offers some of the best viewing real estate in the park. The campsites sit on a sandy hill overlooking many of the most recognized monuments, including the Mittens. The View Hotel nearby is also recommended. The famed Goulding's Lodge is another favorite place to stay and was home for the cast and crew of the movie Stagecoach and other westerns.

In terms of hiking, the land is privately owned and actively used by the Navajo. The Wildcat Trail is the only hike that a visitor can take without a Navajo escort in the park. The trail is a 3.2-mile loop that goes completely around the West Mitten. The trail starts at The View Hotel and once down in the valley is fairly flat. Allow 2 – 3 hours to complete this hike and bring water.

There is also a 17-mile scenic drive on a maintained unpaved road, which is highly recommended. The drive is suitable for most cars and is open for day use only. If you are looking for more immersion, you can take a guided tour. These tours are really the only way to see some of the places within the park. All of the official tour operators are listed here: www.navajonationparks.org/htm/monumentvalleytours.htm

FOUR CORNERS

If there is an anchor to the Grand Circle, it is the Four Corners. It isn't the center of the circle, which is a shame from the standpoint of perfect symmetry, but it is the symbolic center. In this one spot are captured four of the five states that make up the Grand Circle, namely Utah, Colorado, New Mexico and Arizona. Part of the overall allure of the Grand Circle is "Where does that highway lead to?" The answer to this question here is it leads to a magical place where one can stand in four states at the same time.

The park is run by the Navajo Nation and consists of a large marker showing the location of the four corners; suitable for family photos, a four-state game of Twister, and other acts of Tom Foolery. Surrounding this marker on all four sides is a row of vendor stalls. Each stall is run by a local merchant selling the usual collection of jewelry, carved stones, arrows, feathered earrings, dream catchers, and spirit animals. While the initial intent was to have New Mexico crafts on one side and Colorado goods on the other, at this point all of the merchants are for the most part selling Navajo crafts. Sometimes there is some Zuni and Hopi representation as well.

The flea market vibe aside, the merchants are all great folk and perhaps the best part of the monument. They come each day; they all know each other and are worth getting to know a little. Most are willing to share a little of their life with you if you invite them into a conversation. There are Navajo bread and other goodies for sale and basic bathroom facilities, however true to being the center of nowhere, there is no electricity, phone service, or running water here.

There is a $5 entrance fee per person and is cash only. The nearest ATM if 5 miles away at Teec Nos Pos, Arizona. Monument hours are from 8am - to dusk. The Navajo Nation does honor Daylight Savings Time.

WHERE TO GO FROM HERE

This side trip ends pretty much in the middle of nowhere. Since most folks like to be somewhere at the end of the day, it is reasonable to add in a few places to go from here. Fortunately, the road ahead offers multiple opportunities for continuing one's journey.

Going north to Moab puts you into the reaches of Canyonlands and Arches National Park. Heading northeast gets you to Mesa Verde, Durango and the interior of Colorado or you can head south to Albuquerque and the blue desert skies of New Mexico. Finally, you can follow the south road west back into Arizona towards Petrified Forest National Park.

Monument Valley Navajo Tribal Park

Best From

Most visitors make this trip from the South Rim, though the North Rim is closest route for this side trip.

What You'll See

- Antelope Canyon Tribal Park
- Coral Pink Sand Dunes State Park
- Zion National Park
- Springdale, Utah

Why Choose this Side Trip

108

A vacation that includes Grand Canyon and Zion is by far the most popular of the vacation routes in this book and for good reason. With this trip, you get to see the top two most popular national parks in the Southwest. Plus, from Zion, you can continue either to Bryce Canyon National Park or Las Vegas, Nevada.

Zion National Park holds impressive views, with giant 1500-foot red sandstone cliffs, serene waterfalls, record spanning arches and in season, the ability to hike "The Narrows," a slot canyon where the trail you forge is the Virgin River itself. The drive up to Zion is scenic from the moment you start the engine, highlighting some of the best of the southwest. This side trip also includes a stop at the sacred slot canyons of Antelope Canyon and an option to see Coral Pink Sand Dunes State Park.

Allow

- Recommended – 3 to 5 days
- Total Drive Time: 5 hours 45 minutes
- Antelope Canyon: Allow 4 hours for this tour, start to finish
- Coral Pink Sand Dunes: 1 hour to overnight
- Zion National Park, including Springdale: 1-3 days

The ideal use of a week's time would be to split the vacation time equally amongst the two parks with a side trip to Antelope Canyon and Coral Pink Sand Dunes. If you like the outdoors, Zion is one of those places where once you get there you wish you had allocated more time to explore it. With that in mind, if you can add a day or two extra in Zion, do so. The nearby town of Springdale, Utah compliments the hiking and outdoors of Zion well, with great food, drinks, and lodging, right outside the park.

Coral Pink Sand Dunes is listed as an optional leg on this side trip. While you can say you have seen it by doing a drive-by to the park, the signature pink color of the dunes is best seen at sunset and sunrise, making an overnight stay the ideal way to visit these dunes.

Can be combined with

Side Trip 6 - "Rim to Rim and Beyond."

ANTELOPE CANYON

Antelope Canyon is an incredibly picturesque slot canyon, where the rock dances upwards from the canyon floor to the thin slit of the sky above. Please refer to Side Trip 6 – Rim to Rim and Beyond, for details on taking a tour of this Southwest wonder.

CORAL PINK SAND DUNES STATE PARK

The first thing to note about this park is while the color is distinctly different from other sand dunes; it may not be the pink color you envisioned when you first pull up. The color is more of a sandstone red much of the time and requires the right soft and low but direct lighting to bring out the picture-perfect coral color.

The elusive pink color aside, the park is a great stay-over spot within the typical route of the Grand Circle. The park has a nice campground, with 16 tent/RV spots, drinking water, showers, good restroom facilities, and one group site. The park is ATV friendly, which can pose as the only downside if you aren't riding an ATV. One needs to be mindful of these high-speed vehicles in this multi-use area. That said, if you do have an ATV, the area allows exploration into canyons that are very much like Zion NP, but without all the people. For many locals, this is how they see Zion, by riding into the wilderness surrounding it.

There is one other minor but very cool feature of this park. It has an extensive collection of sand from all over the world. Each little jar is labeled with the sand's location. The collection, which takes up an entire wall in the visitor center, started as a ranger's hobby but has grown considerably as tourists have sent in

Footsteps at Coral Pink Sand Dunes

INTO ZION AND UTAH

Zion to Bryce Canyon via Hwy 89
72.4 mi / 116.5 km / 1 hr 21 min

89

ZION
NATIONAL
PARK

○ SPRINGDALE

Antelope Canyon to Zion
112 mi / 180.2 km / 2 hrs 1 min

89

CORAL PINK
SAND DUNES

43

Hancock Rd

UTAH
ARIZONA

89A

ANTELOPE CANYON ◆   109

98

389

← Zion to Las Vegas via Hwy 15
166 mi / 267.2 km / 2 hrs 36 min

89A

North Rim to Zion
123 mi / 197.9 km / 2 hrs 46 min

89

67

GRAND CANYON
NATIONAL PARK

NORTH RIM
GRAND CANYON ◆

GRAND CANYON VILLAGE ○

Grand Canyon South
to Antelope Canyon
137 mi / 220.4 km / 2 hrs 32 min

64

64

N

89

0   10 mi
0   10 km

180

© GONE BEYOND GUIDES 2017

Coral Pink Sand Dunes

SOUTH FORK INDIAN CANYON

Easy – (1.0 mi / 1.6 km), round trip, allow 30 minutes, elev. Δ: 150 ft / 46 m, trailhead at the end of South Fork Indian Canyon Road off Sand Spring Road

This trail leads to some truly amazing pictographs. Formed around 1200 BCE, this rock art was created using natural pigments versus a petroglyph, which is formed by carving into the rock. The pictographs are quite rare and sit behind a protective fence. Bring a zoom lens if you want great pictures. This trail requires a 4WD vehicle that can handle the aptly named Sand Spring Road.

Take Sand Spring Road from Hancock for about a mile through the edge of the dunes and then a little less than two miles up South Fork Indian Canyon to the obvious parking lot for the pictographs. In many ways, this is the gem of the park.

their local samples. It is quite possibly the largest collection of sand in the world and is worth checking out. The visitor center is open during the daylight hours seven days a week during the summer season. There is an $8 entrance fee per vehicle to visit this park. Camping is $20 per night.

110

HIKING IN CORAL PINK SAND DUNES STATE PARK

CORAL PINK SAND DUNES ARCH

Easy – (0.2 mi / 0.3 km), round trip, allow 15 minutes elev. Δ: 50 ft / 15 m, trailhead on Hancock Road

This is by no means the grandest arch you will see but is a welcome surprise for a park whose primary feature is a set of sand dunes. Getting to this arch is easy. At the turnoff from Hancock Road from Highway 89, mark your trip meter and drive 0.8 miles. Drive off the road on your right for about 150 yards, heading towards the obvious lone hoodoo. From here, get out and walk past this hoodoo using the ATV trail on the left and look for two rock outcroppings. Here you will find a small but definite arch.

CORAL PINK SAND DUNES

Easy – (1.0 mi / 1.6 km), round trip, allow 1 - 2 hours, elev. Δ: 100 ft / 30 m, trailhead at campground

The dunes are in easy sight as you pull up and the trailhead is easy enough to find. However, it is recommended to keep along the established route so as not to disturb the fragile flora. Like all dunes, walking in sand can be more tiring than the same distance on hard ground. Also, hiking to the tallest dune, at a 300 feet elevation gain from its base, will add to the time. Look for insect and animal tracks, as well as areas of "plant art," where tall grasses have left their marks in the sand by the prevailing winds.

The one caution with the dunes is that the area is shared with ATV's. Keep an eye out for fast-moving vehicles. The ATV's can be a bit loud, but they are also fun to watch from the tall dunes.

ZION NATIONAL PARK

Zion National Park has a lot of "Wow" factor going for it. The entire Colorado Plateau was once a massive sand dune as large as the current Sarah Desert of North Africa. As with any set of sand dunes, there is one area where the winds are just right, and the dunes are at their highest. For the Colorado Plateau, those highest dunes were where Zion sits today, and as a result, when the mechanics of geology turned those dunes into sandstone, it left the area with some massive chunks of rock to play with. Enter water and wind, which cut into the stone over millions of years, leaving sheer cliffs of epic rock in hues of reds, oranges, and tans. There are many singular words to describe Zion, stunning, humbling, majestic, and even heavenly. Whatever one word that comes to mind, there are really no words that give this place a proper description. You just have to go and see it.

Zion National Park is open year round. The entrance fee is $35 per vehicle for a seven day stay.

HIKING IN THE MAIN PARK

PA'RUS TRAIL

Easy – (3.5 mi / 5.6 km), round trip, allow 2 hours, elev. Δ: 50 ft / 15 m, trailheads at South Campground and Canyon Junction

Pa'rus, which is from the Paiute language, means bubbling, tumbling water. The name describes this trail well as it meanders along the Virgin River. The trail is paved and thus accessible for those with wheelchairs. Pa'rus starts at the visitor center and heads upstream at a very slight incline. The surrounding cliffs and valley open up throughout the journey.

There are several places along the way that provide beach access to the river, and it is not uncommon to see families enjoying the heat of the day by cooling off in the water. Pa'rus trail crosses six bridges as it makes its way to trail's end at Canyon Junction. From here you can hike back (downhill all the way) or pick up the shuttle to your next destination. Dogs and bikes are welcome on this trail.

WATCHMAN TRAIL

Moderate – (3.3 mi / 5.3 km), round trip, allow 2 hours, elev. Δ: 368 ft / 112 m, trailhead near visitor center

If you are looking to get higher up for better views but don't want to climb the 2,000 feet or so to the top of the rim, the Watchman Trail is a good alternative. The trail starts at the Zion Canyon Visitor Center and ends at a mesa top that gives some commanding views of Zion NP and even a glimpse of the Towers of the Virgin and the town of Springdale.

The trail begins by following along the banks of the North Fork of the Virgin River and then juts away from the water to connect to a series of moderate switchbacks that wind their way to the top of the mesa. There is a nominal 368 feet elevation gain, but the views are worth every step. Once at the mesa top there is a half-mile loop that walks around the edge. Note that the loop mileage isn't listed as part of the distance noted in the NPS hiking guide. This is a popular trail due to both the views and the fact it starts at the visitor center.

ARCHEOLOGY TRAIL

Easy – (0.4 mi / 0.6 km), round trip, allow 0.5 hour, elev. Δ: 80 ft / 24 m, trailhead near visitor center

The Archeology Trail is a great hike if you are looking for an early evening stroll. The trail is short, less than half a mile (0.6 kilometers), but climbs steadily to a 1000-year-old prehistoric storage site. While the site requires a fair amount of imagination to piece together the history, this is not the only reason for going.

Virgin River within The Narrows

The site is close to the Watchman campground and rises to a nice vantage point in a very short distance. One can take in phenomenal views both up and down the canyon. You will notice the green riparian corridor of the Virgin River as it meanders through an ever-widening canyon. In all, this is a short but worthwhile trek you can take if you are looking for something near camp.

SAND BENCH TRAIL

Moderate – (7.6 mi / 12.2 km), round trip, allow 5 hours, elev. Δ: 466 ft / 142 m, trailhead at Zion Lodge or Court of the Patriarchs shuttle stops

This long ambling trail follows along Birch Creek before climbing up to a long and decent sized plateau named Sand Bench. The trail does have a 466-foot elevation gain, but the gain is felt primarily as you ascend to the plateau.

Start at the Court of the Patriarchs shuttle stop and pick up the Sand Bench Trail as it follows the Virgin River up Birch Creek. The trail then heads up to and runs the length of the Sand Bench plateau. As the hike unfolds, the Patriarchs, East Temple, Streaked Wall, Sentinel, Mountain of the Sun, and many other peaks can be seen. This trail is shared with horse riders, so be mindful as you take in the views.

LOWER EMERALD POOL TRAIL

Easy – (1.2 mi / 1.9 km), round trip, allow 1 hour, elev. Δ: 69 ft / 21 m, trailhead at Zion Lodge shuttle stop

There are two trails described in the Zion hiking guide that make up the Emerald Pools, the lower pools, and upper pools. Lower Emerald Pools is relatively flat, is paved much of the way, is short in distance and provides incredible views of waterfalls and shallow pools. You do climb a bit on the lower trail, which allows for some nice views of the valley.

The two pools on the lower trail are nice enough, but as is almost always the case, the best pool is at the top. As the canyon is surrounded on both sides by steep cliffs, it will be well into the morning before the sun hits the western side of the canyon. By mid-afternoon, the sun will have passed over the other side, providing more shade. In warm weather, plan to hit the trail either in the early morning or late afternoon to stay cool.

UPPER EMERALD POOL TRAIL

Moderate – (1.0 mi / 1.6 km), round trip from lower pools, allow 1 hour, elev. Δ: 200 ft / 61 m, trailhead at Zion Lodge shuttle stop

Here the trail continues from the Lower Emerald Pool Trail for the final mile. The paved trail is now dirt, and the trail climbs more steeply. If you are hiking this trail in the morning, the sun may have passed over the monolith walls and is now part of the climb up. The views do get better as you gain elevation, and the pool at the top is by far the biggest, sitting at the base of the western cliff faces. It is well worth the effort for the views. These pools are not intended for swimming.

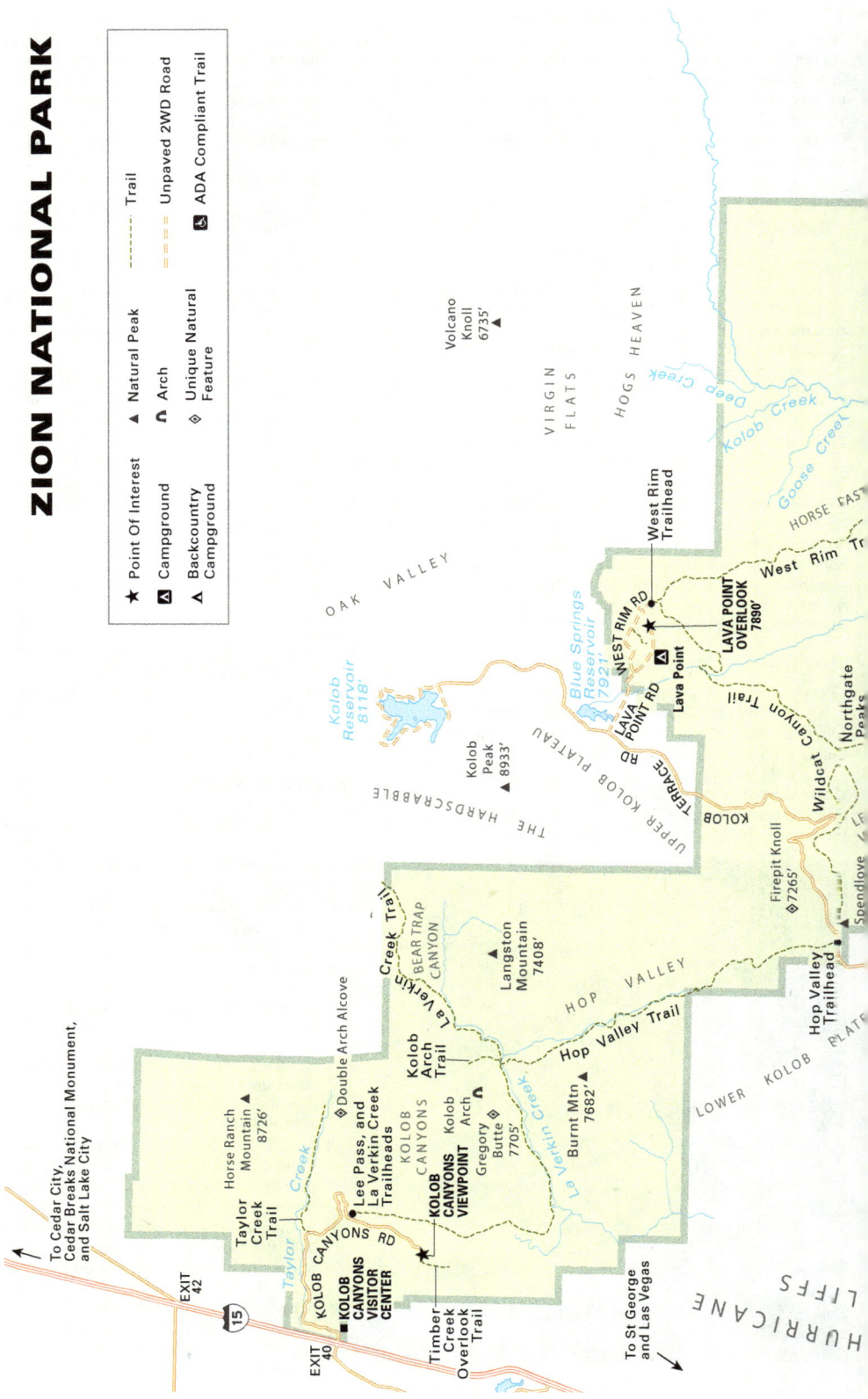

ZION NATIONAL PARK

112

Legend:
- ★ Point Of Interest
- ◢ Campground
- ▲ Backcountry Campground
- ▲ Natural Peak
- ∩ Arch
- ◈ Unique Natural Feature
- ------ Trail
- ==== Unpaved 2WD Road
- 🦽 ADA Compliant Trail

To Cedar City,
Cedar Breaks National Monument,
and Salt Lake City

EXIT 42
EXIT 40
15

KOLOB CANYONS RD

■ KOLOB CANYONS VISITOR CENTER

Timber Creek Overlook Trail

Taylor Creek

Taylor Creek Trail

KOLOB CANYONS RD

★ KOLOB CANYONS VIEWPOINT

● Lee Pass, and La Verkin Creek Trailheads

◈ Double Arch Alcove

Horse Ranch Mountain 8726' ▲

La Verkin Creek Trail

BEAR TRAP CANYON

Langston Mountain 7408' ▲

KOLOB CANYONS

Kolob Arch Trail

∩ Kolob Arch

Gregory ◈ Butte 7705'

Burnt Mtn 7682' ▲

La Verkin Creek

HOP VALLEY

Hop Valley Trail

LOWER KOLOB PLATE

To St George and Las Vegas

HURRICANE CLIFFS

THE HARDSCRABBLE

Kolob Reservoir 8118'

Kolob Peak 8933' ▲

UPPER KOLOB PLATEAU

OAK VALLEY

Blue Springs Reservoir 7921'

LAVA POINT RD

KOLOB TERRACE RD

◢ Lava Point

▲ Lava Point

WEST RIM RD

★ LAVA POINT OVERLOOK 7890'

West Rim Trailhead

West Rim Tr

VIRGIN FLATS

HOGS HEAVEN

Volcano Knoll 6735' ▲

Deep Creek

Kolob Creek

Goose Creek

HORSE PAST

Canyon Trail

Northgate Peaks

Wildcat

Firepit Knoll ◈ 7265'

Spendlove

Hop Valley Trailhead ●

HOP VALLEY PLATE

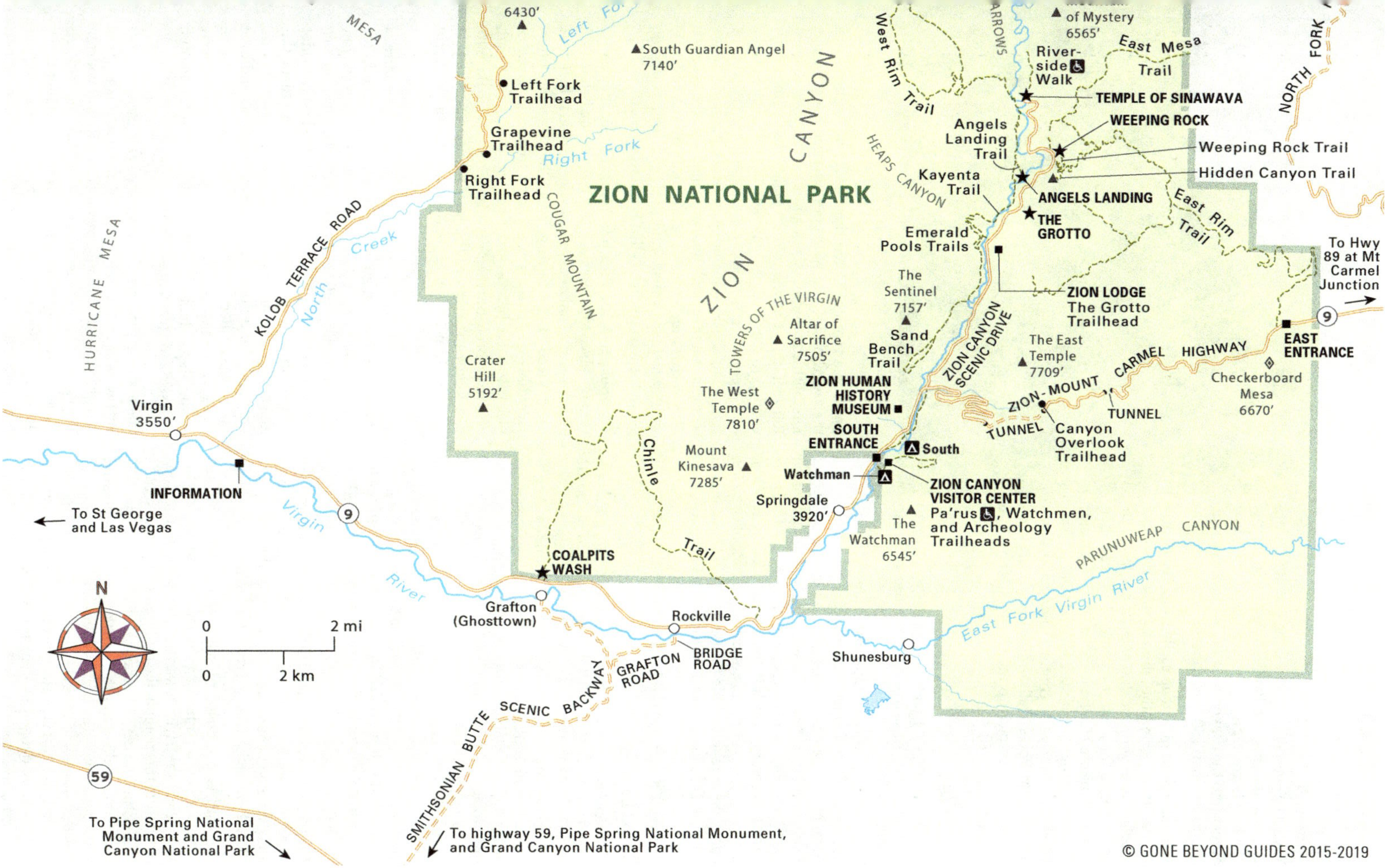

ZION NATIONAL PARK

NORTH FORK

To Hwy 89 at Mt Carmel Junction

(9)

EAST ENTRANCE

Checkerboard Mesa 6670'

of Mystery 6565'

East Mesa Trail

Weeping Rock Trail
Hidden Canyon Trail

TEMPLE OF SINAWAVA

WEEPING ROCK

East Rim Trail

River-side Walk

ANGELS LANDING

THE GROTTO

ZION LODGE
The Grotto Trailhead

ZION - MOUNT CARMEL HIGHWAY

TUNNEL

Canyon Overlook Trailhead

The East Temple 7709'

ZION - MOUNT CARMEL TUNNEL

PARUNUWEAP CANYON

East Fork Virgin River

ARROWS

Angels Landing Trail

Kayenta Trail

West Rim Trail

HEAPS CANYON

Emerald Pools Trails

The Sentinel 7157'

Sand Bench Trail

ZION CANYON SCENIC DRIVE

South

ZION CANYON VISITOR CENTER
Pa'rus, Watchmen, and Archeology Trailheads

South

The Watchman 6545'

Shunesburg

ZION HUMAN HISTORY MUSEUM

SOUTH ENTRANCE

Watchman

Springdale 3920'

113

ZION CANYON

TOWERS OF THE VIRGIN

Altar of Sacrifice 7505'

The West Temple 7810'

Mount Kinesava 7285'

Chinle

Trail

Rockville

BRIDGE ROAD

South Guardian Angel 7140'

ZION

Right Fork

COUGAR MOUNTAIN

GRAFTON ROAD

SMITHSONIAN BUTTE SCENIC BACKWAY

6430'

Left Fork

Left Fork Trailhead

Grapevine Trailhead

Right Fork Trailhead

Crater Hill 5192'

COALPITS WASH

Grafton (Ghosttown)

To highway 59, Pipe Spring National Monument, and Grand Canyon National Park

MESA

KOLOB TERRACE ROAD

North Creek

Virgin River

(9)

INFORMATION

Virgin 3550'

HURRICANE MESA

To St George and Las Vegas

2 mi

2 km

0

0

N

(59)

To Pipe Spring National Monument and Grand Canyon National Park

© GONE BEYOND GUIDES 2015-2019

KAYENTA TRAIL

Moderate – (2.0 mi / 3.2 km), round trip, allow 2 hours, elev. Δ: 150 ft / 46 m, trailhead at Grotto shuttle stop

Kayenta Trail is often hiked along with the Grotto Trail and the Emerald Pools Trail to create a loop. The trail is great, giving some magnificent views deeper into the canyon near the Zion Lodge. The trail has a small 150-foot elevation gain.

The trail can be picked up easily from The Grotto shuttle stop. From the shuttle stop cross the Virgin River via a bridge and follow along its upper banks for a short distance. The trail then enters Behunin Canyon from the Northside before meeting up with the Emerald Pools Trail. To make a loop of it, continue along and down the Emerald Pools Trail until it ends at the Zion Lodge and then pick up the Grotto Trail back to where you started.

THE GROTTO TRAIL

Easy – (1.0 mi / 1.6 km), round trip, allow 30 minutes, elev. Δ: 35 ft / 11 m, trailhead at Grotto shuttle stop

114

The Grotto Trail is a simple flat jaunt that connects the Zion Lodge with the Grotto Picnic Area. Many use it to connect the Emerald and Kayenta Trails to make a 2 ½ mile loop. The Grotto area itself has picnic tables and grates for grilling. It also holds the Grotto Museum, which is the oldest building in Zion. If you are a fan of the historical stonework of the Zion Lodge, be sure to include the Grotto Trail to the mix to see both the museum and the artist in residence house.

ANGELS LANDING VIA WEST RIM TRAIL

Strenuous – (5.4 mi / 8.7 km), round trip, allow 4-5 hours, elev. Δ: 1,488 ft / 453 m, trailhead at Grotto shuttle stop

The views are unparalleled from the unique Angels Landing trail. Built in the wake of the Great Depression by the CCC, it includes a series of switchbacks cut into solid rock. The final half mile is along a narrow knife-edged ridge that uses chains and carved footholds to assist you to the final destination. It is strenuous, but the end result is well worth it. You will have climbed from the bottom of the canyon to close to the top, giving you a view that will most certainly become a life moment. It is a world-famous hike and one of the most popular in Zion.

The trail's name was coined by Frederick Fisher in 1916 when he looked up at the monolith and exclaimed, "only an angel could land on it." With the help of the CCC, Frederick Fisher forged a trail to the top.

The trail is composed of six distinct parts. The first follows a paved path along the river before doglegging west from the river toward a cliff wall. If you look carefully at this point in the trail, you will see the second part of the journey, a series of switchbacks up this cliff. Even from a distance, the switchbacks are impressive if not audacious. The trail builders carved a fairly wide paved trail into solid rock, and while you are indeed climbing up a cliff face, this portion is merely strenuous and no more dangerous than any well-established trail with exposure.

Into Zion Valley

There is a reprieve at the third portion. At the top of the switchbacks, the trail goes between two massive monolithic columns through what is aptly named Refrigerator Canyon. The monoliths climb high enough to block out the sun, and there is a cool breeze that greets visitors as soon as they reach the top of the switchbacks. This lasts for only a short half mile before you arrive at the fourth portion, called Walter's Wiggles. The Wiggles are a series of 21 short but consistently steep switchbacks that wind back and forth until you get to the next respite, called Scout's Lookout.

The lookout is the fifth portion of the journey and a suitable place to take a rest. The Wiggles are below you, and from the lookout, you can see the final half mile pitch ahead of you to Angels Landing. The area offers incredible views. There is also a pit toilet and plenty of places to relax before your final leg. Up to this point, you have been on the West Rim Trail, so make sure you follow the signs to the top of Angels Landing, as the West Rim Trail does continue onward in a different direction.

The final pitch is a bit exciting as it has the adventure of chains that you can grab onto to ensure you get up the last leg. This portion is a razorback ridge. It is narrow with steep drop-offs on either side. The trail is well marked by the chains and crosses the back of the ridge several times as you climb. Many hikers have made this journey, and in the end, it is not as scary as it sounds. That said, this is not a place to test yourself; a handful of people have fallen to their deaths on this trail. I've seen teenagers on this trail but only two children who were in the single-digit age bracket. Use caution, for both yourself and your fellow hikers.

Once at the top, there is a somewhat narrow but flat area to take in the lofty vista. To the north is a grand view of the end of Zion Canyon. You will find yourself gazing at an enormous cul-de-sac of towering rock. As the eye travels from the edge of Angels Landing down the canyon, the citadel of rock stands as one complete sentry extending to the horizon. The red cliff walls meet the green of the desert, culminating in a dense riparian snake of vegetation that surrounds the Virgin River. At times swallows soaring at incredible speeds up to 40 miles per hour (64 km/hour) can be seen. They will soar straight into the cliff walls only to stop at the last second and land in their nests.

If this trail sounds like a must do, be warned that you are not alone. If you want more solitude and less waiting for folks to climb up and down the final pitch, try getting out first thing in the morning or during the dinner hour.

WEEPING ROCK TRAIL

Easy – (0.4 mi / 0.6 km), round trip, allow 30 minutes, elev. Δ: 98 ft / 30 m, trailhead at Weeping Rock shuttle stop

This is a short-paved trail that ends at an alcove called Weeping Rock. True to its name, water seeps through the sandstone and then falls gently like a soft rain once it reaches the overhang. It is possible to stand underneath and watch the magic of water and stone, even on a sunny day. The trail is great for kids and casual hikers looking for a magnificent view of the Great White Throne. There are about 100 feet of elevation gain and some trailside exhibits.

CANYON OVERLOOK TRAIL

Moderate – (1.0 mi / 1.6 km), round trip, allow 1 hour, elev. Δ: 163 ft / 50 m, trailhead near east Zion Tunnel entrance

This is another in the list of "great views without too much effort" category. The trail starts right before the Zion Tunnel as you head into the park. There are parking lots on either side of the Zion-Mount Carmel Highway. The trail gets a fair amount of "impulse hiking" as folks wait for the directed traffic of the tunnel to open up. After all, hiking in Zion does beat out being stuck in traffic in Zion. The hike has a modest 163-foot elevation gain and climbs some steps cut into the sandstone. At the end of the trail is an overlook with a railing at the cliff's edge giving splendid views of the lower portions of Zion Canyon and Pine Creek immediately below, as well as an interesting perspective of the Zion Tunnel.

RIVERSIDE WALK

Easy – (2.2 mi / 3.5 km), round trip, allow 90 minutes, elev. Δ: 57 ft / 17 m, trailhead at Temple of Sinawava shuttle stop

Riverside Walk starts at roads end of the wide main part of the Zion box canyon. From here, the canyon begins to narrow but is still wide enough for the paved Riverside Walk trail that meanders until it reaches The Narrows proper. The trail is fairly flat, with several rolling ups and downs as it contours to the land. There are also a few spots with watery grottoes as well as multiple spots for river beach access. The trail ends at a stonework terrace where you can gaze at the mouth of The Narrows and the various hikers beginning or ending their hike of this landmark trek.

THE NARROWS

Imagine walking up a river flowing clearly and gently around your feet. At times there is no shore, only river and massive sandstone walls that run from the edge of the water and rise swiftly straight up 2000 feet into the sky. There are places where the canyon is wide enough to permit a view of distant sandstone monoliths and other places where the canyon is delightfully slender, only 20-30 feet wide. Each turn gives a different view, all wondrous and grand. For a bit, the river stretches out, allowing a chance to walk on soft sand. You see deer grazing on the banks. Waterfalls come sliding down curved walls from unreachable heights. There is no trail but the river. If you think about it, each step up and down is a step no one has ever taken before in exactly the same way.

Be warned, it is possible that you won't be able to hike the Narrows. If the Virgin River is running too high, either due to winter/spring runoff or to summer flash floods, you will not be able to go on this hike. That said, if the river is running favorably, then make it a point to add this to your vacation planning. The park service actively controls access to the Narrows, which does take the guesswork out of the safety of hiking this trail.

115

Going Upstream from the Bottom of the Canyon

Easy to Strenuous – (9.4 mi / 15.1 km), round trip, allow up to 8 hours depending on distance traveled, elev. Δ: 334 ft / 102 m, trailhead at Temple of Sinawava shuttle stop

The Narrows is found by taking the shuttle to the very end of the canyon via the Riverside Walk Trail. It will take about 40–45 minutes from the campground to the end of the canyon via the shuttle. It will take another hour to 90 minutes to walk the 2.2 miles (3.5 km) needed to complete the Riverside Walk Trail. Make sure you add in this time when you plan your hike.

The Riverside Walk Trail is flat, easy, and paved. The trail follows the Virgin River up along its banks, and there are plenty of places to drop off the trail to explore the river itself. At the end of the trail is a small set of steps down to the river where The Narrows begins and where the hike gets really interesting.

Watchman Mountain and the Virgin River

There are a few trails, but for the most part, you walk in the river itself. You will be walking upstream on uneven ground at times, so be prepared to get wet. Depending on how far up you decide to go, you will need to wade and even swim in some stretches. If you feel confident that the trail will be open, it's best to pick up water shoes beforehand and bring them on the trip for this hike. It will make your hike more enjoyable.

Depending on the time of year, the water may be swift and cold. In the summer, usually by June, the river slows down to a steady but not terribly swift pace, and the temperature is more refreshing than cold.

There are restrictions on how far up you can travel upstream without a permit. There is a tributary creek called Orderville Junction, which is a common destination for most hikers and is the limit of how far up you can travel without a permit. Orderville Junction is about two hours from the trail. That said, it is possible to never make it this far and still have an amazing hike. Each bend offers a distinct experience and new view with another bend at the end that beckons you farther.

Returning will take slightly less time since you are going downstream with the flow of water. If you are doing the hike in the late afternoon, make a note of when you start the hike from the shuttle drop off and how much time you have left before sunset. If you have 3 hours, hike up for 90 minutes and turn around. The Narrows is not an easy hike in the dark especially if you don't have a flashlight.

Going Down-stream from the Top of the Canyon

Note: As this edition goes to press, a portion of the trail that is privately owned has been marked "No Trespassing" by the owner. As a result, the Zion NPS is not issuing permits from the top of the Narrows canyon down.

Strenuous – (16 mi / 25.7 km), one way, full day hike, elev. Δ: 1,400 ft / 427 m, trailhead at Zion Narrows parking area

Going downstream can be done with a National Park Service wilderness permit. Allow a full day for this 16-mile hike. You can find private jeep shuttles that

regularly go up to the drop off spot. This is a strenuous day's hike. There are ample stories of folks that find themselves having to stick it out for the night because they thought it would be an easier hike. Hiking in streambeds is slow work and is more tiring than walking on even pavement. Underestimating this hike in the wrong conditions can be dangerous as well. Flash floods and exposure from the night's elements are serious matters.

Left Fork Trailhead

Strenuous – (7.0 mi / 11.3 km), round trip, allow 5 - 8 hours, elev. Δ: 1,000 ft / 300 m, trailhead on Kolob Terrace Road

The Left Fork of North Creek is most popular for a stretch labeled The Subway, a short and rather amazing section of the creek that looks more like a worm tunnel than a streambed. This is one of the best hikes in the park and is more route than an actual trail. Unlike The Narrows, which can be cooler in the summer heat, this hike is definitely a hot hike when temperatures are high. Start early if it looks to be a hot day.

It is possible to enter from the top and make your way downstream, but this is longer and requires a bit of rappelling and swimming (and carrying your rappelling gear). A permit is required no matter which direction you travel. From bottom to top is described here.

From the bottom, the trail starts by picking one's way down a 400-foot gully starting from the Left Fork Trailhead on Kolob Terrace Road. Once in the creek, head upstream for about two to three hours. The Subway section is a tight section of the creek with several twists and turns right above a cascading set of falls called Red Waterfalls. The Subway itself is spectacular with clear pools and an almost subterranean feel.

It is possible to continue upwards but be mindful of time. Shortly after The Subway, you will be met with large black pools that you must swim to get across to continue exploring the slot canyon. Further up is a soothing little waterfall with a secret natural room behind a watery curtain. Journeying from here requires bouldering and rappelling experience. Enjoy and head back down before dark.

Top Mountain and Shuntavi Butte in the Kolob Canyon District in winter

Like The Narrows, this slot canyon does experience extreme changes in water volume due to flash floods. The permit process helps provide education along the way for this route, but do enter well informed as to the weather for the day.

HIKING IN THE KOLOB CANYON SECTION

NORTHGATE PEAKS TRAIL

Easy – (4.5 mi / 7.2 km), round trip, allow 3 hours, elev. Δ: 50 ft / 15 m, trailhead off Wildcat Canyon trail

If you wondered if you could find a hike that wasn't too hard but also wasn't shared with millions of other tourists, this trail is a good bet. Northgate Peaks Trail is off the beaten path and isn't in the popular NPS hiking brochures, so it doesn't get as much traffic. The hike also shows a different view of Zion, ambling through large ponderosa pine forests found in the higher elevations. The hike is cooler and walks amongst the white Temple Cap monoliths dotting the landscape.

While the name of this there and back hike makes it sound like it climbs some massive Zion mountain, the elevation gain is only 250 feet. The trail ends at a craggy volcanic knob offering views that are distinctively different from the main portions of Zion and the Kolob Canyons. Access to Northgate Peaks Trail is from the Wildcat Canyon parking lot on Kolob Terrace Road.

LA VERKIN CREEK TRAIL (AND KOLOB ARCH)

Strenuous – (14.0 mi / 22.5 km), round trip, allow 8 hours, elev. Δ: 1,037 ft / 316 m, trailhead at Kolob Canyon Road

La Verkin Creek Trail, in the Kolob Canyons section, is a fun trail all around, offering amazing views including Kolob Arch, one of the largest freestanding arches on earth. The hike itself does have some elevation gain, a little over 1000 feet; however, the surroundings are stunning enough to help keep your mind off the inclines. Most folks get a permit and camp overnight; however, it is possible to do this as a long day hike to Kolob Arch.

The trail starts at Lee Pass and crosses in front of the southern portion of the Kolob Canyon cliffs. The trail meets up quickly with Timber Creek and follows along its banks, giving some spectacular views in a pinyon-juniper forest setting. After about two miles, the trail veers away from the creek into the woods as it heads towards La Verkin Creek. The trail then descends into the creek's clear waters, with each step putting you into a more immersive Kolob Canyon experience. Cliffs are now towering over you on either side with the sound of water adding to the magic of this hike.

The end of the trail is Kolob Arch viewpoint where the arch can be seen by hiking up about 150 feet to a viewing area. While the official end of the trail listed here is 7 miles, La Verkin Creek Trail does continue upstream for another two miles. There are many side canyons to explore, some of which require canyoneering techniques that lead to triple waterfalls and other delights. If backpacking, it is possible to connect to the Hop Valley Trail, which leads southeast to the Lower Kolob Plateau.

TIMBER CREEK OVERLOOK TRAIL

Moderate – (1.0 mi / 1.6 km), round trip, allow 30 minutes, elev. Δ: 100 ft / 30 m, trailhead at the end of Kolob Canyon Road

This is one of those trails that could be labeled as "Easy" without much argument; however, the park lists it as moderate. It does have a 100-foot elevation gain but is otherwise a straightforward trail. The trail is picked up at the very end of Kolob Canyon Road. From there the trail follows a small ridgeline to an overlook of Kolob Canyon, looking south. On a clear day, it is possible to see all the way to the north rim of the Grand Canyon.

This trail is located in the Kolob Canyon section. Groups are limited to a maximum size of 12 people at a time. Look for wildflowers in season, which can be abundant on this trail.

TAYLOR CREEK TRAIL

Moderate – (5.0 mi / 8.0 km), round trip, allow 4 hours, elev. Δ: 470 ft / 143 m, trailhead at Kolob Canyon Road

This trail lies within the Kolob Canyons Wilderness and ambles up the Middle Fork of Taylor Creek. This entire area gets less visitation than the main Zion Canyon and this trail has strict limits on prohibiting groups larger than 12 people. Taylor Creek Trail heads into a narrow box canyon of red Navajo Sandstone along a normally gently flowing creek. There is a welcome interplay of the green vegetation, and the red hue of the rocks here and the hike overall is one of delight and wonder. Before the trail begins to fade as it nears the end of the box canyon, look for Double Arch Alcove, an impressive set of alcoves, one on top of the other.

OTHER THINGS TO DO

VISITOR CENTER

The visitors center is located within walking distance of the Watchman Campground and is a great place to start your Zion journey. Here you can get a lay of the land, talk to rangers and, if your kids are interested, pick up a Junior Ranger Program. This is also the hub for finding a shuttle both into the park and out to Springdale.

If the center is closed or overly busy, the NPS has set up some very nice kiosks that allow you to get the information you need. The kiosks list out things to do based on how much time you have in the park and are definitely a terrific way to get started.

The visitor center is open every day except for Christmas Day. Hours are seasonal. Spring: 8:00 a.m. to 6:00 p.m., Summer: 8:00 a.m. to 7:00 p.m., Fall: 8:00 a.m. to 6:00 p.m. and Winter: 8:00 a.m. to 5:00 p.m.

A quick note on the Junior Ranger Programs. If you have younger kids, you likely know about this program. Almost every national and state park offers its own version of the Junior Ranger Program. The program allows children to explore and learn more about the park they are visiting. Each child receives an activity book that asks questions about the animals, plants, geography, and history of the park. The booklets do take some time to fill out, and parents can work with the younger ones to help. Upon completion, kids get a badge or patch and sometimes a park pin. The Junior Ranger Program is a great way to engage your family in the national parks, conservation, and ecology. Depending on the ranger who reviews the completed activity book, the receiving of the official park junior ranger badge can be quite ceremonial with the entire visitor center applauding as the child receives public accolades for his/her accomplishment on becoming a Junior Ranger.

ZION HUMAN HISTORY MUSEUM

The Zion Human History Museum opens one to two hours later than the visitor center and requires taking a short trip on the shuttle. The museum itself is nicely laid out albeit fairly broad and basic in its offerings. The best part of the museum is its grand view located on the backside of the building. The museum was built with the view of the Court of the Patriarchs in mind—

Wildlife in Zion National Park

three immense and stately monoliths named after the biblical figures Abraham, Isaac, and Jacob. Whether the museum is open or closed, the trip is worth the journey for the view alone.

TOOLING AROUND ON THE SHUTTLE

If you read this and find yourself not really wanting to hike a whole lot, take the shuttle and enjoy the view. The shuttle is a wonderful way to explore the park at your leisure. Shuttles are abundant, so it's easy to get off at the various stops, take in the view, explore a bit and then catch the next shuttle. The shuttles are designed to offer clear views of the canyon. The shuttles can get crowded, especially on a summer morning when everyone is trying to head to his/her chosen trailhead while the air temperatures are cooler.

ZION LODGING

ZION LODGE

1 Zion Canyon Scenic Dr, Springdale, UT 84767, (888) 297-2757, www.zionlodge.com/lodging/reservations

Zion Lodge was originally designed by Architect Stanley Gilbert Underwood in 1924 and carries much of the great Southwest character that went into many of his national park lodge designs. The original lodge burned down in 1966 and was rebuilt in 100 days with expedience in mind. In 1990 the lodge was renovated to return the grounds to the look and feel of Underwood's original designs. Today, despite the many visitors, Zion Lodge exudes a feeling of serenity and calm. The grounds are spacious, and the interior is warm and inviting. The lodge is within walking distance of the Emerald Pools Trail, which is an excellent family friendly trail.

Zion Lodge offers twenty-eight cabins with two double beds and twelve cabins with one queen bed. For most families, the cabin offers more privacy and containment

118

than staying at the hotel itself and do book up quickly. All cabins have a private porch, full bath, and a nice gas fireplace and scattered close to the lodge itself.

If double beds aren't cutting it, the lodge rooms may be a better option. Most of the rooms within the lodge have two queen-size beds and a television plus a full bath and private porch or balcony. The rooms are clean but as this lodge is well frequented, expect a little use. There are also second-floor suites and accessible rooms available.

WATCHMAN CAMPGROUND

There are two campgrounds in Zion NP. Of the two, the Watchman Campground has the most amenities for RV travelers. What sets this campground apart is the ability to make reservations during the peak season. For many of the sites, electricity hookups are available. The Watchman Campground is located just ¼ mile (0.4 km) from the South Entrance. There are 162 sites, two that are wheelchair accessible and seven group sites. Of these, 95 have electrical outlets. The remainders are tent and walk-in sites. The group sites are tent only as well. Campsites can be reserved at the Watchman from March through December six months before your date of arrival. Go to www.recreation.gov or call 877-444-6777. Camping is seasonal at Watchman, so check the Zion National Park Service for the latest information.

Some of the sites are shaded but will only accommodate motorhomes that are a maximum of 13 feet (3.69m). Electric campsites in loops A and B run $30 per night. Tent sites in loops C, D, and E are $20 per night. The campground does have relatively clean flush toilet restrooms as well as a slop sink to do dishes in and water stations. Watchman is within walking distance to the visitor center and the shuttle.

SOUTH CAMPGROUND

South Campground has 127 campsites. All sites are first come, first served, and there are no electrical hookups. There are a good number of RV-friendly sites, though, and generators are allowed from 8:00 a.m. to 10:00 a.m. and from 6:00 p.m. to 8:00 p.m. Campsites here are a little less than at Watchman at $20 per night.

South Campground is otherwise the equal of Watchman with one exception, the walk-in campsites. Eight walk-in campgrounds are situated along the banks of the Virgin River. For these, find your designated parking spot, hoof your gear a short distance down to the river and then bask in the glory that you have secured one of the best campsites in the park. Please note that some of these sites do have red ants. There is certainly some consternation in seeing your site's best tent location surrounded by foraging biting fiery red ants. The fact is, these little guys will bed down for the night back at their home far away from your tent and are typically not a problem. Still, if you have small children, these riverside sites might not be your best option.

LAVA POINT CAMPGROUND

This is a first come first serve primitive campground with just six sites. There is no water and no fee to stay at these sites. Getting to this campground is an 80-minute drive from the main section of Zion so check at the Visitor Center to see if they have any update on availability before making the drive. The campground's primitive exclusiveness is a plus for many and offers trailhead entry points that are less frequented. Vehicles over 19 feet are not allowed.

ZION DINING

RED ROCK GRILL

AMERICAN, $$, At Zion Lodge, (435) 772-3213, http://www.zionlodge.com, open daily, 6:30am - 10:30am, 11:30am - 3pm, and 5pm - 10pm

The food is good, views are great. The ambiance is classy, yet accommodating to all. A solid choice if you are in the park and want a sit-down meal. Open year round. Dinner reservations are advised

CASTLE DOME CAFE

AMERICAN, $, At Zion Lodge, (435) 772-3213, http://www.zionlodge.com, open daily in season, 6:30am - 5pm

Castle Dome Cafe offers pizza, burgers, and fries, and grilled sandwiches along with coffee, sodas, soft serve ice cream and beer. While the food is standard quality, the beers are distinctive and refreshing. They offer a choice of local microbrews which can be enjoyed outside on the patio with canyon views in every direction.

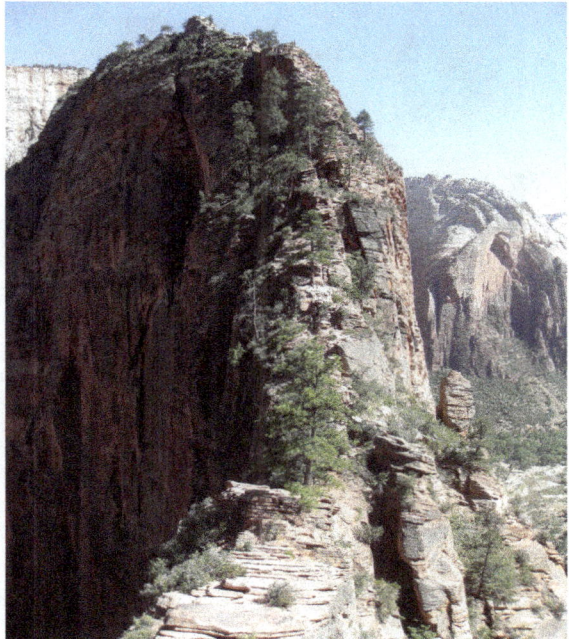

The Final Climb up to Angels Landing

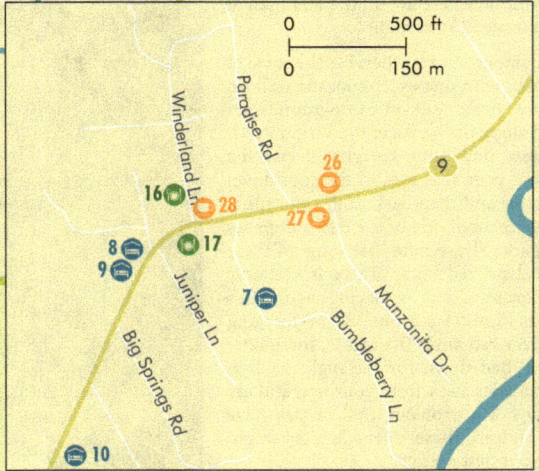

SPRINGDALE

0 ___ 200 ft
0 ___ 609 m

ZION
NATIONAL PARK

120

ZION
NATIONAL PARK

See Inset

ZION
NATIONAL PARK

9
23
1
24
2
3
14 15
25
4
5
6
18
19
11
20
12
9
21
13
22

Inset:

Winderland Ln
Paradise Rd

0 ___ 500 ft
0 ___ 150 m

16
28
26
9
27
17
8
9
7
Juniper Ln
Big Springs Rd
Manzanita Dr
Bumbleberry Ln
10

© GONE BEYOND GUIDES 2019

SPRINGDALE, UTAH

One of the big advantages of Zion National Park is having the town of Springdale, Utah close by. This allows for full immersion into the wilds of Zion National Park during the day knowing you have an adult beverage, great meal, and decent sleeping accommodations waiting for you when you are done. Of course, you can also run things camping or RV style, if you wish, but even within those modes, it is good to know the luxuries of civilization are close by.

Springdale was once a Mormon settlement at the mouth of Zion Canyon and is now a quaint little tourist town. The town has everything for a visitor, including lodging, gift shops, art galleries, restaurants, and ice cream. The spunky village of just 570 inhabitants even has a movie theater. It's a nice alternative to hiking if your family is just not the hiking type or has had enough of the outdoors for now. It is also where you can pick up alternative journeys via jeep tours and mountain biking. The NPS runs shuttle service to Springdale, which can be picked up near the visitor center. Check the visitor center for a schedule.

Looking up from The Narrows

All the lodging AND dining options are listed in order of proximity to the main entrance to the park, from closest to farthest. Also, most establishments vary hours by season. Please check locally for hours of operation. Lastly, menu item prices vary, the prices are a guideline only.

LODGING IN SPRINGDALE

CABLE MOUNTAIN LODGE

147 Zion Park Blvd, Springdale, UT 84767, (435) 772-3366, cablemountainlodge.com

Cable Mountain Lodge's motto is "Steps to Zion," and as the closest accommodation to the park, this is a true statement. What is great about this hotel is that it doesn't hang on its laurels, the rooms, the lodge itself, the staff, the views, everything is done with a high level of service. They offer rooms, villas, and suites, filled with just about every amenity, including a full-size fridge in the villas, and large HDTV's in every room. The villas sleep up to 10 people and can be one of the best options in Springdale if you have a large group.

CLIFFROSE LODGE & GARDENS

281 Zion Park Blvd, Springdale, UT 84767, (800) 243-8824, cliffroselodge.com

One of the lucky hotels that are a stone's throw from Zion National Park, Cliffrose Lodge doesn't disappoint. The rooms are decorated in what could be described as contemporary southwest. The hotel itself is a little dated architecturally, but its proximity to Zion and the heart of Springdale can't be beaten.

121

FLANIGAN'S INN

450 Zion Park Blvd, Springdale, UT 84767, (435) 772-3244, flanigans.com

Flanigan's Inn is so close to Zion, you can walk directly into the park from your room. This 3-star hotel offers one of the best options overall for Zion lodging. The inn has exceptional views, an outdoor pool, and dining at The Spotted Dog Café. All rooms are comfortable, airy, and well appointed. A smart choice.

ZION CANYON BED AND BREAKFAST

101 Kokopelli Cir, Springdale, UT 84767, (435) 772-9466, zioncanyonbnb.com

From the outside, Zion Canyon B&B gives an impression of entering a sprawling but modern hacienda. The interior continues to delight the senses with a southwest style reminiscent of old Mexico. This place is truly a delight to stay in. The rooms are spacious and well-appointed with easy access to the Virgin River to cool off. One can also opt to stay inside and play their pinball machines or simply enjoy the view from your patio.

HARVEST HOUSE BED AND BREAKFAST

29 Canyon View Dr, Box 125, Springdale, UT 84767, (435) 772-3880, harvesthouse.net

Do not be put off by Harvest's House modern architecture. On the outside, this B&B looks like a typical suburban home, but there is much warmth and hospitality once you cross the threshold. The rooms are spacious with private bathrooms and free Wi-Fi. The breakfasts are hearty and delicious.

DESERT PEARL INN

707 Zion Park Blvd, Springdale, UT 84767, (435) 772-8888, www.desertpearl.com/

Desert Pearl Inn is a 3.5-star hotel that offers a warm and modern atmosphere as a backdrop for your vacation. The hotel surrounds a large outdoor pool and cabana area. The rooms are spacious, and each has a kitchenette, complete with dining table, desk and a sofa that converts to a bed. Each room also has a terrace with relaxing views complete with Adirondack chairs to sit in. It's a perfect place for families who are looking to treat themselves while on vacation.

BUMBLEBERRY INN

97 Bumbleberry Lane, Springdale, UT 84767, (800) 828-1534, bumbleberry.com

Bumbleberry Inn is a 3-star hotel within a mile of Zion National Park. The Zion park shuttle system stops at the Inn, making this a convenient base camp. They offer Wi-Fi, air conditioning, fitness room and an outdoor pool. The exterior is dated but this typically the best deal in town. Close to shops and restaurants.

UNDER THE EAVES INN

980 Zion Park Blvd, Box 29, Springdale, UT 84767, (435) 772-3457, www.undertheeaves.com

A very cute B&B on the main drag in Springdale, Utah. Every room is a little different, but overall the decorations are open and warm to the eye. This is a small cottage style house with well-manicured grounds and within walking distance of much the southern part of the town. There is no TV in the rooms, and they offer vouchers for breakfast at local eateries.

RED ROCK INN

998 Zion Park Blvd, Springdale, UT 84767, (435) 772-3139, redrockinn.com

Red Rock Inn is listed as bed and breakfast, but it is unique. Sure, they serve an incredible breakfast, but it is delivered to your own little cottage. They offer four cottages and 2 suites. All offer a private entrance, patio, Wi-Fi, air conditioning, TV, and DVD player. As expected the suites offer more room and a kitchenette for their newest suite. The Red Rock Inn is found on the southern end of Springdale.

HAMPTON INN & SUITES SPRINGDALE ZION NATIONAL PARK

1127 Zion Park Boulevard, Springdale, UT 84767, (435) 627-9191, hamptoninn3.hilton.com

A mid-range hotel with free breakfast, Wi-Fi, and an outdoor pool. Stopping point for the Zion park shuttle. Basic rooms but fairly up to date overall.

Waterfall at Emerald Pools

HOLIDAY INN EXPRESS SPRINGDALE

1215 Zion Park Blvd, Springdale, UT 84767, (435) 772-3200, ihg.com

Holiday Inn Express Springdale is a 3-star hotel with easy access to much of Springdale. Overall, modern, and up to date accommodations inside and out with a large pool and free breakfast. The hotel is very nice and will likely meet or exceed expectations you might have for a mid-range hotel. Zion park shuttle stops right in front of the hotel.

DRIFTWOOD LODGE

1515 Zion Park Blvd, Springdale, UT 84767, (435) 772-3262, driftwoodlodge.net

Driftwood Lodge is a 2.5-star hotel offering many of the same views and comfort of higher-end hotels but at a lesser cost. The grounds offer expansive views into Zion Canyon, giving the feeling that it is just you and the park. The rooms are clean and fresh, yet a little basic. Overall though, this is an excellent value for a visit to Zion.

MAJESTIC VIEW LODGE

2400 Zion Park Boulevard, Springdale, UT 84767, (435) 772-0665, majesticviewlodge.com

Located "downstream" in the southern section of Springdale, Majestic View Lodge offers quaint rooms and its own restaurant, Arkansas Al's Steakhouse. While the restaurant can be hit or miss, the lodge itself does a better job of providing an enjoyable experience. The overall atmosphere is cozy with touches of the Great West.

DINING IN SPRINGDALE

THE SPOTTED DOG CAFE

AMERICAN, $$, 428 Zion Park Blvd, Springdale, UT 84767, (435) 772-0700, flanigans.com/dining, open daily, 7am - 11am, 5 - 9pm, closed in winter

The Spotted Dog Café is located within Flanigan's Inn. The restaurant does breakfast and dinner service. This is a casual yet upscale farm to table bistro, offering locally sourced produce, sustainably harvested seafood, and hormone-free meats. The cafe is a delight to the senses without being a sinkhole for the pocketbook. The wine puts the experience over the top, with one of the best selections in town. This doesn't go unnoticed either. Wine Spectator has given them an Award of Excellence for the last 7 years. In 2016, only 19 restaurants were honored with this award in Utah. This is a contender for the best restaurant in Springdale. Reservations are recommended.

WHIPTAIL GRILL

MEXICAN, $$, 445 Zion Park Blvd, Springdale, UT 84767, (435) 772-0283, www.whiptailgrillzion.com, open daily, 11:30am - 9pm

Small and with a fair amount of invented personality to cover up its low-key location, do not let these first appearances fool you. Whiptail Grill offers a nice menu of mostly Fresh Mex fare. This is a wonderful place for lunch if you just got off a hike and want to satisfy your hunger and settle into a lazy afternoon by the Virgin River.

OSCAR'S CAFÉ

MEXICAN, $$, 948 Zion Park Blvd, Springdale, UT 84767, (435) 772-3232, cafeoscars.com, open daily, 7am - 9pm

The location is prime real estate, which tends to drive the "something for everybody" menu, despite being touted as a Mexican restaurant. For the breakfast crowd, Oscar's offers a mix of the expected selection of breakfast burritos along with the great selection of omelets, pancakes, and French toast. One nice feature is their selection of non-egg offerings. If you are looking for lunch or dinner, Oscar's lightly covers a handful of Mexican dishes, but more than 2/3 of their menu offers the standard array of sandwiches, salads, and burgers. So, while not a true Mexican cuisine only restaurant, the place makes up for it with quick service and tasty food, making it one of the most popular food haunts in Springdale. Oscar's is vegan, gluten-free, and vegetarian-friendly.

MEME'S CAFE

AMERICAN, $$, 975 Zion Park Blvd, Springdale, UT 84767, (435) 772-0114, memescafezion.com, open daily, 7am - 10pm

Located in downtown Springdale, MeMe's Café does a fantastic job of quenching the desire to indulge in something a little bit naughty while on vacation. They serve up a nice assortment of comfort food dishes, such as slow-roasted pork, grilled cheese, and crepes. The ever-changing menu is fresh and delightful, keeping in that comfort food zone whether you are coming for breakfast, lunch, or dinner. Service is friendly and quick in a relaxing atmosphere.

Looking into Kolob Canyon

Temples and the Tower of the Virgin

SWITCHBACK GRILLE STEAK AND FISH

STEAKS AND SEAFOOD, $$$, 1149 Zion Park Blvd, Springdale, UT 84767, (435) 772-3700, switchbackgrille.com, open daily, 5pm - 9pm, Friday through Sunday open until 10pm

This is one of those restaurants where you get the menu and then can't decide what to have because EVERYTHING on it sounds really good. Whatever you choose, it's hard to go wrong. Choices of starters and salads, followed by steaks and sides, a robust seafood selection, special entrees, and desserts. They have a decent wine selection and take reservations. Be sure to ask for a window table for best views. In the same complex is Jacks Sports Grille, which offers more casual fare of wings, burgers, brats, and beer. Both places offer hearty breakfasts as well.

BIT & SPUR RESTAURANT & SALOON

TEX MEX, $$, 1212 Zion Park Blvd, Springdale, UT 84767, (435) 772-3498, bitandspur.com, open daily, 5 - 11pm

Tex-Mex style Mexican is typically heavier on the cheese and includes such dishes as the fajita, nachos and the always fun to pronounce chili con carne, (using a Texas accent of course). Bit & Spur does a fine job with the Tex-Mex name, aiming a little more towards the American side, which allows them to offer a unique variety of dishes. Notables include pollo relleno and carne asada, but they also offer glazed salmon and a solid ribeye. The restaurant has a terrific location, which is more of a warning during the dinner hour, as it is often busy. Their full bar allows one to find ways to fill the time while waiting for their table.

KING'S LANDING BISTRO

AMERICAN, $$, 1515 Zion Park Blvd, Springdale, UT 84767, (435) 772-7422, kingslandingbistro.com, open daily, 5pm - 9pm

Open exclusively for dinner, King's Landing provides a relaxed yet elegant atmosphere to set the mood with amazing views from the patio. Each dish, from the salads to the deserts, are well prepared and delightfully plated. The menu isn't terribly huge, which can be a downside if you don't see the dish you were craving. Overall, King's Landing is a nice place to relax with drinks and friends, with good food and magnificent views.

PARK HOUSE CAFE

AMERICAN, $$, 1880 Zion Park Blvd, Springdale, UT 84737, (435) 772-0100, parkhousecafezion.com, open daily, 8am - 2pm

The Park House Café offers a healthy and fresh menu for breakfast, making it a good pit stop before hitting the trails. One of the best values for breakfast is The Standard, consisting of two eggs, home fries, and toast for 3 dollars. Lunch, however, is where the place really shines, offering a wide variety of American fare that is fresh and tasty. They offer a good selection of sandwiches as well as tacos, kabobs and even a buffalo burger. You can finish things off with a banana split or a root beer float.

ARKANSAS AL'S STEAKHOUSE

STEAKHOUSE, $$$, 2400 Zion Park Blvd, Springdale, UT 84767, (435) 772-0665, majesticviewlodge.com, open daily, 8am - 8pm

There is definitely a correlation with menu prices and value. The higher the price, the higher the expectation. Unfortunately for Arkansas Al's Steakhouse, the quality is inconsistent. Sometimes it's really good, other times not so much. The food is on or slightly below par with other restaurants in the area, but with higher prices.

Trail to Angels Landing

COFFEES AND SWEETS!

PERKS AT ZION

COFFEE, SMOOTHIES, 281 Zion Park Blvd, Springdale, UT 84767, (435) 772-0529, open daily, 6am - 7pm

The baristas here make espresso coffees worthy of praise or at least a decent tip. Quality beans, good microfoam, latte art, and super friendly service. Perks is within a short walking distance to Zion National Park.

CAFE SOLEIL

COFFEE, FULL MEALS, 205 Zion Park Blvd, Springdale, UT 84767, (435) 772-0505, cafesoleilzionpark.com, open daily, 6:30am - 9pm

Best place in town for espresso drinks which is why Cafe Soleil is in this section, but they also offer great food as well. The breakfast menu is fresh and varied with quick service. For lunch, they offer great paninis, sandwiches, salads, wraps, and pizzas. They also offer a delightful choice of fruit smoothies and milkshakes. Café Soleil does a fantastic job of offering healthy fare with a great atmosphere. They support local artists, whose work can be seen on the cafe's walls. This is a great spot to fill the belly after a long hike without feeling too weighed down afterward.

HOODOOS GENERAL STORE & ICE CREAM PARLOR

ICE CREAM, 35 Lion Blvd, Springdale, UT 84767, (435) 772-3101, open daily, 7am - 10pm

The rich maple syrup aroma of Hoodoos is amazing. Large scoops of Blue Bunny ice cream housed nicely into homemade waffle cones. Hoodoos is a straight shooter in the world of great ice cream shops.

SPRINGDALE CANDY COMPANY

ICE CREAM, CANDY STORE, 855A Zion Park Blvd, Springdale, UT 84767, (435) 772-0485, springdalecandycompany. com, open daily, 11am - 9pm, Wed from 3pm - 9pm

Time for something sweet? Springdale Candy Company will have what you are looking for, no matter what that might be. They offer chocolates, caramels, brittles, English toffee, and peppermint bark along with a wide assortment of ice cream flavors and other fun treats. Huckleberry is their signature flavor.

ZION PARK GIFT & DELI

ICE CREAM, 866 Zion Park Blvd, Springdale, UT 84767, (435) 772-3843, zionparkgiftdeli.com, open daily 8:30am – 9pm, Sunday opens at 2pm

Ice cream, fudge, toffees, plus deli sandwiches on freshly home-baked bread. This is a typical tourist-oriented shop but does a good job of delivering treats, souvenirs, and sandwiches.

DEEP CREEK COFFEE

COFFEE, 932 Zion Park Blvd, Springdale, UT 84767, (435) 767-0272, deepcreekcoffee.com, open daily, 6am - 8pm

Deep Creek Coffee is a great local haunt. They offer truly excellent espresso drinks, with rich flavor, fantastic microfoam and with a touch of latte art. The atmosphere is laid back and seemingly distanced from the usual tourist bustle. Deep Creek also offers some awesome breakfast and lunch items. One signature item is the "bro-to," a gourmet breakfast burrito.

125

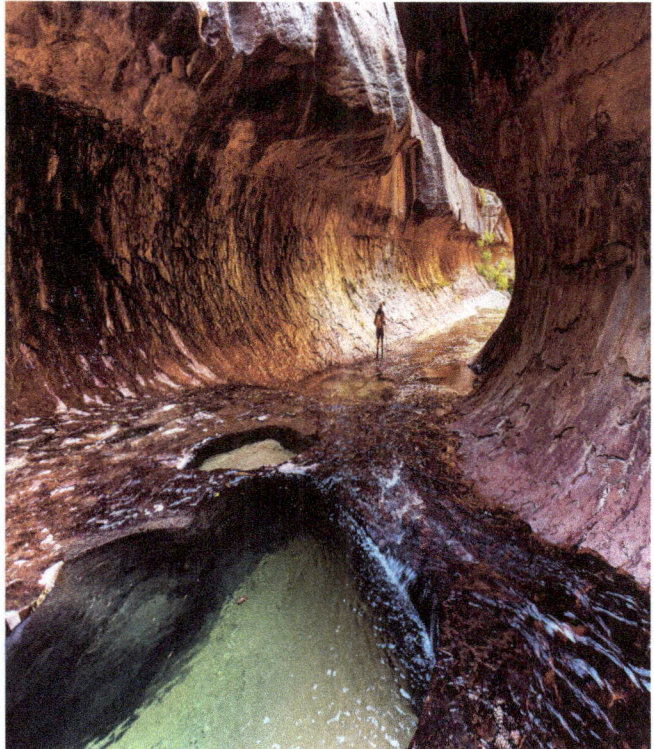

The Subway

Side Trip 9 – The Living Past

BEST FROM

Possible from both North and South Rim. South Rim will be a more direct route.

What You'll See

- Canyon de Chelly National Monument
- Hubbell Trading Post National Historic Site

WHY CHOOSE THIS SIDE TRIP

This is my personal favorite side trip overall. It is the path less traveled, yet filled with destinations worthy of the amazing journey. The trip takes you into the heart of the Navajo Nation which is in many ways like traveling to a foreign country. Here you will see odd rock formations, like Elephants Feet, along with long miles of empty desert landscape, which offers a peaceful, yet forlorn vibe.

The first destination is Canyon de Chelly National Monument, one of the longest continuously habituated areas in North America. This monument is truly unique. It is the only park wholly owned and managed by the Navajo, who charge no entrance fee and offer paid tours of the valley floor. It is a park where indigenous farming practices continue in harmony with the earth. There is no other park quite like it in the United States.

The next stop is Hubbell Trading Post National Historic Site, where again, the traditions of the past merge with the present. This active trading post is both a museum and mercantile, selling locally made baskets, rugs, pottery, and jewelry. From Hubbel Trading Post the journey exits from the world of the Navajo back to the civilization of either Phoenix or Flagstaff, Arizona.

This trip admittedly is aimed at those looking for a little more adventure. The Navajo and Hopi country is within the United States, but in many ways, is completely different. There are long stretches without services and even when available, are often limited. This is also one of the longest side trips, with over 400 miles of total travel.

ALLOW

- Recommended: 3-4 days.
- Driving time: 7 hours
- Canyon de Chelly: 1-2 days
- Hubbell Trading Post: 1-2 hours

The official drive time is about 7 hours; however, time seems to slow down within the Navajo Nation. There is a fair amount of unexpected discovery to be had, so allow a couple of extra hours when driving to Canyon de Chelly and from Hubbell. Allow 2 days at Canyon de Chelly to take one of the guided tours, which are highly recommended. This will require a night of camping, which will also offer up the Milky Way and its blanket of stars under one of the darkest sky areas in the Southwest. If you are stretched for time, you can pull up and have a look down into the villages at the bottom of the canyon from the rim, which would reduce the visit to a day trip.

Can be combined with

Side Trip 1 - "Ancient Lands" and Side Trip 2 - "Mystical Sedona" side trips

CANYON DE CHELLY NATIONAL MONUMENT

Having written about nearly every park in the Southwest, all of them remarkable, there are a few still that are truly unique. Canyon de Chelly is one of these places. The land was established by the National Park Service in 1931 but is not federally owned. Chelly is a Spanish interpretation of the Navajo word Tséyi' which means "inside the rock." This series of finger canyons have been home to a history of people for over 5000 years. Today, 40 Navajo families live and farm the land. In many respects, the ways of the past are the way of the present here. To peer over the edge is to catch a glimpse of the ancient past. To take a guided tour is to bring this past into the present.

Canyon de Chelly is entirely operated by the Navajo Nation and is the only park to be operated in this manner. As it is also home to a living farming community and as such, there are restrictions in visiting the park. In visiting, the most common approach is to take one of the two scenic drives and gaze over one of the ten overlooks. That said, private tours offer a more immersive experience. There are many tour operators

Exterior of Hubbell Trading Post

THE LIVING PAST

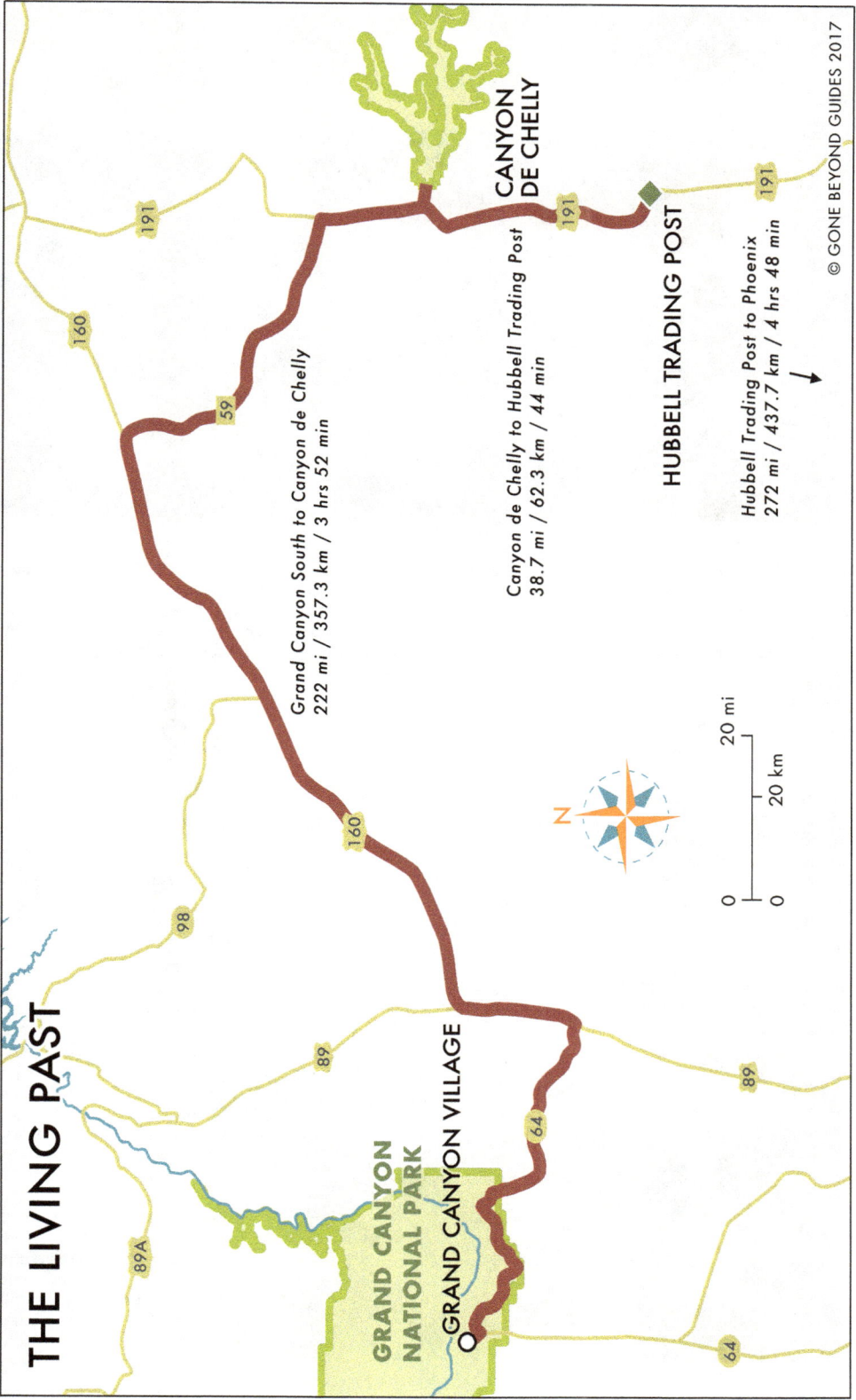

CANYON
DE CHELLY

HUBBELL TRADING POST

Grand Canyon South to Canyon de Chelly
222 mi / 357.3 km / 3 hrs 52 min

Canyon de Chelly to Hubbell Trading Post
38.7 mi / 62.3 km / 44 min

Hubbell Trading Post to Phoenix
272 mi / 437.7 km / 4 hrs 48 min

GRAND CANYON
NATIONAL PARK

GRAND CANYON VILLAGE

20 mi

20 km

© GONE BEYOND GUIDES 2017

127

and many options, including overnight camping, horseback riding, and backcountry backpacking with guide and jeep tours. To ensure you are able to get the tour you want, it is highly advisable to make reservations. There is no entrance fee to the park.

White House Trail is the only established hike in the park. All backcountry travel must have a backcountry permit and be accompanied by an authorized guide. Off-road vehicles are prohibited in the park. All this is to protect the privacy of the residents.

On the subject of privacy, don't be frustrated if you are asked to not photograph the residents and their homes, etc. This is living cultural preserve. To allow a window into the lives of these people is rare enough, enjoy the tour for what it is. If that doesn't help, imagine what your life would be like if you had a parade of people coming to your house in jeeps and horses to watch your activities every single day. It makes sense when you turn this reality around. This is a very unique experience from that context. If you are a photographer, it is very frustrating as there are some amazing shots. That said, be respectful of their wishes.

Camping is available at the park, with 93 tent/RV sites, flush toilets, drinking water, dump station, no hookups, and some pull thru sites. These are offered on a first come-first served basis. The visitor center is open daily from 8am to 5pm, except for major holidays and severe weather.

HIKING CANYON DE CHELLY NATIONAL MONUMENT

As stated above, except for the trail listed below, all backcountry hiking requires an authorized guide and a backcountry permit.

WHITE HOUSE TRAIL

Strenuous – (2.5 mi / 4.0 km), round trip, allow 2 hours

This there and back trail follows a series of switchbacks 600 feet down to the canyon floor. There are one tunnel and a bridge at the bottom to cross, with the end of the trail being the magnificent White House Ruins. What makes this set of ruins so stunning is a large water stained cliff wall that towers above the cliff dwelling and floor ruins. The ruins themselves are well preserved, and some of the exterior walls still have the original plaster. There is a fence at the perimeter of the ruins to help protect them.

White House Ruins Trail

Sunrise at Spider Rock within Canyon de Chelly National Monument

The fresh green colors of mature Cottonwood trees and cacti create an uplifting and peaceful setting against the reds and dark stains of the sandstone that frame them. Bottom line, though there is but one hike in Canyon de Chelly, this one does not disappoint.

HUBBELL TRADING POST NATIONAL HISTORIC SITE

Talk about a unique place, Hubbell Trading Post was created as a center for the Navajo to trade and sell their wares to the outside world. At the center of it all was John Lorenzo Hubbell, who in 1878, purchased the trading post making it a focal point of trade. Ten years earlier in 1868, the Navajo were decimated as a people and in a depression economically. After the Long Walk of the Navajo, a torturous journey where the Navajo were forced to walk 13 miles a day under poor conditions, they returned to their lands to find their fields and cattle stripped. They rebuilt from what they had left and to obtain goods they didn't have, they traded. The Hubbell Trading Post became a major aspect in this part of their history.

Today, the 160-acre Hubbell homestead is protected as a National Historic Park. It includes the trading post, Hubbell's family home, and some outbuildings. Tours of Hubbell's home are given for $5. What is especially amazing is that the park is also a living cultural preserve. The ranch and the trading post are still active. On the ranch, one can see Navajo Churro Sheep, horses, and chickens. The overall vibe of the trading post is similar to a museum where you can purchase the artifacts that you see. Nearly all of the items displayed are available for purchase and are authentic. Auctions of items are also held twice a year. Hubbell's is truly a gem within the Grand Circle.

Hubbell Trading Post is open 8am to 6pm April to September and 8am to 5pm October to March. This is a day use facility, with a visitor center, restrooms, and drinking water.

Hubbell Trading Post

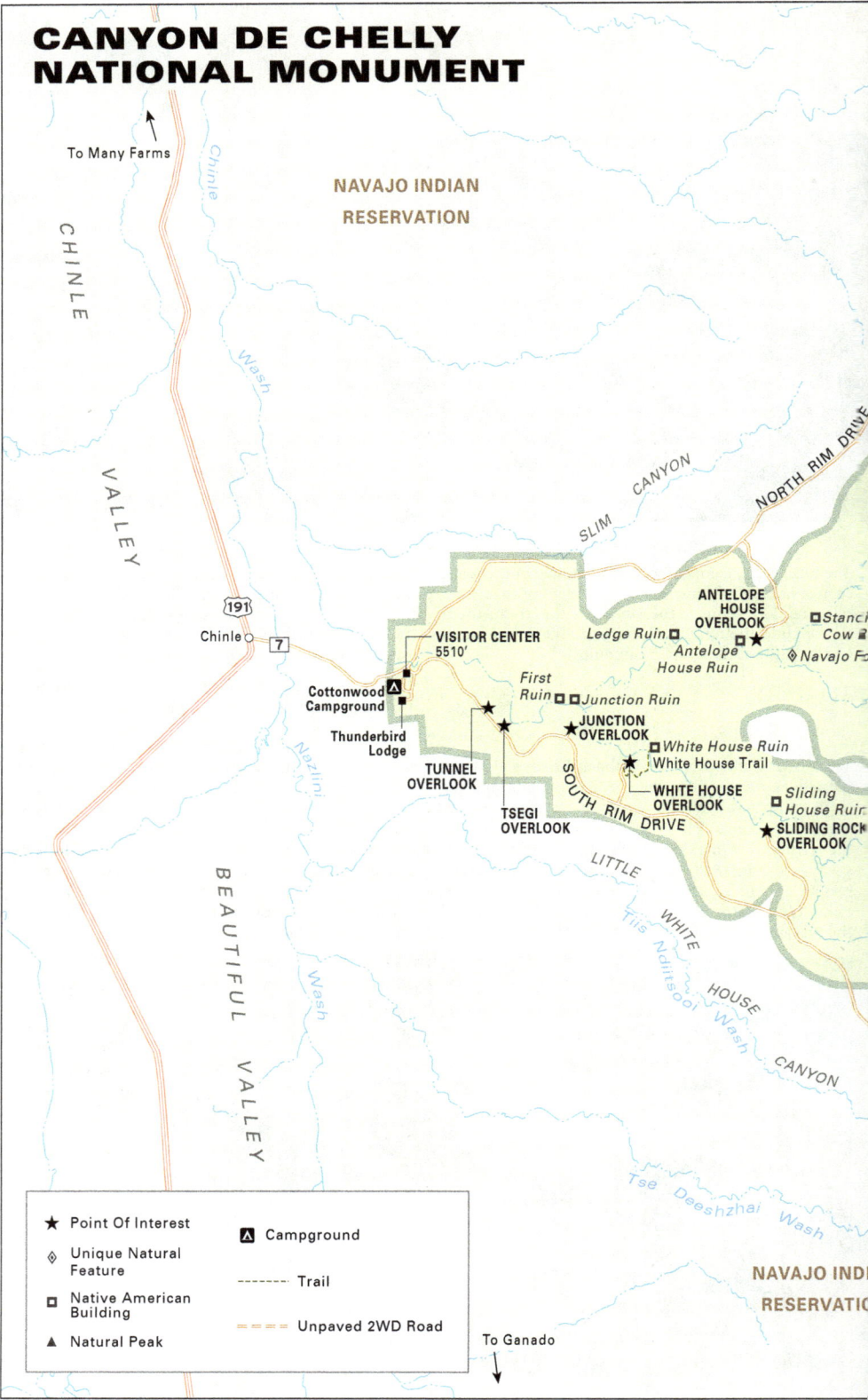

CANYON DE CHELLY
NATIONAL MONUMENT

To Many Farms

CHINLE

NAVAJO INDIAN
RESERVATION

Chinle Wash

VALLEY

130

191

Chinle

7

VISITOR CENTER
5510'

Cottonwood
Campground

Thunderbird
Lodge

TUNNEL
OVERLOOK

TSEGI
OVERLOOK

SLIM CANYON

NORTH RIM DRIVE

ANTELOPE
HOUSE
OVERLOOK

Ledge Ruin

Stand
Cow R

Antelope
House Ruin

Navajo Fo

First
Ruin

Junction Ruin

JUNCTION
OVERLOOK

White House Ruin

White House Trail

Sliding
House Ruin

WHITE HOUSE
OVERLOOK

SOUTH RIM DRIVE

SLIDING ROCK
OVERLOOK

LITTLE

WHITE

Tiis Ndiitsooí Wash

HOUSE

CANYON

Nazlini Wash

BEAUTIFUL

VALLEY

Tse Deeshzhai Wash

NAVAJO INDI
RESERVATIO

Legend

★ Point Of Interest

◈ Unique Natural
Feature

□ Native American
Building

▲ Natural Peak

🅰 Campground

------- Trail

==== Unpaved 2WD Road

To Ganado

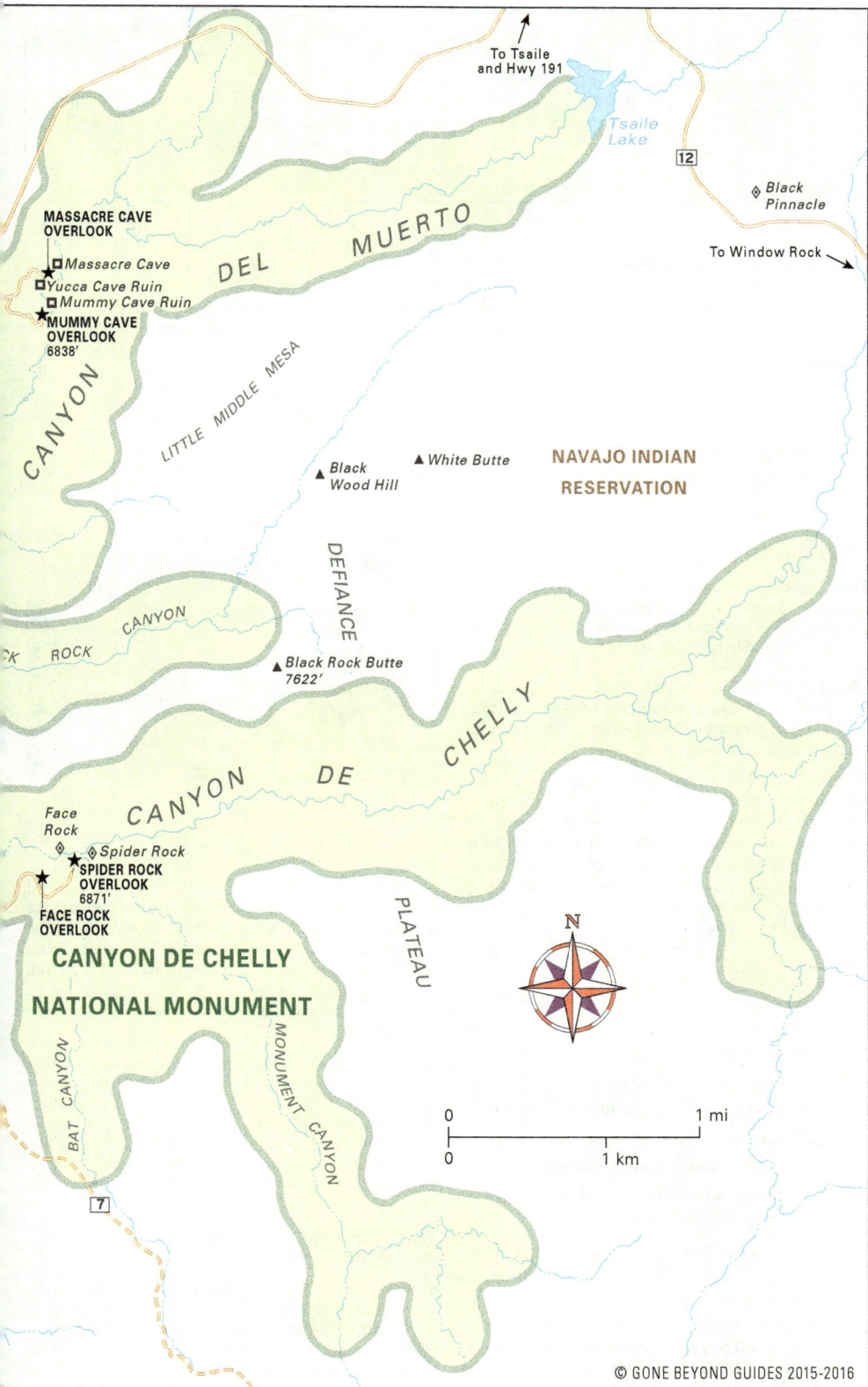

To Tsaile
and Hwy 191

*Tsaile
Lake*

12

◇ *Black
Pinnacle*

To Window Rock →

CANYON DEL MUERTO

**MASSACRE CAVE
OVERLOOK**
★
□ *Massacre Cave*
□ *Yucca Cave Ruin*
□ *Mummy Cave Ruin*
★ **MUMMY CAVE
OVERLOOK**
6838'

LITTLE MIDDLE MESA

▲ *Black
Wood Hill*

▲ *White Butte*

**NAVAJO INDIAN
RESERVATION**

DEFIANCE

ROCK CANYON

▲ *Black Rock Butte*
7622'

CANYON DE CHELLY

*Face
Rock*
◇ ◇ *Spider Rock*
★ **SPIDER ROCK
OVERLOOK**
6871'
★
**FACE ROCK
OVERLOOK**

CANYON DE CHELLY

NATIONAL MONUMENT

PLATEAU

BAT CANYON

MONUMENT CANYON

7

N

| 0 | | 1 mi |
| 0 | | 1 km |

Side Trip 10 – Vegas Baby!

BEST FROM

This leg can be done from either the South or North Rim of the Grand Canyon. Like all the side trips in this book, this trip is listed in order of appearance of parks coming from the Grand Canyon. If you are flying into Las Vegas, consider making this side trip in reverse as you head towards Grand Canyon National Park.

WHAT YOU'LL SEE

- Hoover Dam
- Valley of Fire State Park
- Las Vegas

WHY CHOOSE THIS SIDE TRIP

This is a classic vacation route. You get to gamble, drink, see shows and go clubbing. You get to peer over the edge of the Hoover Dam, maybe hike among some pretty rocks, and to top it off, you get to see that big hole in the ground everyone keeps talking about. Now that's what I'm talking about! Plus, if you do Vegas as the first stop, you may just get so much hard-core partying in that finding some peace at the Grand Canyon is just what the doctor ordered.

This route offers up an unlikely combination of nature and nightlife, but as both destinations are fun and as fun is really what vacationing is all about, this side trip has a lot to offer. On this journey, you get to do it all, from waking up married to a complete stranger and that unexplainable bobcat in the bathroom to contemplating the meaning of life as the sun sets over one of the most beautiful spots in the world. It's Vegas and the Grand Canyon, what could possibly go wrong with a trip like this?

ALLOW

- **Recommended – 3 days**
- Driving time: 6.5 hours to Las Vegas, including all described stops along the way
- Hoover Dam: Allow 2-3 hours
- Valley of Fire State Park: Allow 2-4 hours minimum for scenic drive and day hike, overnight camping is possible
- Las Vegas: Allow a minimum of 2 days, Vegas at night is completely different than during the day and worth seeing.

As hinted at above, this side trip is best done starting from Las Vegas. You can do day trips to both Hoover Dam and Valley of Fire State Park using your hotel in Vegas as a base camp. From there, head to the Grand

Canyon after you've finished with Vegas. If you are coming from the Grand Canyon, your best bet is to leave early enough to take the Hoover Dam tour find a campsite at Valley of Fire State Park or hotel in Las Vegas. Alternatively, if you skip Valley of Fire, you can cut about 90 minutes of drive time off getting to Las Vegas. This is the most popular decision. However, the Valley of Fire is an exceptional park, so if possible, try to find a place for it in your travels.

CAN BE COMBINED WITH

Side Trip 1 - "Ancient Lands" and Side Trip 2 - "Mystical Sedona."

Hoover Dam

HOOVER DAM

Hoover Dam was built over a five-year period beginning in 1931 and impounds the manmade Lake Mead, which when full, is the largest reservoir in the United States. The dam was built for hydroelectric power, flood control, and irrigation water. The design and construction of Hoover Dam were unprecedented in its size and it was the largest concrete structure to be built for its time.

The Hoover Dam facilities are still in operation today, and tours are given of both the dam itself and the power plant. They also have a visitor center that offers restrooms, maps, displays, a 10-minute film to watch on the Hoover Dam, food, and a gift shop. If you take one of the tours, you can enjoy the visitor center for free. However, if you don't take one of the tours, there is an admission fee of $10.

The visitor center is open from 9am - 5pm Pacific Standard Time. Parking is $10.

There are two tours, the first is a 30-minute tour of the power plant. The Powerplant Tour includes a 70-second elevator ride that takes the visitor over 500 feet down to the Penstock Viewing Platform where you stand on top of one of four 30-foot diameter pipes that are able

VEGAS BABY!

GRAND CANYON NATIONAL PARK

64

64

40

GRAND CANYON VILLAGE

N

0   10 mi

0   10 km

Grand Canyon South to Hoover Dam
248 mi / 399.1 km / 3 hrs 57 min

40

40

40

93

95

Hoover Dam to Valley of Fire
67.2 mi / 108.1 km / 1 hr 31 min

ARIZONA
NEVADA

VALLEY OF FIRE

HOOVER DAM / LAKE MEAD

NEVADA
ARIZONA

Valley of Fire to Las Vegas
53 mi / 85.3 km / 1 hr 2 min

167

15

15

15

LAS VEGAS

NEVADA
CALIFORNIA

15

133

to transport an incredible 90,000 gallons of water per second from Lake Mead to the generators. The tour also includes a viewing of the some of the actual generators in use. Cost per person is $12 for seniors, US military, and children ages 4-16. Adults are $15 and children under 4 are free. This tour is wheelchair accessible. The tour is not suitable for folks who suffer from claustrophobia or have a pacemaker or defibrillator.

The Hoover Dam Tour is a 1-hour guided tour of the dam itself and is $30 per person. Children under 8 are not allowed on this tour and groups are limited to 20 people total per tour. This tour includes everything you would see on the Powerplant Tour plus a navigation through tunnels to uncover historical insights and take a peek out air vents in the dam itself called inspection galleries. The guides offer an entertaining mixture of explanation, anecdotes, and history to bring about a full picture of this engineering feat.

Due to heightened security, be prepared for a TSA level of personal scrutiny before you are allowed to begin the tour. Cameras, purses, small daypacks, and tripods are okay but will be scanned. Knives and weapons of any kind are strictly not allowed. Also, no food is allowed on the tours, including chewing gum, though water bottles are okay.

VALLEY OF FIRE STATE PARK

What a park! If you are flying into Las Vegas, you have likely flown over Valley of Fire State Park as you make your final descent. It is the beacon of intriguing red sandstone that stands out amongst the dry landscape of the Mojave Desert just before landing. As amazing as it looks from the air, Valley of Fire SP is even more magnificent up close. If you can pry yourself away from the gaming tables, this park will not disappoint. Arches, slot canyons, petrified wood and candy caned striped rock formations greet the visitor. It's a no-brainer as to why this was Nevada's first state park because it is one of the coolest places in the Southwest!

The park is open each day from sunrise to sunset, except for the campground, which is open 24 hours. There is an entrance fee of $10 per vehicle. Camping is $20 per night or $30 if you use a site with RV hookups. Amenities include a visitor center, drinking water, showers, RV dump station, and restrooms. There are two campgrounds plus 3 group sites offering 72 tent/RV spots, some with power and water hookups. These are offered on a first come-first served basis.

Driving around Valley of Fire State Park is enjoyable, offering a range of jaw-dropping scenic views. For the hiker, the park also offers a great selection of trails to choose from. This park can get very hot in the summer, so plan to head out early in the morning if it's a hot day.

HIKING VALLEY OF FIRE STATE PARK

Valley of Fire State Park can get very hot in the summer and is prone to flash floods. Take all of the usual precautions when traveling or hiking in this park.

OLD ARROWHEAD ROAD

Moderate to Strenuous – (6.8 mi / 10.9 km), round trip, allow 1 hour

The Old Arrowhead Road follows the remains of the first all-weather road connecting Salt Lake City to Los Angeles, by way of Las Vegas. There is a little historical marker dedicated to this "milestone of progress." The Arrowhead Road started in 1914 and began receiving motorists in 1915. This was a novel time for the automobile; roads were being built as fast as trains were declining as the means to get around the country. It was a time when the personal freedom of being able to "hit the road" and go anywhere your car could take you was a new thought. By 1924, Highways 91 and Interstate 15 took over as the main routes. This hike encompasses some beautiful scenery. Most walk the short extension near Elephant Rock and leave the longer trail for folks who can drop one car at one end and shuttle back to the other.

Valley of Fire State Park

VALLEY OF FIRE
STATE PARK

Legend:
- ★ Point Of Interest
- ⏷ Campground
- ◈ Unique Natural Feature
- ∩ Arch
- ■ Historical Site
- --- Trail

To Interstate 15

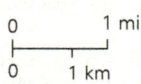

169

VALLEY OF FIRE

STATE PARK

White Domes Loop Trail
White Domes
◈ *Gibraltar Rock*
Fire Wave Trail
Fire Wave

Prospect Trail

WHITE DOMES RD

FIRE CANYON RD

★ **FIRE CANYON OVERLOOK**

Rainbow Vista Trail

★ **RAINBOW VISTA**

Mouse's Tank/ Petroglyph Canyon Trail

∩ *Ephemeral Arch*

Pinnacles

Loop Trail

Pinnacles

VISITOR CENTER

Balancing Rock Trail

Seven Sisters

Cabins

Natural Arches Trail

Elephant Rock Loop Trail

∩ **Entrance Station**

VALLEY OF FIRE HWY

Elephant Rock

Atlatl Rock
Arch Rock ∩

Old Arrowhead Road Trail

Petrified Log

Charlie's Spring Trail

Firecave ⏷

Petrified Logs

Petrified Logs Loop Trail

◈ *Beehives*

⏷ **Group Camping**
(by reservation)

To Interstate 15

■ **Entrance Station**

N

0   1 mi
0   1 km

167

LAKE MEAD

NATIONAL

RECREATION

AREA

To Las Vegas

Lake Mead

PETRIFIED LOGS LOOP

Easy – (0.3 mi / 0.5 km), round trip, allow 15 to 30 minutes

This short interpretive trail is described for one reason; petrified logs are downright awesome. Simply put, this area was once part of a supercontinent called Pangea that sat near the equator. Mind you, this was 225 million years ago, but still, nothing puts context that there used to be an ancient pine forest here than the physical testimony of petrified logs. There are two locations where the logs can be viewed and interpretive signs along the way.

Along the Fire Wave Trail

136

PINNACLES LOOP

Moderate to Strenuous – (4.5 mi / 7.2 km), round trip, allow 1 hour

This is a great remote hike, with possibilities of seeing no other hiker. From the trailhead near the Atlatl Rock parking area, head up the main wash, following marked signs. You'll enter into an area of sharp pinnacles, with tons of exploration possibilities. There is some scrambling, and the trail does get faint in areas as you make your way through the pinnacles and back down an alluvial fan to the parking lot.

PROSPECT TRAIL

Moderate to Strenuous – (4.6 mi / 7.4 km), one way, allow 2-3 hours

The Prospect Trail is another there and back trail with one end starting at the White Domes parking area and the other end at Highway 169 near the Petrified Logs area. This trail is best done with two cars and is easier, (downhill) if you start from the White Domes parking lot. Prospect Trail gives a sense of deep immersion into the park's wilderness and is one of the best hikes for feeling remote and "away from it all." It starts by following nearly half of the White Dome Trail before continuing south at the White Dome/Prospect Trail fork. From here, the trail continues to navigate through cross channels and small canyons. There is some scrambling at a few stretches along this part, but nothing major. For the last stretch, the trail empties into an alluvial fan that will need to be crossed to connect to the Valley of Fire Highway 169.

BALANCING ROCK

Easy – (0.1 mi / 0.2 km), round trip, allow 15 minutes

If you make a stop at the visitor center, be sure to take this short trail to a large precariously tilted square shaped rock that looks as if at any moment it will fall over, crushing any and all in its path. Great photo op!

MOUSE'S TANK

Easy – (1.4 mi / 2.3 km), round trip, allow 30 minutes

Mouse's Tank and Atlatl Rock together hold some of the largest concentrations of petroglyphs in Nevada comprising of historical markings by different cultural groups, with some being 3,000 years old.

The trail is quite sandy and typically very busy. Either try to go at sun up or just as the sun is setting to minimize crowds. Petroglyphs tend to be more noticeable in indirect light such as an overcast day and with a fair amount of patience. Missing the less obvious ones is easy. Pay particular attention to the north face of canyon walls, there are literally thousands of various symbols and artistic figures. Some are closer to eye level, while others are high up on cliff faces, as if as a test of bravery.

The trail ends at a natural round stone tank that holds water year-round in all but the driest of years. It is named after a Southern Paiute Indian named "Little Mouse," who used this location to hide out in the 1890's. Little Mouse was known for thievery and general local nuisance. going on occasional drunken bouts of craziness. He hid out in the area because he was accused of murdering two prospectors. Whether he actually did or not is not actually known, though it is known he was surrounded a few miles away and in refusing to give up, was shot and killed.

RAINBOW VISTA

Moderate – (2.1 mi / 3.4 km), round trip, allow 1-2 hours

Most take this hike to get a great view of Fire Canyon from the overlook at the end of this there and back trail. This trail offers full immersion up a small canyon, with stunning rock formations along the way. The trailhead itself is a great pull off spot to take pictures of the landscape to the north, which can be quite inviting under mixed lighting conditions, especially in the spring after a storm. The one downside to this hike is that the trail floor is deep sand, making the going a bit harder. Once inside the canyon and towards the end of Fire Canyon overlook, there are caves and other nooks and crannies to explore.

WHITE DOMES LOOP

Moderate – (1.0 mi / 1.6 km), round trip, allow 45 minutes to 1 hour

The White Domes Loop highlights the diversity of the park's contrasting rock, with just about every color in the sandstone palate. There is a bit of minor rock scrambling involved that leads to a little slot canyon. The slot canyon is just 0.25 miles long but is pleasantly narrow. As you make your way back on the loop, look for an arch.

The one other aspect of this trail is the ruin of a stone building, which was used in the 1966 movie, "The Professionals," starring Lee Marvin and Burt Lancaster. The movie was about a kidnapped wife of a Texas millionaire, who hires four rough and tumble characters to get her back. It was nominated for three Academy Awards.

FIRE WAVE TRAIL

Moderate to Strenuous – (1.3 mi / 2.1 km), round trip, allow 1 hour

This hike is certainly one of the top picks in terms of great hikes. It is the unique sandstone formations that really make this hike outstanding, which is saying something, as there are many unique rock formations in Valley of Fire. The highlights of the hike are swirls of red and white rock layers that have then been eroded into graceful curving formations of slickrock. The rocks here defy the imagination and are a photographer's dream. While the hike itself can be done in an hour or less, give yourself more time to take in the vividly crisp colors of rock as natural art.

NATURAL ARCHES

Moderate – (5.0 mi / 8.0 km), round trip, allow 2 to 4 hours

The first thing to know about this trail is that the main attraction, a natural arch that looked like a dragon feeding her young, collapsed in 2010. It fell from natural causes, and no one was hurt. Now just the broken remnants remain. The good news is the views on this hike are stunning in their own right. The trail is on the trail map but isn't given much attention in the brochure covering the main hikes, making Natural Arches a great hike to get away from it all, even during crowded weekends.

The trail follows a sandy wash of pink and white canyon sand, deep enough in spots to test the hiker. Heading up the canyon, the wash narrows after about a mile with a few short scrambles. This portion is not well marked, but is obvious enough, despite a couple of side canyons that quickly become dead ends if you should take a wrong turn. The trail gives the hiker ample views of this amazing landscape, and while the showcase dragon arch is gone, there are a few arches to be seen that are cool in their own right. There is a humongous balancing rock 2.4 miles in that makes for a pleasant stop before heading back.

ELEPHANT ROCK LOOP

Easy – (1.2 mi / 1.9 km), round trip, allow 30 minutes

This is a super family-friendly trail that is fairly flat and easy to navigate for all ages. It is 0.4 miles round trip if you just want to see the Elephant Rock or 1.2 miles for the whole loop. The rock is just off the main highway, but parking is non-existent here, so head first to the East Entrance parking lot. From there, hike from the self-pay station and about 0.1 miles of the trail take a left to lead you right on up to Elephant Rock. The loop continues parallel to the road before bearing right and looping back around past some interesting rock formations.

CHARLIE'S SPRING TRAIL

Moderate to Strenuous – (6.7 mi / 10.8 km), round trip, allow 3-4 hours

This trail is seldom traveled and leads to a nice watery oasis fed by an underground spring. You will see tamarisk and cattails downstream of the spring before the water is reclaimed by the earth. For the most part, the trail follows an obvious wash, with one small dry waterfall and an equally small slot canyon before the reveal of the watery oasis. A one-half mile into the trail is a large memorial for John Clark, an honorably discharged Sergeant who died in route to Salt Lake City in 1915, presumably from thirst.

The journey to the spring is 2.75 miles. From here, you can either turn around or continue up the wash and bushwhack your way back. To do the latter, continue up the wash until you reach a power line road on your right coming into the wash. Take this road and continue until you see the road cross on your left and follow it up a hill and over to the next wash north of you. Continue on this wash in a northwesterly direction looking for a large solitary sandstone monolith as a marker. Once you see this outcrop, head towards it back to the highway. Head left on the Valley of Fire Highway back to your car.

LAS VEGAS

Las Vegas Welcomes You

Beyond the gambling, incredible resort hotels, nightlife, and extravagantly produced shows, you can do pretty much anything in Vegas, from shooting an AK47 assault rifle to visiting a museum entirely dedicated to the atomic bomb. The place is complete madness or completely magical, depending on one's personal sentiment towards general debauchery.

Most of the attractions, hotels, and restaurants listed here can be found in the main section of Las Vegas, referred to as The Strip. There are a few places that are just too good to not write about that are "off strip" and are certainly worth considering.

In the town's formative years, Vegas was known for its adult nightlife, centered primarily around gambling. Today, the town has something for everyone, and while it still attracts an adult crowd, there are plenty of things to do for all age groups and for families as well. The town's attractions are like movie ratings, they offer things to do that would be rated G to XXX. In keeping with the overall spirit of the book, some of the more popular "G – PG-13 attractions" are listed below. Also note that the Las Vegas shows, such as The Beatles Love and Penn and Teller (two of the author's favorites) are not listed due to space and revolving availability.

LAS VEGAS

- 🔵 Lodgings
- 🟢 Restaurants
- 🟠 Coffee and Sweets
- ⭐ Things to do

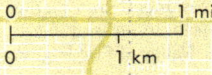

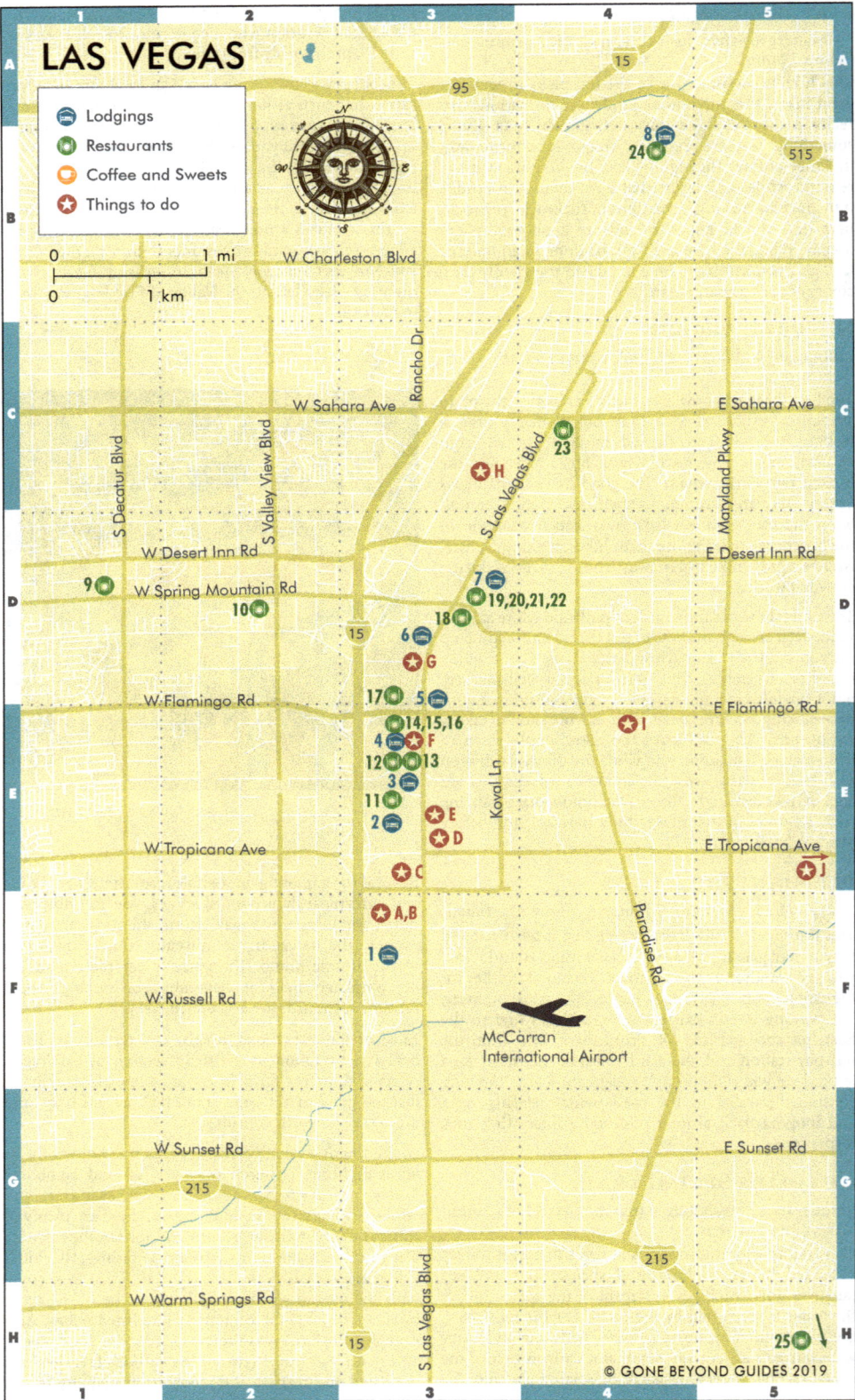

0   1 mi

0   1 km

95

15

515

W Charleston Blvd

W Sahara Ave   E Sahara Ave

Rancho Dr

S Decatur Blvd

S Valley View Blvd

S Las Vegas Blvd

Maryland Pkwy

23

H

W Desert Inn Rd   E Desert Inn Rd

9

W Spring Mountain Rd

10

7
19,20,21,22
18
6
G
15
17   5

W Flamingo Rd   E Flamingo Rd

14,15,16
4   F
12   13
3
11
2
E
D

Koval Ln

I

W Tropicana Ave   E Tropicana Ave

C

J

A,B

1

Paradise Rd

McCarran
International Airport

W Russell Rd

W Sunset Rd   E Sunset Rd

215

215

W Warm Springs Rd

15

25

S Las Vegas Blvd

© GONE BEYOND GUIDES 2019

138

Friendly Attractions in Vegas

Tournament of Kings

3850 S. Las Vegas Blvd. Las Vegas, NV 89109, (702) 597-7777, www.excalibur.com

A fun choice is the medieval jousting and dinner at the Tournament of Kings. Held at the Excalibur Hotel, this is a cool dining experience ("wenches" serve up "dragon's milk," and you have to eat your three-course meal entirely with your hands). In addition to the tasty fare, you get to enjoy a very entertaining show. Your seat location doubles as the country you represent as you watch the knights of each territory battle it out for one victor and then rally their efforts against an invading army that has a dragon on its side. The whole event, with fireworks, swordplay, and flamethrowers is quite a spectacle.

M&M's World

3785 S Las Vegas Blvd, Las Vegas, NV 89109, (702) 736.-7611, www.mmsworld.com

M&M's World is four stories of M&M chocolate paradise. Each story has a different theme, and there is something for everybody. Sure, there are logo T-shirts and, of course, there are M&M's themselves, but there is much more at M&M's World. We are talking logo Frisbees, dice, laptop covers, pens, socks, lip gloss, luggage, aprons, beachwear, and even M&M's spatulas and measuring cups. You start wondering how your kitchen would look if you just went crazy with an "M&M's Everything" theme.

You can get your own personalized M&M's candy, up to eight characters and two lines on every candy. You can choose from a wall of 22 M&M's dispensers and even watch the World's main characters, "Red" and "Yellow," in a free 3D movie that runs throughout the day called "I Lost My M in Vegas." The show combines live actors with a movie and runs about 10 minutes.

Titanic: The Artifact Exhibition

3900 S. Las Vegas Blvd. Las Vegas, NV 89109, (702) 492-3960, www.luxor.com

The intention of this exhibit is simple, to bring the history of the Titanic to life. With more than 300 artifacts and large replicas of portions of the ship, the visitor is swept back in time. The items include personal effects from the passengers as well as their emotional stories. The largest and most impressive item on display is the "Big Piece." Part of the ship's hull, this is the largest item retrieved from the wreckage. Weighing two tons, it took two days just to get the hull into its present location at the Luxor Hotel.

To make the journey even more interactive, both children and adults are given a keepsake that characterizes an actual passenger who was on the ship during its fated voyage. The keepsakes represent all manner of passengers both rich and poor. After the tour is over everyone can learn whether his or her passenger lived or was one of 1523 folks who did not make it.

139

M&M World

Las Vegas

Lodging

1 Mandalay Bay Resort.....................F3
2 Monte Carlo Hotel and Casino..................E3
3 ARIA Resort & Casino.......................E3
4 Bellagio Hotel and Casino...................E3
5 Flamingo Las Vegas.......................D3
6 The Mirage..........................D3
7 Wynn Las Vegas.......................D3
8 Golden Nugget Hotel & Casino.................D4

Things To Do

A Titanic The Artifact Exhibition..............F3
B Bodies...The Exhibition..................F3
C Tournament of Kings....................E3
D CSI: The Experience.....................E3
E M&M's World.......................E3
F Fountains of Bellagio...................E3
G Mirage Volcano......................D3
H Adventuredome Theme Park............C3
I The National Atomic Testing Museum........E4
J The Gun Store.......................E5

Restaurants

9 Raku................................D1
10 Chengdu Taste.......................D2
11 Bardot Brasserie.....................E3
12 Beauty & Essex.....................E3
13 Jaleo..............................E3
14 Harvest by Roy Ellamar...............E3
15 Le Cirque..........................E3
16 Picasso............................E3
17 Restaurant Guy Savoy................D3
18 Morels French Steakhouse & Bistro....D3
19 Costa Di Mare......................D3
20 SW Steakhouse.....................D3
21 Mizumi.............................D3
22 Andrea's...........................D3
23 Bazaar Meat by Jose Andres...........C4
24 Vic & Anthony's Steakhouse...........B4
25 Kaiseki Yuzu........................H5

The Bellagio

high-ceilinged dome with natural lighting that is itself impressive. The place has just about everything you would expect to find in a theme park, including thrill rides, laser tag, miniature golf, clown shows, bumper cars and other assorted carnival rides. Be sure to try El Loco, which ascends 70 feet before diving downward and backward at 1.5 Gs.

MIRAGE VOLCANO

3400 S. Las Vegas Blvd. Las Vegas, NV 89109

The Mirage volcano operates nightly starting at 6pm running until 11pm on the hour. This attraction has been around since 1989, and it may seem a bit trite, but the Mirage has done a great job of keeping this free attraction relevant. In 2008, they did a $25 million redesign, leveraging WET, the same team responsible for The Fountains of Bellagio. They even hired ex-Grateful Dead drummer Mickey Hart, who, along with composer Zakir Hussain, created a soundtrack made specifically for the event. It's well worth watching and still impressive after all these years.

THE FOUNTAINS OF BELLAGIO

3600 S. Las Vegas Blvd. Las Vegas, NV 89109

This free attraction, found in front of the Bellagio Hotel, has become one of the most recognized and filmed attractions on the strip. It is not unusual to find yourself lost in the choreography of water as it shoots and dances in the air in unison to more than 30 songs. The lake itself is an impressive 375,000 square feet, equivalent to eight football fields. The amount of water in the lake could fill 2,000 swimming pools. There are 1,214 fountain shooters, capable of jetting higher than a 24-story building. At the peak of the fountains display, there are more than 17,000 gallons of water in the air. Impressive stuff and a must-see attraction. The fountain runs more often on the weekends, running every 15 minutes from 7pm to midnight.

SHOOTING THE AK 47

Bring cash and a drivers license to The Gun Store (2900 E. Tropicana. Las Vegas, (702) 454-1110, thegunstorelasvegas.com) to shoot anything from a machine gun, AK47 or any number of other firearms, assault or otherwise. They even have a ladies' night on Friday's and Saturdays, where if you rent one firearm, your special someone gets one free rental of her choice.

THE ATOMIC BOMB MUSEUM

The Atomic Test Museum (755 E Flamingo Road, Las Vegas, (702) 794-5151, nationalatomictestingmuseum. org) houses over 12,000 artifacts dedicated to atomic testing, atomic bomb development, how radiation is checked, and other mind-blowing facts. It's typically open from 10am – 5pm and costs $22 for adults, $16 for ages 7-14 and free for those under $7. Best bet is to get the family pack (which admits 2 adults and 3 children) for $65.

BODIES...THE EXHIBITION

3900 S. Las Vegas Blvd., Las Vegas, NV 89109, (702) 492-3960, www.luxor.com

Okay, yuck right? Who wants to see a bunch of exhumed bodies stretched out in odd poses? Well, not so fast. The attraction displays a very tasteful and unique view of well, you. If you were ever the slightest bit curious as to what you might look like on the inside, then come see Bodies. More than just a science lab gone wrong, the many examples of the internal human in 3D are highly educational just by viewing them. Alongside the visual are equally interesting quick facts on the wall.

There are exhibits on the nervous system showing the extensive set of nerves that make up our body. There is also a smoking exhibit that shows the lungs of a smoker compared to those of a non-smoker. The smoking exhibit is so motivational, the Luxor put a bin to throw out your cigarettes next to it, should you choose. There are nine rooms in total, representing different parts of the body, including the circulatory, digestive, muscular, nervous, and respiratory systems. Off in its own private area is a section devoted to fetal development. Visitors can see the different stages of fetal development from eight weeks old to eight months. As this is a sensitive topic, the section is housed in a private area that can be bypassed at the visitor's discretion.

CSI: THE EXPERIENCE

MGM Grand, 3799 S. Las Vegas Blvd., Las Vegas, NV 89109, (877) 660-0660, www.mgmgrand.com

Have you ever watched a murder mystery on TV and thought you would have made a good crime investigator? CSI: The Experience puts that thought to the test. You are given forensic evidence and other clues to help you solve a case. This is a real hit with the younger kids; teenagers may find the clues a bit too straightforward.

ADVENTUREDOME AT CIRCUS CIRCUS

2880 S. Las Vegas Blvd., Las Vegas, NV 89109, (800) 444-2472, www.circuscircus.com

Adventuredome, the largest indoor theme park in the United States, should get your family's attention. The five-and-one-half-acre complex starts with a

Lodging

MANDALAY BAY RESORT AND CASINO

3950 Las Vegas Blvd. South, Las Vegas, NV 89119, (702) 632.7777, mandalaybay.com

Mandalay Bay is the best hotel because of the pools. With three pools and several hot tubs, the quantity alone is fun for kids and adults alike to explore. But what really sets Mandalay Bay apart are the wave pool and the lazy river. The wave pool is 1.6 million gallons of artificial wave fun, though bodysurfing the small waves is best for the little ones.

The shore of this beach is lined with real sand. Yes, you can build sand castles in Vegas. There also is a wading pool for little ones off to the side of the wave pool area. The layout for this section is nice as it allows small children the ability to have fun without parents worrying about them drifting into the deep end.

The lazy river is almost a quarter mile (0.4 km) of gently flowing water. You can rent or buy an inner tube and float to your heart's content. There are a vast number of pool chairs to be had, though the ones closest to the "beach" and lazy river are prime real estate, so arrive early if you want those.

PARK MGM LAS VEGAS

3770 Las Vegas Blvd. South, Las Vegas, NV 89109, (702) 730-7777, montecarlo.com

The Monte Carlo Resort pools are a close second to those of Mandalay Bay. The Monte Carlo also has a wave pool and a 400-foot long lazy river. Also, there is a kiddie/wading pool for the smaller children. A special treat for the kids in this area is lounge chairs that are right-sized for them.

The downside of Monte Carlo is its size. The lazy river is about 1/3 the size of Mandalay Bay's. This reduction in size is an overall trend for the resort's pool area but feeling cramped is perhaps its only complaint. If Monte Carlo has a resort pool, Mandalay Bay has a resort water park.

It must be said for both resorts, on a hot day the lazy river can turn into a "crazy river" by mid-morning. Be prepared to leave the notion of serenely gliding alone along blissfully cool waters at the pool gates.

Mandalay Bay

THE MIRAGE

3400 S. Las Vegas Blvd, Las Vegas, NV 89109, (702) 791-7111, mirage.com

The Mirage breaks from the waves and lazy rivers, offering a combination of lush foliage and waterfalls instead. The feel is tropical and relaxing and yet still includes a separate family pool with a small waterslide. At the Mirage, the kids will thoroughly enjoy themselves at the pool while parents unwind amongst the illusion of island tropics. Two other pluses: the pools are heated and stay open an hour later (until 8pm) than the pools at Mandalay Bay and the Monte Carlo.

What tips this over the edge as the choice for many parents are Siegfried and Roy's Secret Garden and Dolphin Habitat. Both attractions are favorites with kids. If you have a budding dolphin trainer or zoologist in your group, staying at the Mirage puts you closest to this attraction.

GOLDEN NUGGET HOTEL AND CASINO

129 E. Fremont St, Las Vegas, NV 89101, (702) 385-7111, goldennugget.com

There are two outdoor pools at the Golden Nugget, the Tank, and the Hideout. As you may have guessed, the Hideout is for folks 16 years and older. The Tank, however, was made for kids and grownups who still have a bit of kid in them.

141

The Tank allows you to slide three stories down a transparent waterslide through a 200,000-gallon aquarium. While the biggest attractions within the aquarium are full sized sharks and rays, there are over 300 species within the ecosystem. The Tank is the centerpiece of the pool area; the pool sits around the aquarium. The waterslide tunnel put the Golden Nugget on the map for cool pools and was listed as one of American's Most Amazing Hotel Pools" by CNN. The pool is heated year-round.

THE FLAMINGO

3555 Las Vegas Blvd. South, Las Vegas, NV 89109, (702) 733-3111, caesars.com

The Flamingo has 15 acres of pool and wildlife habitats webbed in a labyrinth of water slides and footpaths. The Flamingo's swimming area is like that of Mandalay Bay, a water park. There are pools, waterslides, waterfalls and creature comforts at the nearby Club Cafe. The lush, picturesque grounds are home to silver pheasants, penguins and, of course, flamingos, which visitors discover as they walk among the maze-like layout of the pool area. The paths themselves are invitations to explore and, once done, there are ledges to claim and relax on within this multilevel area.

If your children love waterslides, finding every one of them is as much fun as sliding down them. The mazes and the waterslides provide hours of fun, and the secluded grottos allow for equal time to just unwind and relax. There is a small but secluded wading pool for the little ones as well.

ARIA RESORT & CASINO LAS VEGAS

3730 S Las Vegas Blvd, Las Vegas, NV 89158, (866) 359-7111, aria.com

Aria Resort is a 5-star hotel and one of the newer properties in Las Vegas. It is chic, hip and modern, expressing a seen and be seen atmosphere. Amenities include 3 pools with cabanas, including the Liquid Lounge for adults only that hosts a DJ, signature drinks and a plethora of single folks trying to be not-single, if only for a brief period. The resort also hosts a hair salon, spa, and a sizeable collection of mostly fine modern art. Aria offers eleven dining options that range from bakery to buffet to fine dining.

WYNN LAS VEGAS

3131 S Las Vegas Blvd, Las Vegas, NV 89109, (702) 770-7000, wynnlasvegas.com

Wynn Las Vegas is one of the highest rated 5-star hotels in the world, and it shows. From shopping, dining, or just walking the grounds, it is an experience in over the top elegance. The resort sits on over 200 acres and is, in fact, two hotels, the Wynn Las Vegas and Encore Las Vegas, both owned by Wynn Resorts Limited. While they both share many of the same amenities and standards of excellence, Encore offers larger rooms.

The property houses shops, salons, fitness centers, pools, some of the finest dining in town, golf packages at the nearby Wynn Golf Club, and spas at both Wynn and Encore. There is far too much to list everything here, but just within the subject of shops, we are talking the biggest name shops like Cartier, Dior, and Lois Vuitton. Again, the entire experience is designed to be over the top best of the best. The best way to take advantage of a stay at either resort is to make a reservation with their concierge services. This will allow you to make the most of your experience.

BELLAGIO HOTEL AND CASINO

3600 S Las Vegas Blvd, Las Vegas, NV 89109, (888) 987-6667, bellagio.com

Bellagio is almost soothing in its approach as a 4-star resort experience, offering over eleven restaurants, spa, golf packages, pools, bars, and more. The ambiance is Mediterranean meets luxury making the hotel one of the top destinations in Vegas. Bellagio is centrally located to many of the other casinos and attractions on the strip.

Restaurants include Harvest by Roy Ellamar, Le Cirque, and Picasso (described below), the small Italian plate style offering of Lago, fine Sichuan (Szechaun) and Hunan Chinese cuisine at Jasmine, modern Japanese at Yellowtail, along with several other dining establishments worthy of a visit

As mentioned before, there is also the watery elegance of the Bellagio Fountains, which are worth seeing even if you don't stay at the hotel. The Bellagio is one of the first in high end elegance at Las Vegas and has held up well, providing a timeless architecture and experience.

Because of the backdrop of the hotel and its fountains, Bellagio also continues to be a favorite for weddings as well. It's always fun to watch young couples in love.

Restaurants

CHENGDU TASTE

SICHUAN CHINESE, $, 3950 Schiff Dr, Las Vegas, NV 89103, (702) 437-7888, chengdutastelasvegas.com, open daily 11am - 3pm, and 5pm-10pm

Mung bean jelly noodle with chili sauce, cumin lamb, and twice cooked pork are just some of the delicious menu items at Chengdu Taste. Located just off The Strip in a mini-mall in Vegas' Chinatown, this is the best Sichuan Chinese in Las Vegas. It will leave you wishing your local Chinese takeout place was as good!

RAKU

JAPANESE, $$, 5030 Spring Mountain Road, Las Vegas, NV 89146, (702) 367-3511, raku-grill.com, open Monday thru Saturday 6pm - 3am, closed Sun

Aburiya Raku is Japanese for "Charcoal Grill House Enjoyment," which is exactly what chef Mitsuo Endo serves in his small restaurant. Raku is a completely different side of Japanese cuisine. Do expect a wide choice of sakes and authentic Japanese dishes cooked over a charcoal robata grill. Don't expect to find sushi here. The plates are small and start at $3, so come with an expectation to order a wide variety of foods to enjoy. You'll feel like you are feasting like an emperor!

COSTA DI MARE

ITALIAN, $$$$, 3131 Las Vegas Blvd S, Las Vegas, NV 89109, (702) 770-3305, wynnlasvegas.com, open daily 5:30 - 10pm

From the moment you walk inside Costa di Mare, you know a special experience lies ahead. The décor is absolutely magnificent, done in a hip Mediterranean style. Located within the Wynn, Chef Mark LoRusso offers homemade pasta and a selection of over 40 fish that are locally caught off Italian shores and flown in. The service matches the incredible ambiance. A good place to spend some of your winnings if you love seafood.

ANDREA'S

ASIAN FUSION, $$, 3131 S Las Vegas Blvd, Las Vegas, NV 89109, (702) 770-5340, wynnlasvegas.com, open daily 6 - 10:30pm, Friday and Saturday until 11:30pm

Andreas is another of the Wynn Las Vegas restaurants. Here the lively ambiance of nightclub pair with an Asian fusion menu, offering an assortment of spicy and savory dishes. From oysters, sushi rolls, steaks, seafood, seared foie gras, and even spicy Jidori fried chicken, there is something for everyone. The amazing centerpiece of the restaurant is an oversized photograph of eyes, the eyes of Steve Wynn's wife, Andrea Hissom.

BARDOT BRASSERIE

FRENCH/STEAKHOUSE, $$$, 3730 Las Vegas Blvd S, Las Vegas, NV 89158, (702) 690-8610, aria.com, open Monday thru Friday 5:30 - 10:30pm, Saturday and Sunday 9:30am- 10:30pm

Located in Aria Resort, Bardot Brasserie offers a country French bistro menu that is a collective best of the best in Parisian dining. Here you can relax with a selection of cheeses, with walnut mustard and seasonal jams or up level to a meal of Prince Edward Island mussels in garlic butter, tarragon, and vermouth. They also offer steak and chicken alongside a wide selection of champagnes, wines, and signature cocktails.

BAZAAR MEAT BY JOSÉ ANDRÉS

STEAKHOUSE, $$$$, 2535 Las Vegas Blvd S, Las Vegas, NV 89109, (855) 761-7757, slslasvegas.com, open daily 5:30 - 10pm, open to 11pm Friday and Saturday

Bazaar Meat is a steakhouse reinvented. Chef José Andrés truly went above and beyond with his selection of shared plates, from a full raw bar of oysters, abalone, and caviar, to well-prepared steak and salmon tartares,

carpaccios, and fire-roasted meats. Recommendations include the "Vaca Vieja" Ribeye tasting and for a lighter fare, try one of his signature airbread sandwiches, especially the Reuben.

BEAUTY & ESSEX

AMERICAN, $$$, 3708 Las Vegas Blvd S, Las Vegas, NV 89109, (702) 737-0707, beautyandessexlv.com, open daily 5 - 11pm, open until midnight Thursday thru Saturday

Beauty & Essex, located in The Cosmopolitan, is the work of famed chef Chris Santos, who is best known on the TV show Chopped. Chris has two other restaurants of the same name in New York and Los Angeles. The dining experience is highly upscale comfort food, that is well prepared and plated, served within an elegant ambiance. Here you can find items like Caesar toast with creamy garlic and crispy chicken skin, Thai pork belly lettuce cups, and oven-braised chicken meatballs, just to name a few items. A meal here is a unique experience to the senses and satisfying to the spirit.

MORELS FRENCH STEAKHOUSE & BISTRO

STEAKHOUSE, $$$$, 3325 Las Vegas Blvd S, Las Vegas, NV, 89109, (702) 607-6333, morelslv.com, open daily for B, L, D, hours vary

CarneVino's puts one into a very difficult place. On the one hand are their steaks, with offerings of dry and wet aged steaks along with all the classic fixings for a great steak dinner . Then there is the selection of country French dishes to consider, robust, hearty, and flavorable. Whatever you decide, be prepared for a memorable dining experience!

HARVEST BY ROY ELLAMAR

AMERICAN, $$$, The Bellagio, 3600 Las Vegas Boulevard South, Las Vegas, NV 89109, 702-693-8865, bellagio.com, open daily 5 - 10pm

Health conscious, farm to table, seasonal, sustainable, all words to describe what Roy Ellamar has created with Harvest. Let's start with the Snack Wagon, which features "creations of the moment" from invited chefs. These are served tableside, creating an atmosphere of personal attention in the most culinarily delightful way. His menu items are fresh, light, and robust in flavor. Try the Yellowtail Poke, spice rubbed lamb chops or the duck confit buns.

Model of the Titanic

JALEO

SPANISH/TAPAS, $$$, 3708 Las Vegas Blvd S, Vegas, NV 89109, (877) 293-2003, jaleo.com, open daily 12 -11pm, open until midnight Friday and Saturday

Chef José Andrés take the robust flavors of Spanish cuisine to Las Vegas with Jaleo. José serves a wide selection of tapas, paellas and an unforgettable skirt steak that will take you to another level of contentment. If you want to raise the bar even higher, reserve one of the chef's multi-course meals where you will be taken on an incredible tour of both traditional and modern Spanish cuisine.

KAISEKI YUZU

SUSHI/JAPANESE, $$, 1310 E Silverado Ranch Blvd #105, Las Vegas, NV 89183, (702) 778-8889, yuzukaiseki.com, open Monday thru Thursday 11:30am - 3 pm and 5:30 - 10:30pm, open Friday and Saturday 5pm - 1am

Chef Kaoru Azeuchi is a master in the art of kaiseki, a style of authentic Japanese cuisine of small and intricate dishes. Menu items include sushi, sashimi, nigiri, and hot and cold plates. For a full experience, order one of the Omakase, which is a selection of menu items selected by the chef. This once hidden gem is getting harder to get into, so reserve well in advance.

LE CIRQUE

FRENCH, $$$$, 3600 Las Vegas Blvd S, Vegas, NV 89109, (702) 693-8100, bellagio.com, open Tuesday thru Sunday 5 -10 pm

Located in the Bellagio, Le Cirque offers a French cuisine of fine dining, with unparalleled service and courses. The menu is a selection of prix-fixe options ranging from 3 to 10-course meals, including a pre-theater menu for those seeing Cirque du Soleil. Chef Wilfried Bergerhausen's delightful offerings have put Le Cirque on multiple award lists, including Michelin. Le Cirque also has two sommeliers on staff offering an impressive 900 wines.

PICASSO

FRENCH, $$$$, 3600 South Las Vegas Boulevard, Las Vegas, NV 89109, (702) 693-7223, bellagio.com, open daily except for Tuesdays 5:30 - 9:30pm

Picasso is located near Le Cirque in the Bellagio and also offers French cuisine from chef Julian Serrano. The menu is less encumbered by the often rigid and stuffiness of traditional fine French cuisine, mixing in Spanish offerings into a newer French menu. One huge differentiating aspect is you get to dine with actual Picasso paintings near your table. Picasso also has an outstanding selection of 1500 varieties of wine.

RESTAURANT GUY SAVOY

FRENCH, $$$$, 3570 Las Vegas Blvd S, Vegas, NV 89109, (702) 731-7286, www.guysavoy.com/en/, open Wednesday thru Sunday 5:30 - 9:30pm

Modeled after Guy Savoy's restaurant of the same name in Paris, this counterpart offers the most traditional menu within fine French dining in Vegas. If French is the finest of all food preparation, Restaurant Guy Savoy is the best of the best in town within that celebrated realm. Attire is formal here. This is an incredible experience in the art of food.

SW STEAKHOUSE

STEAKHOUSE, $$$$, 3131 Las Vegas Blvd S, Vegas, NV 89109, (888) 320-7110, wynnlasvegas.com, open daily 5:30 - 10pm

There are a lot of steakhouses in Las Vegas. If you are looking for a great steak combined with the best service for any steakhouse, head to SW Steakhouse in the Wynn. Chef David Walzog knows his way around aged Nebraska corn-fed beef but also offers Japanese Wagyu Kobe along with lamb and seafood. The ambiance of the restaurant overlooking Wynn's Lake of Dreams is a big plus.

MIZUMI

JAPANESE/KOREAN, $$$$, 3131 South Las Vegas Boulevard, Las Vegas, NV 89109, (888) 352-3463, wynnlasvegas.com, open daily 5:30 - 10pm

Sushi and sashimi along with a full Teppan menu (think Benihana, i.e. food cooked on an iron griddle). Chef Devin Hashimoto was named one of the top chefs in Vegas. Try the braised American Wagyu short ribs.

VIC & ANTHONY'S STEAKHOUSE

STEAKHOUSE, $$$$, 129 E Fremont Street, Las Vegas, NV 89101, vicandanthonys. com, (702) 386-8399, open daily 5 - 11pm

The Mirage

Located in the Golden Nugget Hotel and Casino, Vic & Anthony's is the preferred steakhouse of Vegas locals. This is a perfect steakhouse and seafood experience, in every way. The only thing missing is the "Vegas Strip premium." This is our number one choice for steak in Vegas.

145

Hiking to Havasu Falls

Side Trip 11 – Havasu Falls

BEST FROM

South Rim Grand Canyon is your best bet for this side trip. Tack on an added 3-hour drive if coming from the North Rim.

WHAT YOU WILL SEE

- Havasu Falls and Mooney Falls

WHY CHOOSE THIS SIDE TRIP

Havasu Falls is one of the absolute gems of the Southwest. The hike itself is through lightly wooded red rock canyons, leading to pools of strikingly sublime turquoise colored water, with a refreshing set of waterfalls endlessly cascading and replenishing them. The light blue colors of the water are almost dreamlike, and it honestly seems to defy belief that a place like this can exist. This is a place of legend and magic and is thus a bucket list "must do" place to visit for many.

However, with anything that is compared with paradise, there is always a catch. Here the catch is that it can be very difficult to get a reservation to hike to the falls. As described below, reservations for the season start on February 1 and require a decent amount of luck, tenacity, and patience to obtain. If you want to go, plan ahead to ensure you get a permit.

One unique aspect of this side trip is that its sole destination includes a strenuous 24-mile backpacking trip to get there. Those considering a hike to Havasu Falls should be in good physical condition and plan for a two-day backpacking trek minimum.

ALLOW

- Recommended: 2- 3 days.
- Driving time: 7.2 hours, including the exit to Las Vegas. It is 3.5 hours to Supai Trailhead parking from the South Rim Grand Canyon.

- Havasu and Mooney Falls: The hike to the falls is 12 miles each way.

CAN BE COMBINED WITH

Side Trip 1 - "Ancient Lands," Side Trip 2 - "Mystical Sedona" and Side Trip 10 - "Vegas Baby!"

HAVASU FALLS

Within the entirety of the Grand Circle, Havasu and Mooney Falls is an oasis that defies belief. Here in the middle of the desert are pools of serene turquoise water with cascading falls feeding into them. The contrast of surrounding red sandstone canyon walls and the hypnotic blue of the water itself is truly special. Havasu Falls is arguably the soul of the Southwest, willing to accept all those that travel to it and echoing a humble sacredness. If ever there should be a place go to the Southwest, this is that place.

Not to oversell on the expectations though, this destination is a popular one. You will share whatever magic and experience you uncover with others, especially during the peak summer season. The area weather can be quite hot, to the point that the Supai have the policy to close the trail if it gets above 115°F. While it doesn't usually get that hot, it does commonly get over 100°F. Given the length of the hike, it will be hard to fully escape the heat, but do plan to leave early in the morning if it is hot out. The other way to playback this section of guidance is if you are one who does not like crowds or heat, aim for the shoulder seasons of early to mid-spring and late fall.

Before stepping one foot on the trailhead, you'll first need to get reservations at www.havasupaireservations.com. Pricing for 2018 is as follows and include all necessary permits, fees, and taxes:

- One Person, 2 Days / 1 Night: $140.56
- One Person, 3 Days / 2 Nights: $171.11
- One Person, 4 Days / 3 Nights: $201.67

Horses on the trail to Havasu Falls

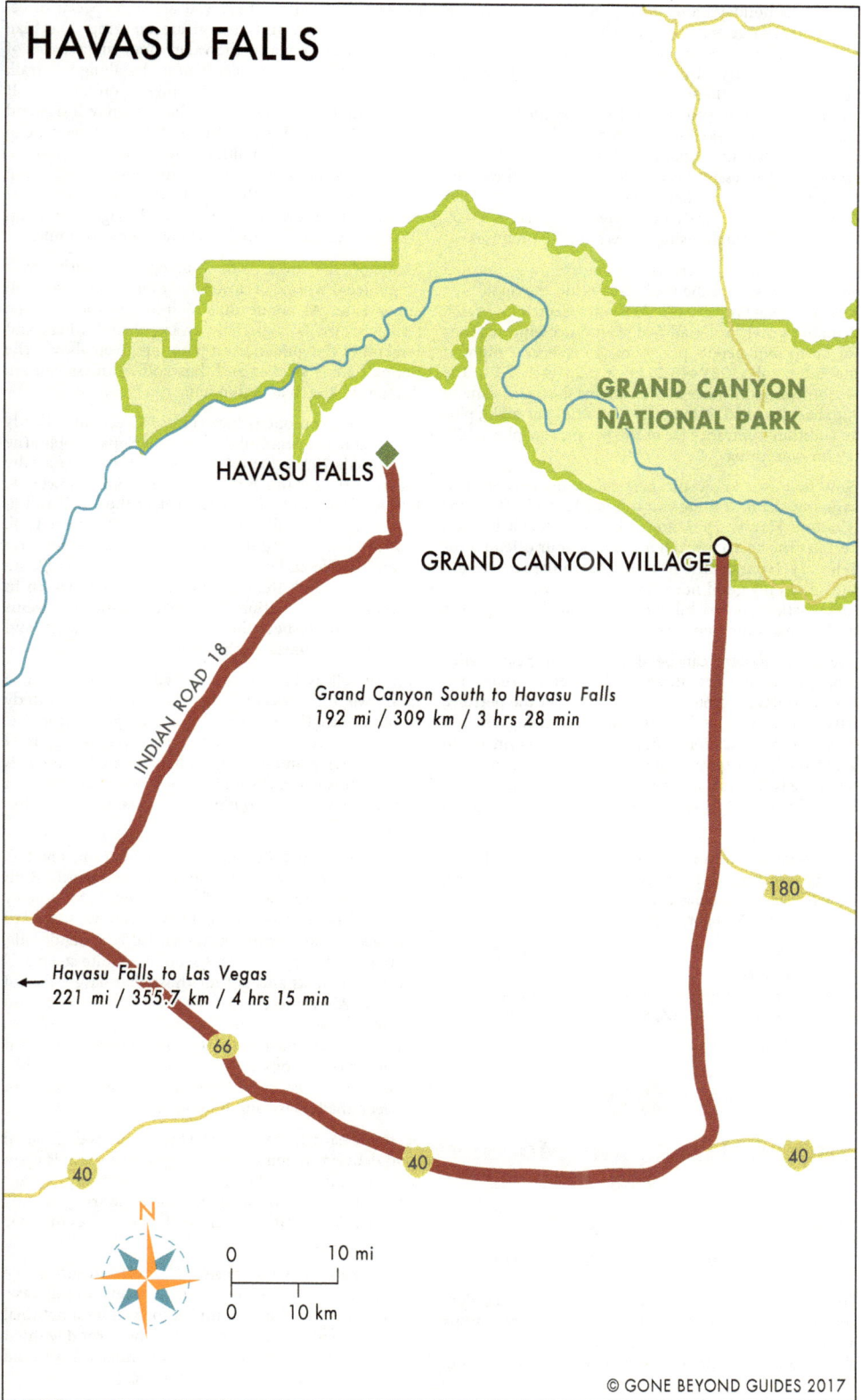

HAVASU FALLS

HAVASU FALLS

GRAND CANYON
NATIONAL PARK

GRAND CANYON VILLAGE

INDIAN ROAD 18

Grand Canyon South to Havasu Falls
192 mi / 309 km / 3 hrs 28 min

← Havasu Falls to Las Vegas
221 mi / 355.7 km / 4 hrs 15 min

180

66

40

40

40

N

0   10 mi

0   10 km

Weekends, holidays, and spring break nights carry an additional charge of $18.34 per night. The season opens on February 1st at 8am Arizona time, and 300 permits are given each day. The campground is closed December and January. There are no refunds and fees are collected at the time you make the reservation. If there isn't you will be asked to hike the 8 miles back to the trailhead. Also, the Supai can close access to the falls, typically for excessive heat or flash floods. In these cases, they will try to reschedule your reservation to a later date. Drones are strictly prohibited and carry a $1000 fine if you are caught using one within the premises.

For non-campers, there is the Supai Lodge located about 8 miles from the trailhead within the Supai Village. The lodge is basic but does offer electricity, Wi-Fi, drinking water, a shared fridge, and accommodations for up to four people per room. To reserve a night at the lodge, call (928) 448-2111 or (928) 448-2201. The village also has a store and a café for food and general supplies. As of 2018, lodge fees are $175 per night, plus an additional entrance fee of $90 per person, plus a 10% tax on everything.

Now that you know the particulars on permits and camping, the next thing you will need is luck. The word is out on Havasu Falls, and it is very difficult to get a permit. The best approach is to mark your calendar for February 1st and then head to the online reservation site. The only good news here is this is the same process whether you are hiking alone or are booking for a professional tour company.

The online system can be slower during peak traffic, especially in the first three weeks after February 1st. If you do have a group helping you to get the permits, have a plan A, B, and C for dates and make sure you have a communication system for when you finally do get through. The season usually books out within weeks but there is always hope that there will be a cancellation if you don't want to wait until next February to get in line.

Additional details can be found at the Havasupai Reservations website. All that said don't get too discouraged, as with planning, tenacity, luck, and eventuality, you will get a spot. You got this!

The recommended reservation process is through their online portal at www.havasupaireservations.com/. You can also contact the Havasupai Tourism offices by mail at P.O. Box 160 Supai, AZ, 86435, and by phone: (928) 448-2121.

HIKING HAVASU AND MOONEY FALLS

HAVASU AND MOONEY FALLS

Strenuous – (24.0 mi / 38.6 km), round trip, 2-day backpacking trip

Located within the Havasupai Reservation, the trip does get a lot of visitors during peak season. Start by finding a parking spot near the trailhead, which is situated about 1,000 feet off the canyon bottom. Right from the trailhead, you will see you are in a special place. The views down and around are amazing. The hike heads steeply down to the valley floor via a series of switchbacks. There are plenty of mules along this trail, and one needs to be especially diligent on this part. If you see mules coming, stick to the canyon wall side and not the cliff side. The mules often travel at a decent clip giving the backpacker little time to react. Hugging a wall in these instances tends to fair better than clinging to the edge of a cliff. This is especially true in a narrow section further on. The mules have the right of way on this trail. Respect the mules. Do not taunt the mules.

Most of the hike travels along the wash, with magnificent views of towering orange-red walls on either side. At about mile 7 into the journey, the trail narrows. Be especially aware of mules here and remember the guidance on taunting given above. The hiking here is shadier and thus cooler unless you are doing this stretch at high noon.

The slot canyon opens into Havasu Creek and shortly after that to the peaceful village of the Supai People. The town holds 208 residents, give or take, and is officially the most remote inhabited community in the lower 48. Besides flying in by helicopter (or as the locals call it, "cheating"), the only way in is via the Havasupai Trail. It is the last community in the United States to have its mail delivered by mule. Some of the village folk are more open to all these tourists than others, which in looking at the situation from their perspective seems fair enough. Respect the Supai and their village, and they will most likely do the same to you.

Havasu Falls is 2 miles from the village of Supai. These final two miles deeper into the canyon are utterly inspirational. The water is a light blue-green turquoise. The distinctive hue comes from the strong reflection of the underlying limestone creek bed. It's not just the falls that are this color, the entire creek from Supai on is a gem like color of a Southwestern version of paradise found.

Havasu Falls and Mooney Falls further on are tall, roaring sheets of water and simply beyond words. Both are amazing, and both must be seen. Getting to Mooney Falls requires a Class 3 descent to the bottom, some 210 feet below. Aids include a tunnel, ladders, handholds, railings, and footholds. This section is quite steep and exposed in areas and not for those that have a fear of heights. Also, these areas become bottlenecks, and one may have to stand in place as they wait for folks to come up or down. Finally, it should not be attempted when the conditions are wet or otherwise unfavorable, as sections can get very slippery. The campground is in between the Havasu and Mooney Falls.

As stated earlier, the US Postal Service does their Supai mail delivery by mule. Since the postal service is open to anyone, it is possible to send off a letter or postcard from the village, knowing part of its journey was by mule, the last community in the United States to move mail in this manner.

If you do want to send a postcard home from Supai, note that the post office is closed on weekends. In this case, some locals are willing to mail it for you for a nominal fee. Given you are hiking around in their world without a care and they get their mail by pack mules, this would be a good opportunity to be generous.

Side Trip 12 –
The Secret Grand Canyon

BEST FROM

North Rim Grand Canyon

WHAT YOU WILL SEE

- Pipe Springs National Monument
- Zion National Park
- Snow Canyon State Park
- Grand Canyon-Parashant National Monument
- Valley of Fire State Park
- Las Vegas

WHY CHOOSE THIS SIDE TRIP

The Secret Grand Canyon is an excellent choice if you have decided to see the Grand Canyon via the North Rim and have an adventurous spirit. This side trip includes Zion National Park, one of the most popular parks of the Southwest. You also will have the opportunity to visit multiple other parks along the way that are spectacular and unique. The trip includes Pipe Springs National Monument; a Mormon pioneer fortified ranch, as well as excellent day hike possibilities within Snow Canyon and Valley of Fire State Parks.

For the adventure minded, this side trip includes the Grand Canyon-Parashant National Monument. This park is a rugged and isolated million-acre wilderness with no visitor center, campgrounds, or paved roads. Grand Canyon-Parashant is only recommended for those that have a 4WD high clearance vehicle, camping gear, and good backcountry skills. If you are more of a casual visitor and find this park a bit too wilderness and survival, no worries, as you can check out the other parks and still have a great side trip.

ALLOW

- Recommended: 4-6 days.
- Driving time: Over 11 hours, including the final stop in Las Vegas.
- Pipe Springs National Monument: allow 1.5 – 2 hours for a tour and visit
- Zion National Park: Recommended minimum is two days, though add a day here if possible
- Snow Canyon State Park: Allow 2-3 hours for a pleasant day hike and visit

- Grand Canyon-Parashant National Monument: Assuming you have a high clearance 4WD and good backcountry skills, recommended minimum is two days, add a day here if possible.
- Valley of Fire State Park: Allow 2-4 hours minimum for scenic drive and day hike, overnight camping is possible.
- Las Vegas: allow overnight stay minimum.

CAN BE COMBINED WITH

This is already a pretty loaded side trip, but if time allows, take a look at Antelope Canyon in Side Trip 8 - "Into Zion National Park."

PIPE SPRINGS NATIONAL MONUMENT

Pipe Springs was first discovered in 1858 by Jacob Hamblin, a Mormon missionary on an expedition to the Hopi mesas. Two years later, James M. Whitmore and a group of fellow pioneers created a homestead and cattle operation near the spring. Building a group of homes in the Navajo territory was one thing, keeping it was another. Once the Apache, Navajo, Utes, and Paiutes joined forces to start the Black Hawk War in 1866 that was primarily aimed at the Mormons, things came to a boiling point. After a raid of the Pipe Springs homesteads, the families decided to build a fort on the location.

This fortified ranch house was laster purchased by Brigham Young in 1872 for the Church of the Latter-Day Saints (LDS). Brigham sent Mormon Bishop Anson Perry Winsor to run the ranch, and he renamed it Winsor Castle. The ranch became a haven for travelers passing through and even acted as a refuge for polygamist wives during the late 1800's. In the end, the ranch's ties to polygamy would be its downfall, and the LDS lost ownership of the property in 1887.

Pipe Spring National Monument

THE SECRET GRAND CANYON

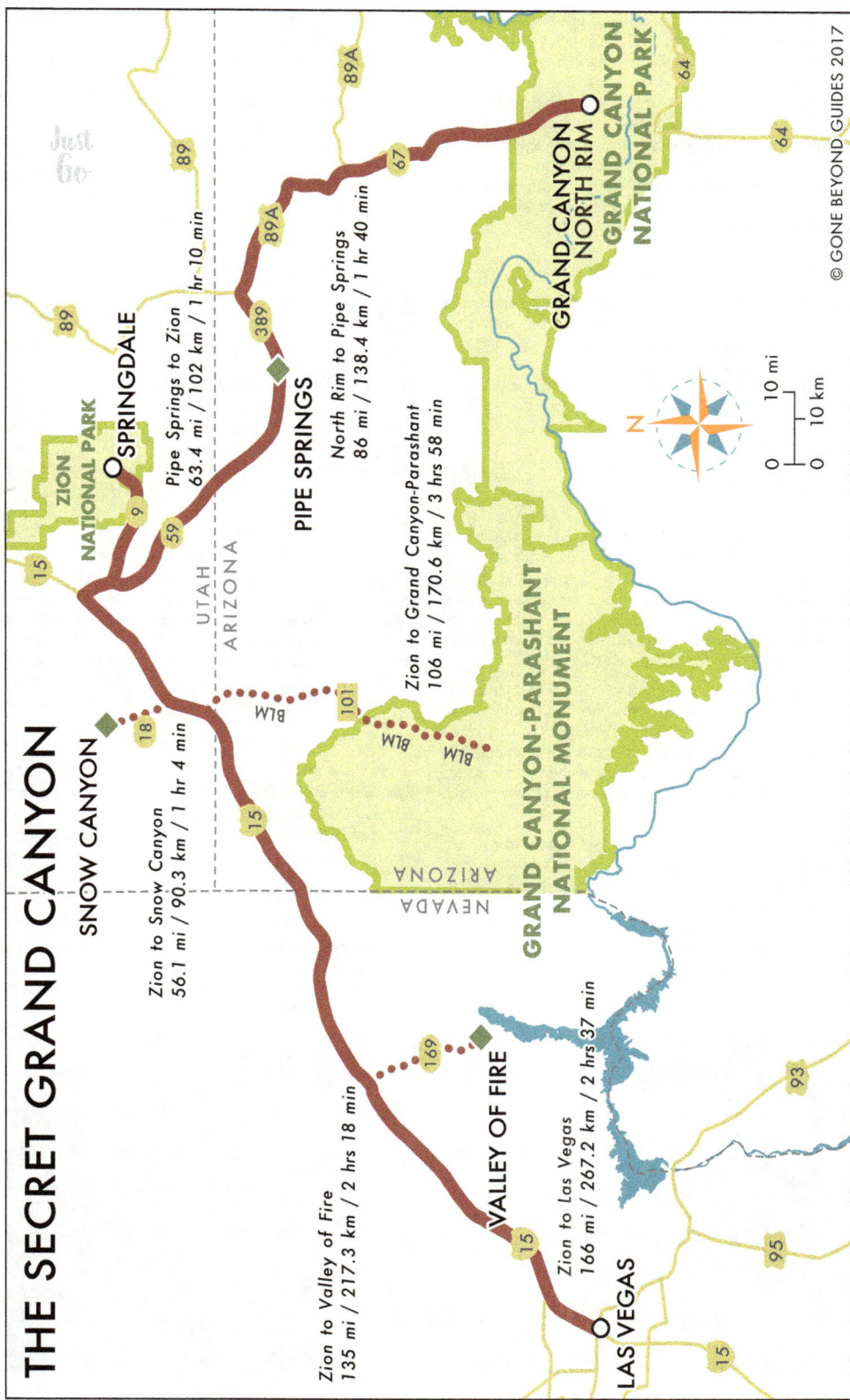

SNOW CANYON

SPRINGDALE

ZION NATIONAL PARK

Zion to Snow Canyon
56.1 mi / 90.3 km / 1 hr 4 min

Pipe Springs to Zion
63.4 mi / 102 km / 1 hr 10 min

PIPE SPRINGS

UTAH
ARIZONA

North Rim to Pipe Springs
86 mi / 138.4 km / 1 hr 40 min

Zion to Grand Canyon-Parashant
106 mi / 170.6 km / 3 hrs 58 min

BLM

GRAND CANYON-PARASHANT
NATIONAL MONUMENT

GRAND CANYON
NORTH RIM

GRAND CANYON
NATIONAL PARK

ARIZONA
NEVADA

Zion to Valley of Fire
135 mi / 217.3 km / 2 hrs 18 min

VALLEY OF FIRE

Zion to Las Vegas
166 mi / 267.2 km / 2 hrs 37 min

LAS VEGAS

Just Go

© GONE BEYOND GUIDES 2017

151

N

10 mi

10 km

Today the monument is a cultural preserve, offering a 30-minute ranger-led tour of the ranch house and an extensive museum and visitor center. It is also possible to take a self-guided walk amongst the out buildings, corral, and garden areas. Pipe Spring National Monument offers an informative and interesting step back in time; especially if you take the ranger-led tour. Pipe Spring's is a day use park, open from 8am – 5pm from May to August and 8:30am – 4:30pm from September through April. There is an entrance fee of $10 per person to visit this park.

ZION NATIONAL PARK

Zion National Park offers some of the tallest sandstone cliffs and longest arches in the world. The scenery is stunning, allowing for incredible hiking opportunities, camping, lodging, and food within the park and just outside in the town of Springdale. For a full description, please refer to Side Trip 8 - Into Zion National Park.

SNOW CANYON STATE PARK

Snow Canyon State Park has some amazing views, even as you pull up. From a distance, the broad panorama of red and white sandstone, with a hint of lava-capped adventure in the background, is simply breathtaking. One's eye, just on the approach, can gaze merrily for hours, sweeping back and forth along broad brushstrokes of white to red sandstone. It is, even on the horizon, a place of sandstone as art.

This natural display intensifies as one draws in and onto the trail. There are sand dunes, hoodoos, fins, razor-thin labyrinths, and canyons that beckon with their twists and turns to hike around just one more bend. The rock is bright with color, and the possibilities for hiking seem endless. There are petroglyphs and other evidence of use before modern times as well.

Snow Canyon is a place of slickrock magic to be sure, but there is more to the park than just carved sandstone. There is also a section where lava has covered over the sandstone, creating a different exploration. Within this area are lava tubes, caves, and lava flows with some cool features to discover. In fact, the park's tallest feature is a cinder cone.

Snow Canyon offers camping and a lot of established trails. Given that it is close to St. George and Ivins, Utah makes this an enjoyable day hiking spot for travelers that don't want to camp. Snow Canyon Campground offers 31 tent/RV spaces, drinking water, flush toilets, showers, hookups, dump station, some pull thru sites, call visitor center for reservations.

With the exception of the campground, Snow Canyon State Park is open from 6am - 10pm daily. There is a day use fee of $10 per vehicle. Camping is $20 per night or $25 for sites with hookups.

HIKING SNOW CANYON STATE PARK

JOHNSON CANYON

Easy – (2.0 mi / 3.2 km), round trip, allow 1 hour

This trail is closed from March 15 to October 31 to protect nesting bird populations. When open, this is considered one of the top hikes in the park. Easy and level, the trail passes by a natural spring and ends at a monstrously thick arch spanning 200 feet.

WHIPTAIL TRAIL

Easy – (6.0 mi / 9.7 km), round trip, allow 3 hours

Whiptail is a paved, there and back route popular with the locals. There are plenty of bikers, joggers, and walkers on this trail. The trail sits at the base of Snow Canyon's red (and white) rocks, giving a nice backdrop for all users. There is a small elevation gain, but the trail is wheelchair accessible. This is a popular hike, especially on weekends.

JENNY'S CANYON

Easy – (0.5 mi / 0.8 km), round trip, allow 30 minutes

This trail is closed from March 15 to June 1 to protect nesting bird populations. Jenny's Canyon is a short level hike that ends at an interesting slot canyon and is great for kids.

SAND DUNES

Easy – (0.5 mi / 0.8 km), round trip, allow 30 minutes

A quick and easy jaunt to a small set of sand dunes. The trail is a great family hike with fabulous scenery from every angle. If you have small children, this is a perfect place for playing in the dunes.

Snow Canyon State Park

SNOW CANYON STATE PARK

Legend:
- ★ Point Of Interest
- ◈ Unique Natural Feature
- ▲ Natural Peak
- ⚑ Campground
- ------ Trail
- ===== Unpaved 2WD Road

To Veyo

Cinder Cone Trail

Cinder Cone ▲

Whiterocks Ampitheater Trail

RED CLIFFS
NATIONAL
CONSERVATION
AREA

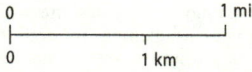

Whiterocks Trail

■ Park Entrance

N

★ OVERLOOK

Lava Tubes ◈

Lava Flow Trail

★ OVERLOOK

Lava Flow Trail

Butterfly Trail

Petrified Dunes Trail

RED CLIFFS
NATIONAL
CONSERVATION
AREA

SNOW CANYON DR

Three Ponds

West Canyon Trail

Whiptail Trail

0   1 mi
0   1 km

18

Hidden Pinyon Trail

■ PARK HEADQUARTERS ⚑

Whiptail Trail

Pioneer Names Trail

Sand Dunes Trail
◈ Sand Dunes
Jenny's Canyon Trail

Whiptail

■ Park Entrance | Johnson Canyon Trail

SNOW CANYON

STATE PARK

TUACAHN DR

CENTER ST

Ivins ○

SNOW CANYON PKWY

400 E

To W Old Hwy 91 and Hwy 18

To St. George and Interstate 15

© GONE BEYOND GUIDES 2015-2019

153

Petrified Dunes - Snow Canyon State Park

Pioneer Names Trail

Easy – (0.5 mi / 0.8 km), round trip, allow 30 minutes

Pioneer Names Trail takes a somewhat sandy but otherwise ambling and quick path to a red rock alcove. Within it are the names of several Mormon pioneers from 1881. Getting to the alcove and up close to the pioneer graffiti requires a short but steep climb up slickrock at the end. The surroundings are a pleasing mix of red sandstone and the green of the desert pinyon-juniper woodlands.

West Canyon Trail

Moderate – (8.0 mi / 12.9 km), round trip, allow 4 hours

This trail is an old dirt road that leads up into the main canyon in the park. The hike itself is level for the most part and offers splendid views into all of the side washes, sandstone hills, and cliff faces. The trail offers a lot of opportunity for adventure, with plenty of slickrock to explore. The canyon is wide and inviting, traveling much of the time through grasslands. Stay on the trail whenever possible and avoid walking on undisturbed soil.

Hidden Pinyon

Moderate – (1.5 mi / 2.4 km), round trip, allow 1 hour

Stunning views are found all around you on this hike. Great hike to capture the essence of the park in a short amount of time. Hidden Pinyon is also an interpretative trail that describes the geologic features and native flora in the park.

Three Ponds

Moderate – (3.5 mi / 5.6 km), round trip, allow 2 hours

The hike is primarily through a sandy wash with some slick rock. The trail follows through a twisty wash with deep "slog worthy" sand to the mouth of a large canyon. The trail ends at the first of three potholes that seasonally fill with water. There are two other pools further on. While hiking to murky, stagnant water may not be for everyone, the surroundings along the way are very nice and are sure to please.

Petrified Dunes Trail

Moderate – (1.0 mi / 1.6 km), round trip, allow 45 minutes

Here is another trail taking the hiker to "sand dunes frozen in time." Geologically speaking, much of the Grand Circle was a vast sand dune, so in effect, all the redrock you see falls under this moniker. That said, this is one of the nicest hikes in the park. The sandstone here is unique, odd, and beautiful, all at the same time.

Lava Flow Trail

Moderate – (2.5 mi / 4.0 km), round trip, allow 1 - 2 hours

Lava Flow is an easy to follow trail with some caves near the trailhead. Bring your headlamps. The trail itself is uneven throughout as it heads up into an ancient lava field. This trail can be very hot in the summer but does show a different side of the park.

Whiterocks Amphitheater

Moderate – (4.0 mi / 6.4 km), round trip, allow 2 hours

Whiterocks Amphitheater is a straightforward trail into the main white sandstone area of Snow Canyon. The trail starts out in moderately deep sand but quickly hits the slickrock for an ascent of about 100 feet. The trail officially ends at a bowl of white rock, surrounding the hiker in amphitheater fashion, on three sides. Scrambling to the top for better views is possible. Some sections require Class 3 level scrambling. At the top, the hiker is rewarded with some fantastic views of the park.

There is a shorter trail of about one mile in length located north of the junction of Snow Canyon Drive and SR18 (north of the junction 0.5 miles).

Cinder Cone Trail

Strenuous – (1.5 mi / 2.4 km), round trip, allow 1 - 2 hours

Hiking up cinder cones can feel like you are going nowhere fast, but the trail does reach the top. The trail corkscrews up with an elevation gain of 500 feet. Once at the top, there is a view of the crater and the park's gorgeous views.

Grand Canyon -Parashant National Monument

GRAND CANYON-PARASHANT NATIONAL MONUMENT

If isolation and solitude are what you are looking for, Grand Canyon-Parashant is the answer. This national monument is a large park at just over one million acres, yet the park has no paved roads, lodges, or visitor center. Grand Canyon-Parashant is a land where two sets of spares are the norm, and the extra tanks of gas bloted to the top of your rig are not just for show. The park contains the north-western edges of the Grand Canyon as well as high plateau forests and desert grasslands that surround the canyon. The park holds three large wilderness areas, multiple plateaus, deep canyons, and many washes offering a vast array of backcountry hiking and travel opportunities. There are a few maintained trails, which are listed below.

🥾🚶 HIKING GRAND CANYON-PARASHANT NM

For all of these hikes, bring a topo map of the area to be hiked (and surrounding area), a good high clearance vehicle and the ability to self-sustain in the desert. Most of the hikes described below are remote, and some of the routes to them are not maintained. Check with the BLM monument manager before any trip in this area to sync on local conditions. The BLM St. George office phone is (435) 688-3202.

GRAND WASH BENCH TRAIL

Strenuous – (20.0 mi / 32.2 km), round trip, full day trip or 2-day backpacking trip

The Grand Wash Bench Trail travels along a bench north to south within the 36,300-acre Grand Wash Cliffs Wilderness. Area scenery includes narrow canyons, two sets of towering cliffs and sandstone buttes. Ecologically, this hike travels through a transition zone and holds varied wildlife including bighorn sheep, the Gila monster, and the desert tortoise. Flora includes pinyon-juniper forests and desert grasslands.

MOUNT TRUMBULL TRAIL

Moderate – (5.0 mi / 8.0 km), round trip, allow 4 hours

A pleasant hike to the top of an ancient shield volcano. The gradient up is mild after the first ascent. The trail becomes a route about 2/3 of the way up as the solid ground turns to deep cinders. Follow the paths of others and use a zigzag pattern to help make progress. There is a register at the true top of this 8028-foot peak and no register at the false summit. From the top, there are sweeping views in every direction.

HELL HOLE – MOUNT LOGAN TRAIL

Easy – (1.0 mi / 1.6 km), round trip, allow 1 hour

This trail takes the hiker to the top of Mount Logan. Great majestic views into western Grand Canyon as well as southern Utah. The summit also gives a commanding view of Hell Hole, which is the northern end of Grand Canyon's erosional artwork.

NAMPAWEAP ROCK ART SITE

Easy – (1.0 mi / 1.6km), round trip, allow 30 minutes

Once thought to be a travel corridor, this short hike leads to hundreds of boulders containing thousands of petroglyphs left by ancient travelers over a 10,000-year period. Nampaweap means "foot canyon" in Paiute.

MT. DELLENBAUGH

Strenuous – (6.0 mi / 9.7 km), round trip, allow 4 hours

Like Mount Trumbull, this is another ancient shield volcano. The trail follows up an old converted jeep road to the top of this 7012-foot peak. The peak has an interesting tie to the John Wesley Powell expedition. Three of Powell's team, William Dunn, and brothers Oramel and Seneca Howland, decided they had enough of trying to be the first group of men to navigate down the Colorado River and thus left Powell. They hiked north through Separation Canyon and onto the Shivwits Plateau. William Dunn climbed Mount Dellenbaugh to get his bearings and inscribed both his name and year onto a rock. The local Shivwits killed the three men shortly after that. The historical graffiti can still be found with some exploration.

While this hike is one of two "official" hikes in the park (the other is Mount Trumbull), do not let that fool you. Getting to the trailhead requires traveling on dirt roads for nearly 90 miles. As repeatedly stated, Prashant is a remote land. However, for many, that is the point.

VALLEY OF FIRE STATE PARK AND LAS VEGAS

Valley of Fire offers dramatic red rock views, hiking, and camping near the city of Las Vegas. For a full description of both Valley of Fire and Vegas, refer to Side Trip 10 – Vegas Baby!

ACKNOWLEDGMENTS

First off, I want to thank MRoy Cartography for their wonderful map making, headed by Molly Roy. I came in with a request to make these the best maps out there and she fully delivered.

I am extremely thankful to George Trager and Ernest Doucette, who have helped as a second pair of eyes, sounding board, and fellow Southwest wilderness enthusiast.

I want to thank Verde Valley School in Sedona, Arizona, whose teachers were not only the catalysts for creating these books, but continue to support me decades later. If your child is looking for a full education, one that teaches cultural diversity, respect for all people, and compassion, along with a full STEM oriented curriculum, there is really no better school than Verde Valley School.

A special thanks to the National Park Service and its employees. There has never been a time when you weren't able to support this effort, which is remarkable given how much you all do. I truly appreciate all that you do for us as a nation and for all the help and assistance you have given me. To NPS - - thank you!

I also want to thank those within the states of Utah, Arizona, New Mexico, Colorado, and Nevada that strive for a balance between preservation and utilization. Each of you protects some of the best and most remote lands in the United States.

Most of all, I wish to thank my loving wife Angela and two boys, Everest and Bryce. The time you have given me to create these books is a true blessing, both in the adventures we have taken and in the many hours writing and editing you have given me.

ABOUT THE AUTHOR

Eric Henze began his writing career at the age of twelve with a sci fi short titled "5:15", tackling a plot around a timepiece that could end the world. His passion for hiking started in Sedona, Arizona where he lived in his youth. It expanded to peak bagging in the Sierra Nevada Mountains and then the Andes of South America, where he lived as a Peace Corp volunteer for two years, climbing many of the peaks of Ecuador and Peru. A highlight was climbing Sangay, an active volcano that often shoots VW size rocks at climbers to maintain their attention. In his own words, "It was a delight".

His passions for writing, hiking, and adventure have led to a series of guidebooks for both the National Park Service and the California State Parks. A portion of the proceeds of all of his books will go towards directly supporting these parks.

By day, the intrepid author works for Microsoft helping large healthcare providers and payors at the executive level navigate towards, within and beyond the digital revolution.

His children have noted that his last words will be while driving through the Southwest and seeing some point of interest. As he pulls over the car yet again and starts heading towards some rock, canyon, or bush in the far distance, these last words will be, "I'll be right back, I'm going go check that out".

You can reach the author through our FaceBook page:

www.facebook.com/GBG.GoneBeyondGuides

ISBN-10: 0-9971370-5-3

ISBN-13: 978-0-9971370-5-7

www.ingramcontent.com/pod-product-compliance
Lightning Source LLC
Chambersburg PA
CBHW062117040426
42336CB00041B/1445